O CANADA CROSSWORDS

BOOK 13

100 Daily-size & Weekend-size Crosswords

GWEN SJOGREN

D1399029

NIGHTWOOD EDITIONS

Nightwood Editions
P.O. Box 1779
Gibsons, BC
V0N 1V0
www.nightwoodeditions.com

Library and Archives Canada Cataloguing in Publication

O Canada crosswords.

Bk. 13 written by Gwen Sjogren.
ISBN 978-0-88971-272-0 (bk. 13)

1. Crossword puzzles. 2. Canada—Miscellanea.
I. Sjogren, Gwen, 1962–

GV1507.C7H35 2000   793.73'2   C 009-10576X

Contents

Capital Places

Important Canadian cities

1

ACROSS

1. Céline's first single: "Ce n'était qu'un _____"
5. Metrical foot
9. River in Stratford ON
13. _____ and ends
17. Spanish cheers
18. Toronto Harbourfront street: Queen's _____
19. 2011 women's French Open champ
20. Telegram
21. Beijing Olympics golden Canadian team: _____ eights
22. Mine entrance
23. Hyena's hunt type?
25. *Titanic*, for example
28. Neck and neck
29. Henpeck
30. Audition
31. Gentleman in Granada
33. Skate, say
35. Snake that suffocates
36. Toronto NHLer Phaneuf
38. Old Russian space station
39. Tempo
40. Sphere
41. Libya city
43. Attack
46. Crimean port
49. HBO rival, for short
50. British North America _____
52. Canadian band Rush, for example
53. Santa's transport
55. Sept-_____ QC
58. Surprised cry
60. Pound sound
61. **Capital near the Northumberland Strait**
65. _____ Pérignon
68. Santa _____ winds
69. Jazz improv
70. Unkempt, in appearance
74. NL-born NHLer Pardy
76. Go from brunette to blond, say
78. US airline regulator (abbr.)
80. Mink wrap
81. Dennis' danger?
83. Fido's freshwater catch?
87. Dodge truck type
88. "Sometimes When We Touch" singer Dan
89. Deface
90. Clay and sand soil
92. Island east of Ellesmere
93. Andean animal
95. Acid type
97. Eucharist jug
99. Consume
100. Breadth
102. McGraw-Hill Ryerson business
105. Appetizer, Italian style
108. National symbol: Maple _____
109. On the briny
110. Mackerel
111. "Cut it out!"
112. Anti-fur org.
113. Baby birds' home
114. John A. Macdonald banknotes
115. Posted
116. Top spot
117. Aide (abbr.)

DOWN

1. Pitcher Sergio or quarterback Tony
2. Voting district description, in Canada
3. Like a respected retiree
4. Work of writing
5. **Capital in a territory**
6. They monitor public spending
7. Key street in Winnipeg?
8. Computing memory units
9. Shortened moniker for Montréal's CFL team
10. **Capital on an island**
11. Red TV studio words
12. Narthex neighbour
13. Oprah's network
14. Governor General, say
15. Apprehension
16. Former Montréal Canadiens star Savard
24. Nips at the finish line
26. Move one's head in agreement
27. San _____, Italy
32. Common soccer score
34. Final
35. Canadian comedy: *Trailer Park* _____
37. _____ *obstat*
39. Triviality
42. Marco's shirts?
44. Richard or Rocky
45. Chop off
47. Quirk
48. Turkish title (var.)
51. Red Cross bed
54. "Messiah" composer
56. And more, for short
57. Employees
59. Hooting birds
62. Sunbeam
63. Sell online, say
64. Olivia Newton-John hit: "If _____ for You"
65. Coquitlam or Revelstoke, in BC
66. Wordsworth work
67. NYC borough
71. Aquatic mammals
72. Simplicity
73. Hamilton-born *Ice Road Truckers* star Rick
75. Harm

8

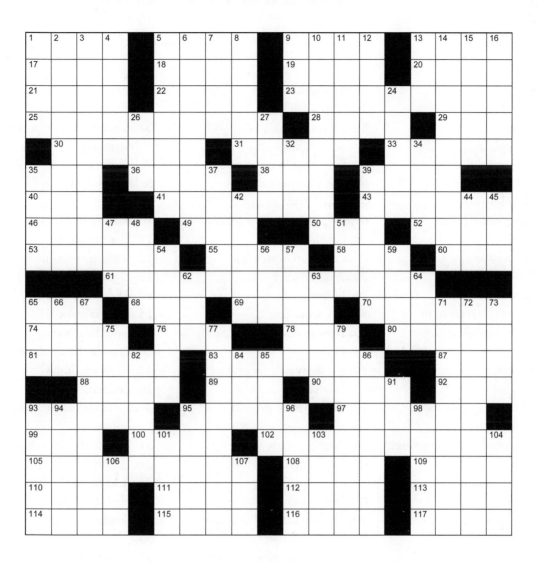

77. Capital on the North Saskatchewan

79. Recently

82. Hold

84. Paddle's kin

85. See 82-D

86. Capital with an Atlantic port

91. Pas' partners

93. Smallest amount

94. Jouster's spear

95. Butter up?

96. *Mea* _____

98. Accra's country

101. Kicking Horse _____

103. Honk

104. World Trade Organization predecessor (abbr.)

106. Psyche sections

107. Choose

House Hunting

Wacky real estate

ACROSS

1. Phi _____ Kappa
5. Hover over a weaver?
9. Old-style pulpit
13. Wet blanket?
17. Served like Serena?
18. Debate side
19. *The Young and the Restless*, for example
21. Current regulators
23. Fertilizer (var.)
24. Like some bath mats
25. Clayoquot or Howe in BC
27. 19th-C. Canadian retailer Timothy
28. Beaver State constabulary (abbr.)
29. *Lord of the Rings* creatures
30. Pen contents
31. **Non-serious buyer's showing?**
36. Sis-boom-_____
37. *Dangerous Liaisons* star Thurman
40. Montréal actor Toufexis of *Smallville*
41. Mere
42. Pregnancy procedure
44. Cheery tune
45. Eye component
46. Diplomatic building
47. Land formation in Florida
48. Hermit or king
49. '72 April Wine hit: "_____ Side of the Moon"
50. Transactions at the till
51. **How an aloof realtor might act?**

55. Venomous snake
58. Ump's call
59. Canadian-born NHLers Sakic and Thornton
60. Caribbean music genre
63. Arsonist, perhaps?
66. Towel inscription
67. Ex-prime minister Martin
68. City in Australia
69. Canadian-born actor Raymond
70. Pianist's piece
71. Immediately
72. Pea container
73. **How to encourage a sale?**
75. Fitting
76. It follows one–two–three– in a Feist song
77. Third-person pronoun
78. Slack-jawed
81. Port _____ BC
82. Mythological lady with a box of evils
87. Tale tellers
89. Oliver Cromwell nickname
91. _____ photography
92. Number of ladies dancing
93. Stole fur
94. Juno Award winner Jordan
95. Bride's covering
96. Mercury and Mars
97. Notices

DOWN

1. Canadian retailer: Bulk _____
2. '80s Canadian hit: "_____ Beach"
3. Young driver of Canada?

4. Fusses
5. Not quite on time
6. Borrowed by prospective purchasers
7. PEI-born NHLer Steve
8. Montana's "Garden City"
9. Per se
10. Kvetches
11. Not hirsute
12. Make up one's mind
13. Orate
14. After deductions, in Dorchester
15. Three-ply cookie
16. Sound the alarm
20. **Popular floor plans?**
22. Vegas machines
26. Bacchanalia
30. Canadian singers Tamblyn and Thomas
31. TV bandleader Lawrence
32. "I cannot tell _____"
33. A Munster's bloom?
34. Nestlé bar: Kit _____
35. Singly
36. _____ vivant
37. River in Kazakhstan
38. Pal
39. "My Cup Runneth Over" singer Ed
42. Fountain fool?
43. Happy
45. Dot-com's address
46. Savannah or Siamese
48. **How to discourage a sale?**
49. Track action
51. '80s Headpins hit: "Don't It Make You _____"

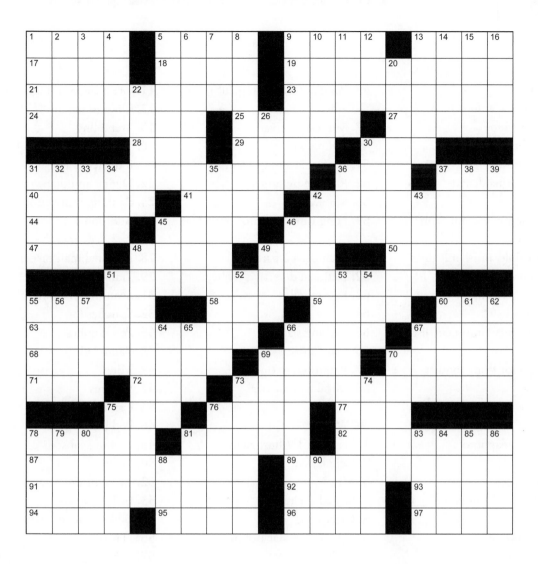

52. Unexploded explosive
53. Exchange letters
54. "_____ Got the Whole World in His Hands"
55. Statement of dislike: "I'm not _____"
56. Queen of Carthage
57. 14th Ontario premier
60. Canadian author: John Ralston _____
61. African antelope
62. Sheltered

64. 06/15/11 Vancouver event
65. Elaborate
66. Rushing
67. Evening mtg. at school
69. One bit per second, in computing
70. Ties the score
73. Tidbit
74. Scottish lords
75. After, in Alma
76. Persian language
78. Termites' relatives?

79. Greek earth goddess
80. Upper limbs
81. Optimism
83. Darkens
84. *Garfield* pooch
85. Calgary Stampeders kicker Paredes
86. Requests
88. Hebrew letter
90. _____ de Janeiro

Canada Cornucopia 1

ACROSS

1. National law enforcement org.
5. Margarine type
9. Union foe
13. Spring flower
14. _____ formaldehyde
15. Not fresh
16. Common fabric, for short
17. Get ready
18. Permissible, in Islamic diets
19. Oklahoma tribe
21. All that remains?
23. Difficult
25. Canadian environmentalist Suzuki
26. Conqueror from another country
30. Canadian Ben Heppner, et al.
33. Ensnare
34. Sashes in Sapporo
36. Rajah's wife
37. Coop queen
38. 1983 federal legislation: _____ Act
40. NHL surface
41. BlackBerry message
43. High-_____
44. Ian Millar's equipment

45. Popular Canadian quaff in the '60s
47. Musical intervals
49. Sailing, say
51. Food thickening agent
52. Remove by surgery
55. Maturation
59. Long-time Toronto sports bar: _____ Moose
60. Archipelago part
62. Fictional detective Wolfe
63. Less moral
64. Lions' den
65. Lacking slack
66. Some insects
67. Bathroom fixtures
68. Metal containers?

DOWN

1. Daytime TV host Kelly
2. Canola, say
3. Mrs. Mulroney
4. Get all excited
5. Great Lake
6. '70s hockey star Bobby
7. Club dues
8. Recorded
9. Endurance
10. Scottish, to a Roman

11. Great Big Sea singer Doyle
12. Ontario region: Nickel _____
15. Trembling
20. 1961 Hockey Hall of Fame inductee Day
22. Digital audiotape (abbr.)
24. Banking transaction
26. Additional
27. _____ de menthe
28. National mail carrier
29. Transfix
31. Scouting mission, for short
32. Searches for
35. Pelvic bones
38. Band-Aid
39. Mites
42. Seizures
44. Capital of Ontario
46. Pod bit
48. Roofing substance
50. Listing
52. *Fantastic Four* star Jessica
53. Bellyache, say
54. Biblical Jacob's twin
56. Have on
57. "The _____ North strong and free"
58. Cinnamon candies: Red _____
61. Pearson or Trudeau (abbr.)

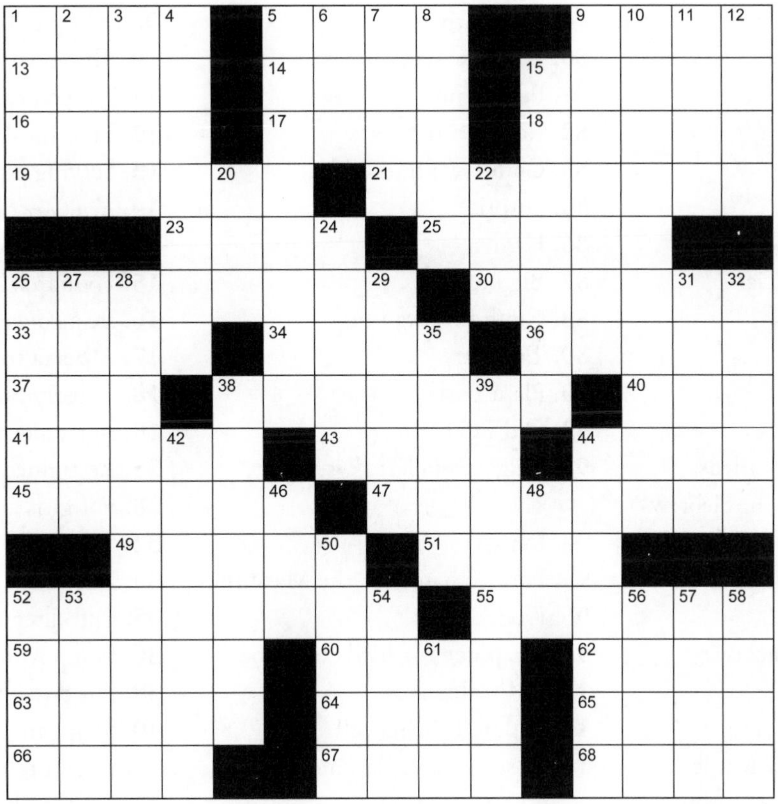

Solution on page 208

4 Bird's-eye View

A puzzle for the flighty

ACROSS

1. Canadian capital
7. Most frosty
14. Ford model since '76
20. Pureed fruit sauce
21. Editor, say
22. Sort of
23. Off the beaten path
24. Your chattels?
26. Inquire
27. Non-binding judicial pronouncements
29. Colour
30. Melodies
31. Refusals
33. **SK place for crazy birds?**
37. Beth's predecessor, in Hebrew
39. Chatter, in the Outback
41. Water pitcher
42. Gullible one
43. History Television show: _____ *Pilots NWT*
46. Sent in a résumé, say
48. Canadian Country Music Association inductee Osburne
49. Reticent
50. Chunk of dirt
51. "You must _____ of your mind!"
52. Say nay
53. That woman
54. Leaves for lunch?
55. "Put a lid _____!"
56. Support a gambler?
58. Without a care
60. Tactic, in Toledo
62. Blank look
64. Years (Fr.)
65. Toasted sandwich type, for short
66. **MB town for fast flyers?**
69. Garland film: *For Me and My _____*

72. It separates Mar. and May
73. *The Divine Comedy* poet
74. Physics particle
76. Combative
80. Window section
81. Pueblo pot
82. Romanced
83. Compass point (abbr.)
84. Surprise
86. Firm
87. Big heads
88. Cloth for cleaning
89. Tar's tie?
90. Plant parts
92. Old PC platform
93. Calgary's tallest skyscraper: The _____
94. Repast
95. Former name for the Maritimes
96. Dodge
98. **BC place for birds that soar?**
100. Miscalculates
103. Spore-bearing cell
105. Estrogen Replacement Therapy (abbr.)
107. Chemical element B
109. Stripper's scarf
110. Naval renegade
115. Get off-line
117. Books, in Baie-Comeau
118. Dandy drawing?
119. Stimulate interest
120. Middle East dignitaries (var.)
121. Confronts
122. Stings an intellectual?

DOWN

1. Pacific _____
2. Abdomen locale
3. **Ontario place for gobblers?**
4. Carte start
5. Breeze
6. Tall perennial

7. Toronto NBAer
8. Oasis song: "D'You Know What _____?"
9. It's larger than a *lac*
10. Those with social connections
11. Tokyo's former name
12. Elvis hit: "Return to _____"
13. Serving platter
14. *King Lear* line: "_____, foh and fum . . ."
15. Foot arch
16. Be a consumer?
17. **Alberta town for trumpeters?**
18. Calgary Stampeders QB Drew
19. Agreements at sea?
25. Restrained a Rottweiler
28. For girls and boys
32. Gesture to a general
34. Not fatty
35. Off kilter
36. Gunpowder holder
38. Put down the law?
40. Soupçon
44. Cape Breton resource
45. Toronto hotel, colloquially: King _____
46. Weapon of mass destruction
47. Kind of code
48. NYC opera mecca, for short
49. Farmer who knows ewe?
50. *To Tell the Truth* panellist Peggy
52. Scornful
53. Antivenins
54. Sight or smell
56. Declares
57. EU member
58. Rabbit's relative
59. Large spoon
61. Increased
62. Playing with a full deck
63. Wile E. Coyote explosive
67. Banff's _____ and Basin National Historic Site

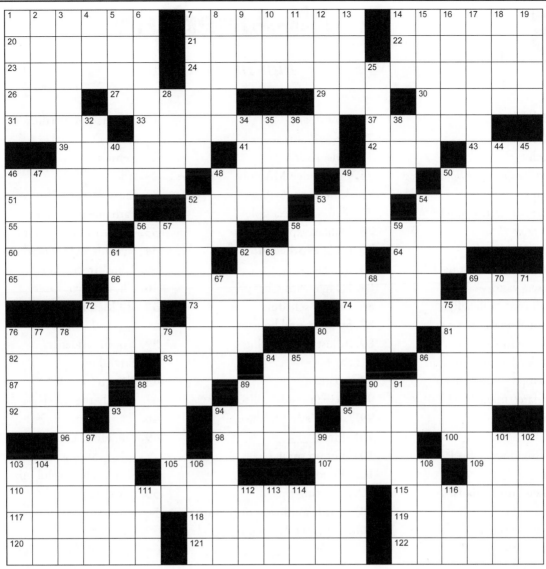

68. + or - item
69. Manitoba town for seabirds?
70. '80s sitcom: *Kate &* _____
71. Guides
72. War god
75. Louse
76. Bowled over
77. Belinda Carlisle, for example
78. Newfoundland enclave for honkers?
79. Marine plant
80. _____ money on
84. Fly in the ointment

85. Booth fee
86. Unhappy
88. TSN commentator Black
89. Hawaii high point: Mauna _____
90. Mark for life
91. Canadian "Eyes of a Stranger" band
93. Street musician
94. Canadian measurement system
95. Cancels a takeoff
97. Filthy _____
99. US film critic Roger

101. Get out of bed
102. Hits the spot
103. _____-bodied
104. Slender
106. *Babylon 5* character Antono
108. Canadian comedian Macdonald
111. Donkey
112. Chapel Hill university (abbr.)
113. Prefix with classical
114. '80s TV drama: *Emerald Point* _____
116. _____ few rounds

Solution on page 208

5 All-American

Fun in the USA

ACROSS

1. Foundation
6. Beseech
11. Canadian *Bye Bye Blues* actress Jenkins
18. Sheila McCarthy movie: _____ *of Singing Birds*
19. Nettle shrub
20. Margin of Mickelson's '04 Masters victory
21. 1,760 yards, officially
23. National anthem
24. Japanese robes
25. Actor's advocate, for short
26. Desktop option: Screen _____
27. Standard time (abbr.)
28. Vicinity
30. Lose
33. '81 Rosanne Cash #1: "Seven Year _____"
37. **Massachusetts dads?**
40. Mine yield
41. Bar at the beach?
43. Female lobster
44. Cyst liquid
45. Volcano in Sicily
46. Golden wine
49. Encountered
50. Ponies up, in poker
51. Horace treatise: _____ *Poetica*
52. Infant's word
53. Shania Twain hit: "Whose Bed Have Your Boots _____ Under?"
55. Bodily joint
56. Clever remark: Bon _____
57. **Pennsylvania ESP?**
60. College cheer, say
63. Aussie gemstone export
65. "If it _____ broke . . ."
66. Murmur
67. Play for a sap
68. Stick with the blame?

70. Play a part
71. Great Plains state
73. Swiss river
74. Cambridge MA univ.
75. *Maude* star Arthur
77. Shares, for example
78. Halifax explosion ship
79. **Ohio expression?**
83. Sunday seats
84. Haggle with Cheney?
86. Behind schedule
87. Stereo sound booster
89. Adjusts text spacing
91. Satchel
92. Accidents
97. Pacific islands, collectively
99. Not pleasing to the eye
101. Hard-_____
102. Group speak
103. Bouquet
104. Relaxing rub
105. Town southwest of Brampton
106. Margaret Atwood book: *The Edible _____*

DOWN

1. Enjoy the glory
2. Against
3. Coal site
4. That _____ say
5. Smarted
6. Magician's exclamation
7. Unlawful exit
8. Kuwait, for example
9. Jet wing component
10. Become more intense
11. Outback animals, colloquially
12. Sets up troops' tents
13. MTV cartoon series: _____ *and Butt-head*
14. Labourers of old
15. **North Carolina dessert?**
16. Northern catch: Arctic _____

17. Alberta public education union (abbr.)
22. Lenin's _____
29. Add
31. He composed "Rule, Britannia!"
32. Parliamentary yeses
33. Tea growing region in India
34. "Cuchi-cuchi" entertainer
35. **Texas firecrackers?**
36. Chow down
38. '89 Meryl Streep film: _____-*Devil*
39. Not in residence
42. Errand boy
45. U-turn from WSW
47. Muddy the waters
48. _____-partisan
49. Canadian retailer: M&M _____ Shops
50. Sheep/rabbit wool mix
53. UK citizen
54. Dusk, in poetry
55. Door opener
58. Three-syllable metrical foot
59. Winter coat?
61. Off-centre
62. Warms up
64. 19th-C. scribe Edgar Allan
68. Settled one's debts
69. Neil Diamond hit: "_____ Said"
70. Garlic, in Gatineau
71. Edinburgh "no"
72. Egyptian snake
74. '69 Joni Mitchell song: "Chelsea _____"
75. Plant related
76. Chic
79. Abdominal bulge
80. _____ rasa
81. Plum type
82. Leave off
85. English Romantic poet John

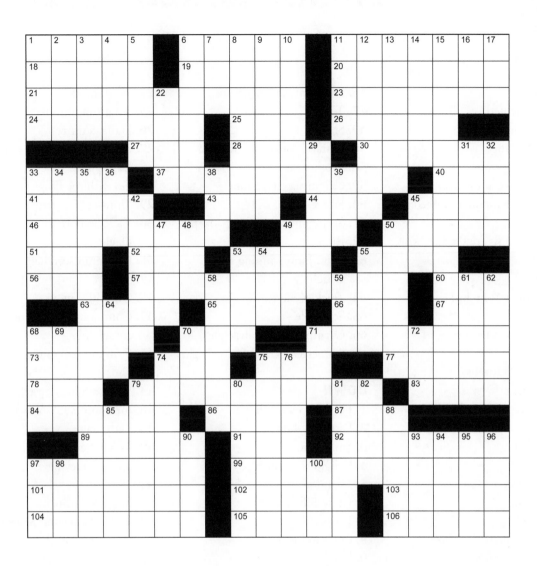

88. "Poppycock!"
90. Wise old man, say
93. Terry Fox, to many
94. Molecule component

95. Arizona Natives
96. MRI, for example
97. 19th-C. German physicist Georg

98. It employs operatives (abbr.)
100. Bigheadedness

Solution on page 209

6 Canada Cornucopia 2

ACROSS

1. Supplemented
6. Lost a lead, say
10. Small change?
14. Glittering stone
15. Distinctive ambiance
16. Cookie that's often dipped in milk
17. Canadian figure skating "king" Stojko
18. VIA _____
19. '74 Guess Who hit: "Star _____"
20. Carp ON museum
23. Rages
24. Baghdad citizens
28. Decadent
31. '72 Edward Bear hit: "Last _____"
33. G8 mbr.
34. Rubes
35. Ladder steps
36. Screw up
37. Smooch
38. Edible aquatic delicacy
39. Emerge victorious
40. Table scrap
41. Poker pot
43. Rattan furniture repairer
44. American Native
45. "500" race won by Jacques Villeneuve in '95
46. Ship's forward structure
47. Tossed
49. Stare at
50. Ontario tourist attraction
56. Mother deer
59. California city: Santa _____
60. Freeze
61. Springhill-born singer Murray
62. Ruin
63. 1982 Juno-winning singer Ulrich
64. Track event
65. Squabble
66. Olympic silver bobsleigh winner Upperton from Calgary

DOWN

1. Long in the tooth
2. Pastrami shop
3. Small bird
4. Religious teachers, say
5. Abandons in the Arabian?
6. Underhill's arrows?
7. Poi party
8. Ontario town
9. Strolling
10. Snake that strikes
11. MLB pitcher's stat
12. Federal regulator headquartered in Calgary (abbr.)
13. Little poodle's plaything?
21. Maiden name indicator
22. Work units
25. Kingston university
26. Haifa country
27. French existentialist author Jean-Paul
28. Go with the flow?
29. Third-_____-fifth
30. Victoria-born producing icon David
31. Like a birdseed ball
32. Sole
35. On CPP, say
39. Common chiropractic complaint
41. Fruit or bird, in New Zealand
42. Guts
43. What a rancher might reel in?
46. It monitors US Airways (abbr.)
48. Early stage
49. Saskatchewan Meech Lake-era premier Devine
51. Slime
52. Largest continent
53. *Boston Public* star Sharon
54. Persuade a pike?
55. Michael J. Fox sitcom: _____ *City*
56. Brilliant or Mica, in BC
57. '74 hit by 61-A: "Just _____ Look"
58. Compass heading (abbr.)

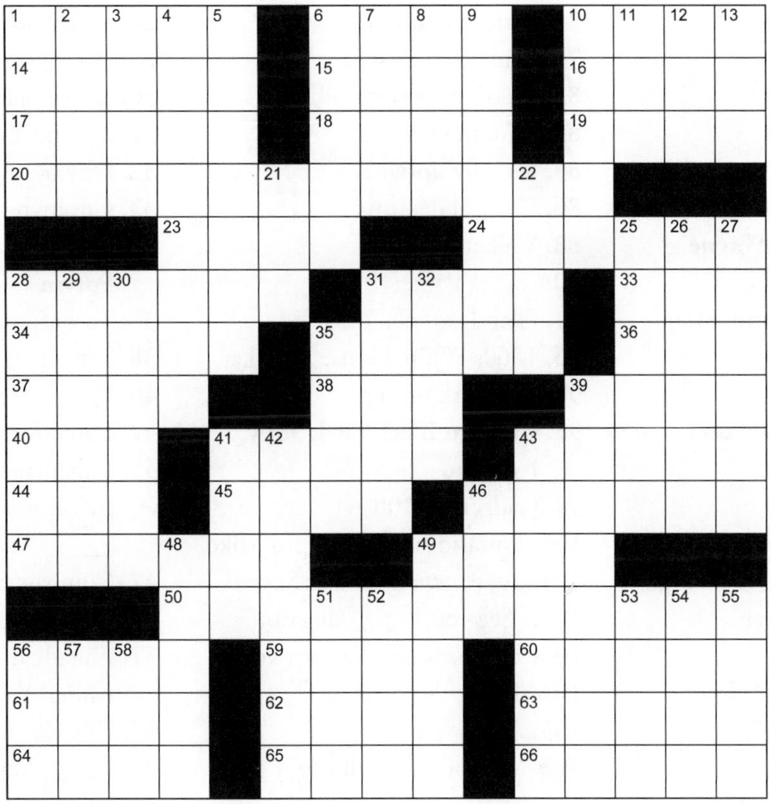

Solution on page 209

By the Numbers

Famous players, famous jerseys

ACROSS

1. Stonecrop, say
6. Fruit type
10. "Sure …"
14. French possessive
17. Get _____ out of
18. Desert-like
19. Type of bonding
20. Genre
21. Edmonton Oiler Wayne Gretzky
23. Montréal-based band: Simple _____
24. Noon, to Nero
25. Cleaned one's hands after an oil change?
26. Rumple
27. School fundraising grps.
28. Get into the _____ of things
29. Long-winded speech
31. Bark a.k.a.
35. '89 Cerrone song: "Never _____ Day Go By"
36. Remember the good old days
39. Music star from Napanee Lavigne
41. Latin dance
43. Giving in
44. Started a tennis game
46. Tilted
49. Guys and gals
50. Checks for size in a fitting room
52. Wood Buffalo National Park herd
54. Invaders in *Mars Attacks!*, for short
55. Toronto Maple Leaf Darryl Sittler
59. On behalf of
62. Frasier's sibling, on TV
63. Building
65. Walking sticks
70. Former Calif. NFL club
73. Wall light type
74. Duet parts
76. Plant tissue
78. African animals
79. Wine connoisseur
82. Wood preserving oil
84. Seldom seen
85. Morally upright
86. Corneal deposit
88. William's missus
90. _____ Parker
91. Glands in men only
96. 1860s White House moniker
97. Pitchfork prong
98. Chicago Blackhawk Tony Esposito
99. Gadget for 100-A
100. Ontario-born PGA pro Mike
101. *Say Anything …* star Skye
102. "See you _____ alligator"
103. *Ed's Up!* Canadian network
104. Tolkien soldiers
105. Assns.
106. Without smooth edges

DOWN

1. Beach grains
2. 18th-C. Iroquois enemy
3. "_____-Dong! The Witch Is Dead"
4. Cybercafé patron
5. Doles out punishment, say
6. Johnny-jump-ups
7. Blue Monopoly avenue
8. Crossword, perhaps?
9. African language group
10. Adulterated
11. Fir native to Canada
12. Rubber band
13. Montréal Canadien Guy Lafleur
14. Pittsburgh Penguin Mario Lemieux
15. Oscar-winning director Kazan
16. Crazy Canucks' equipment
22. Jolly boat
26. *SCTV* hoser Rick
27. _____ *and Prejudice*
30. Single bills, in Baltimore
31. Squander
32. Obvious
33. Gin ingredient
34. New York Islander Denis Potvin
37. Toronto fair since 1879 (abbr.)
38. Some Lat. abbrs.
40. "_____ we forget"
42. Cared for kids
45. Canadian Smart's '45 book: *By Grand Central Station I Sat _____ and Wept*
47. Compass point (abbr.)
48. Bird of peace
51. Canadian 2011 Grammy winner Young
53. '90s Canadian/German cartoon: _____ *Newt*
56. Nunavut Library Association (abbr.)
57. In few words
58. 1982 Genie acting award winner Mancuso
59. 2002 Nelly Furtado single: "Trynna _____ Way"
60. Take place
61. Oscar-winning actress Witherspoon
64. Boston Bruin Bobby Orr
65. AB Jack Singer Concert Hall grp.
66. "_____ we there yet?"
67. Colorado Avalanche Joe Sakic
68. Overact
69. Frosh, next year
71. Literary figure of speech
72. Playing legato, say

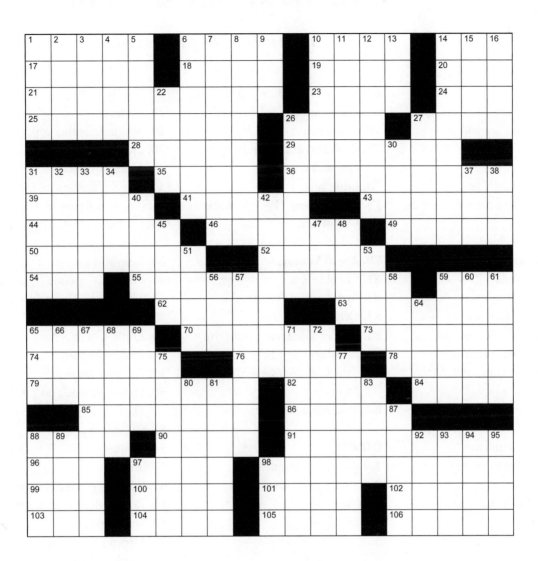

75. More glossy
77. Songs after curtain calls
80. Like Marilyn or James
81. Eye surgeons' instruments
83. Burst of wind

87. Canadian decor publication:
_____ *at Home*
88. *The Green Hornet* role
89. Biblical sibling of Seth
92. Miles away
93. Michael Jackson sibling

94. He preceded McGuinty in
Ontario
95. See 18-A
97. **Buffalo Sabre Tim Horton**
98. Male relative in Madrid

8 Give Yourself a Hand

. . . if you like to play cards

ACROSS

1. Hungarian horseman
7. Looks out for oneself, say
12. Mrs. Sinatra #2
15. Complete
16. Mrs. Jean Chrétien
17. Ex-premier of New Brunswick Bernard
19. **King of hockey?**
20. Deep shade
22. Works with lace
23. Fishing aid
25. *My Little Chickadee* star W.C.
26. '70s CTV show: *Stars on _____*
27. Petro-Canada product
28. Directional sense
31. Douglas fir, say
32. Serious point (var.)?
36. Ian _____ Sylvia
37. Renter's document
38. Quatrain rhyme scheme
41. Lean to?
44. Canadian Union of Students (abbr.)
45. *South Pacific* song: "Bali _____"
47. Way back when
48. **Jack of clubs?**
50. **Queen of Mean?**
52. Spanish soccer chant
53. Superlative suffix
54. See 23-A
55. Punted?
56. Mental acuity
58. Bits of Greek?
60. US rock band: _____ Speedwagon
61. Inability to get results
67. Read rapidly
68. Wray of *King Kong*

69. Contraction often heard at Christmas
70. Crash pad
71. Canadian entertainers: _____, Lois and Bram
73. Little lady?
74. Sinatra song: "I _____ Kick Out of You"
75. Leader of the pack
79. **Ace of Ventura?**
81. Islamic royal
82. Arctic marine mammal
83. Orbit's high point
84. Former Canadian politicians Broadbent and Schreyer
85. "The Greatest Canadian" Douglas
86. Transmit again

DOWN

1. Like busy schedules
2. Remove one's sneakers
3. New York's _____ Island
4. Biblical wrongs
5. _____ de Triomphe
6. Foxy name?
7. Truth
8. "Xanadu" rock grp.
9. Bit of licorice?
10. Kind of "fingerprint"
11. _____-cleaning oven
12. Birth province of 68-A
13. Court sport
14. "He's in for _____ awakening"
18. From, in Frontenac
21. Children's rhythm: Ta ta _____ ta
24. Edmonton Symphony Orchestra (abbr.)

27. Kindly
28. Matures
29. Michael Collins' grp.
30. Prepared potatoes
33. Military vehicle
34. Winter illnesses
35. _____ scaloppine
39. US Pulitzer-winning writer James
40. Juno-winning guitarist Liona
41. Old CTV sitcom: _____ *Job*
42. 1953 Leslie Caron film
43. Vinegar ingredient
44. Limit
46. Pushes forward
49. "In your dreams!"
50. Howie Mandel, on *Deal or No Deal*
51. Anon
54. Risqué
57. Trappers
59. Black or green beverage
60. Rocky Mountaineer component
62. Seth's first son
63. Hagen of the stage
64. Come to light
65. Shiny fabric
66. Hung around
67. Embarrassment
71. Place to sweat it out?
72. Salamander
73. CFL trophy: _____ Cup
74. NL national park: _____ Morne
76. However, for short
77. Head covering in the Highlands
78. North Dakota arboreal emblem
80. Bananas consumer

Canada Cornucopia 3

ACROSS

1. _____ A Sketch
5. Put up
10. 1977 hockey comedy: _____ *Shot*
14. Waiter's handout
15. Take exception to
16. Perfume resin
17. British hot springs city
18. Suggest
19. Float in the water?
20. God with a bow
21. Venetian blind strings
22. Way off
23. Uncooked
24. Toronto's Degrassi, for example
25. Countertop component
26. Used a besom
28. Yellowknife street: Ragged _____ Road
29. Alberta national park
30. Israel's Sharon
32. *Battle of the Blades* star Jamie
34. *Enola* _____
35. Clump
37. CBC Radio listening: *The Vinyl* _____
39. Long-running TVOntario show: *Polka* _____ *Door*
42. Appear menacingly ahead
44. Peggys in NS, et al.
47. Not vacant, like a lav
49. '60s war country, for short
51. Flinch, say
53. _____ precedent
54. Block and tackle component
56. Ex-Toronto Maple Leaf Domi with the most penalty minutes
57. Age (var.)
58. African river or country
59. Chick's utterance
60. Polar explorer Richard
61. Citizen of Muscat
62. Ex-federal justice minister McLellan
63. Salacious look
64. Got carried with the current
65. Reddish purple
66. Scandinavian mythology source
67. Lab work, say
68. *Planet of the* _____

DOWN

1. Fire remnants
2. New Zealand group
3. Top Toronto tourist attraction?
4. Interjections of inquiry
5. Order of the court?
6. Suckerfish
7. Victoria harbour hotel
8. Dead-end rue?
9. Lovers' rendezvous
10. Baked bread dish
11. Lazing about
12. Cattle fodder
13. Decay
24. Canadian cheese company: Tre _____
27. Old CTV show: *The* _____ *and Whistle*
29. Earlier
31. Toilet, in Tottenham
33. Fond-du-_____ SK
36. Geniality, at the Québec Winter Carnival?
38. 1973 Constance Beresford-Howe offering: *The Book of* _____
39. Put out of commission
40. Like a Cyclops
41. Gave academic assistance
43. Dionysus' female followers
45. Destroyed, colloquially
46. Ontario _____ Centre
48. Nepean-born *Grey's Anatomy* star Oh
50. Attractive piece of metal?
52. Conical tents (var.)
54. 1948 Canadian golden Olympian Barbara Ann
55. Annuls
59. Perry Como song: "_____ Loves Mambo"

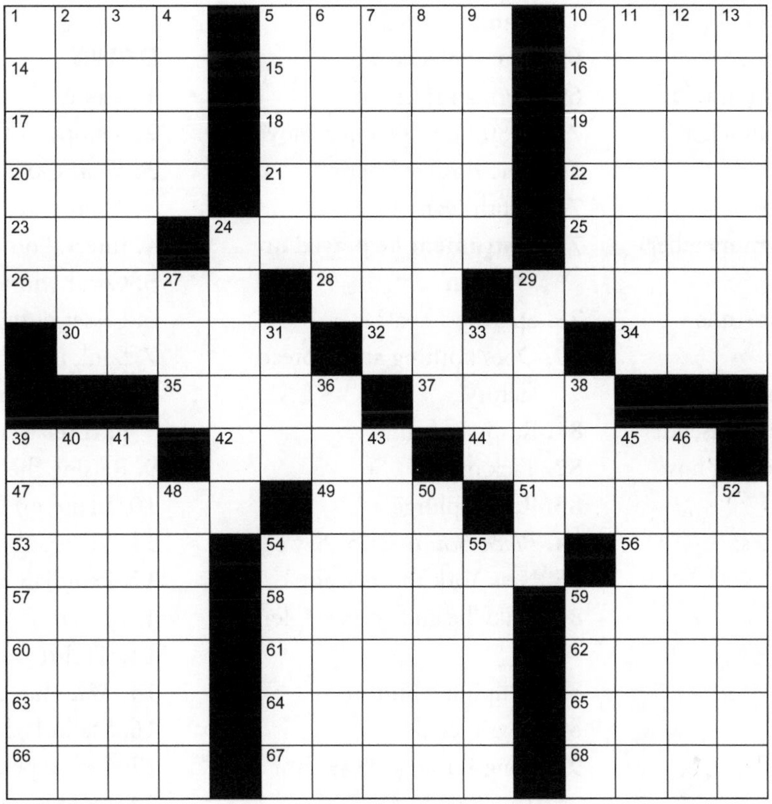

Solution on page 210

10 His Own Way to Rock

A Burton Cummings bio

ACROSS

1. Spring mo.
4. Eliza Doolittle's abode?
7. Org. for US lawyers
10. Plan detail, for short
14. '84 Bruce Cockburn hit: "If _____ a Rocket Launcher"
18. Bovine call
19. Troglodyte
21. Toronto sports team member, for short
22. Ending for glass or stone
23. Marsh
24. Cut more than once?
25. American pioneer's godsend?
26. *Project Runway Canada* host
27. Glacier slides
29. Incorrigible cobblers?
31. With poise
33. Flourishes
34. Grin
35. Capo's chick
36. Alumna bio word
37. Meat cut
38. Sensory organ
42. Not polite
45. Hurled
46. Touched
47. Drink garnish
48. French military boat
50. Took top spot
51. de Gaulle phrase: "_____ le Québec libre"
52. Glossy fabric
53. Makes a case for
55. **Canadian award he won for "You Saved My Soul"**
56. International accord signed by Canada in 2002
57. Acid neutralizers
58. Swiss capital
59. Myanmar money
60. "_____ thou slain the Jabberwock?"
61. **Band for which he was front man**
65. Sound of a crowd
69. German river
71. 1980 Dom DeLuise movie
72. Blue-flowered herb
74. Relish (var.)
77. **Instrument he played on "Undun"**
78. Sparrows' spas?
80. Does nothing at the bread factory?
81. Raspy breath
82. Tack on
83. Retail splurge
84. *Black Beauty* scribe Sewell
85. New York sports team
86. Oakville golf course: Glen _____
88. Cellphone button
89. Bovril, et al.
91. Long-serving US senator Thurmond
92. Brief life story?
94. Rat who rats?
95. Music type: Heavy _____
96. Some mealtimes
100. Lizard with a crest
103. Live's partner
104. Overabundance of food?
105. Rice-A-_____
106. 18th-C. Spanish painter
108. Declare, from the bench?
110. '50s White House resident, for short
111. BC broadcaster Rafe
112. Black, poetically
113. Messenger on a bike
114. Spat, in Shropshire
115. Some keyboard keys
116. Biblical no-nos
117. Dynamite AC/DC song?
118. Want _____
119. Navy member (abbr.)

DOWN

1. Scope
2. Snoopy or Odie, say
3. *Royal Canadian Air Farce* star Abbott
4. Interval on the ivories
5. Oscar winner Matlin
6. Lesser of two _____
7. Soul, in Sainte-Foy
8. **His long-time songwriting partner Randy**
9. Raising the stakes
10. Island off Nova Scotia
11. Mavens
12. Freudian milieu
13. Invent
14. **'78 hit from *Dream of a Child***
15. *Mad Men* star Jon
16. Sea in Uzbekistan
17. Refuse permission
20. Double-curved letter
28. **Top-ten 1980 song**
30. Tundra beast
32. Bitter or bass quaff
34. Excommunicates, say
35. Free-for-all
37. Tart plum
38. Rave or pan
39. Yugoslavian president (1953–80)
40. Skip over
41. Loverboy lead singer Mike
42. Indian royal family member (var.)
43. Soft palate part
44. Circular plates
45. Rinse with Listerine, say
46. Helsinki residents

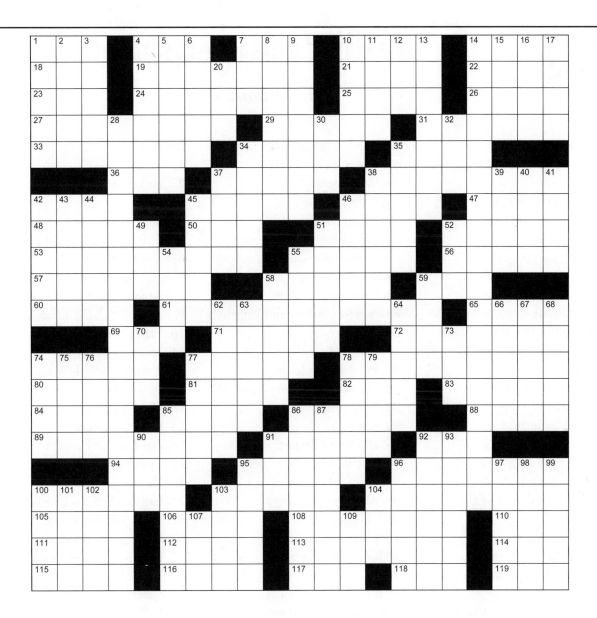

49. Western Canada natural resource

51. Left-hand page

52. Heavens above?

54. Throes

55. Some Canadian birds

58. Picture _____ AB

59. Watering hole at the farm

62. Some musical keys

63. Ancient Europeans

64. *Tess of the d'Urbervilles* scribe Thomas

66. Improper

67. White with fear

68. Destroyed, in Dulwich

70. Woman with a ring

73. *60 Minutes* network

74. Thick piece

75. First-class

76. Wind measurement device

77. Weird one

78. City northeast of Tehran

79. Word in a footnote

85. Households, in Honfleur

86. Magnetize?

87. MB university that gave him an honourary degree

90. Gabrielle Roy novel: *The _____ Flute*

91. NL band: Great Big _____

92. Took in water, nautically

93. Lollygaggers

95. Wherewithal

96. Fourth Estate

97. Blazing

98. Canadian territory

99. Oodles

100. _____ *La Douce*

101. Objective of hockey?

102. Military group

103. William _____ Mackenzie King

104. _____ oak (var.)

107. *Star Wars* character: _____-Wan Kenobi

109. What some chins do

11 Willie's Shoemaker

Awl about shoes

ACROSS

1. _____ Spring Island BC
5. Italian auto
9. Staunchly maintain
13. Aria singer's milieu
18. Assortment
19. _____ in the bucket
21. Remove, for short
22. Retail revenue source
23. Watercraft
24. Canadian boreal forest
25. Composer of 95-D Carl
26. Garbage
27. Desert description
28. Rock band from 86-A: _____ of a Deadman
30. **His seasonal plant?**
32. Some dressings
34. Golfer's par putt, often
36. Get more *Canadian Geographic*
37. NAFTA partner
40. Canadian Automobile Association's Australian counterpart (abbr.)
41. Held back info, say
42. Hope or Dover, in Ontario
43. **His sandwich bread?**
46. Mare's mouthpiece
47. Chart topper
50. Pharaoh's beetle
51. Feet "piggies"
52. Tried to get elected
53. Belleville-born NHLer Matt
55. New York state canal
56. "Do _____ others . . ."
58. Author's achievement
60. Previous perfect score, in gymnastics
61. Jim Carrey film: _____ *Ventura: Pet Detective*
62. Lift?
65. Southern Alberta river
66. Jabs at

68. Former Calgary MP Hanger
69. Room, in Rimouski
71. Wave the flag?
74. Trojan War hero
77. Vintage auto
78. Philadelphia org. featured on *Parking Wars*
81. Going back in
83. Criminal, for short
85. Actresses Arthur and Benaderet
86. BC place
87. Early hour
88. Proofreader's instruction
90. Former federal Tory Stanfield
92. Web browser entry
93. Revolver, colloquially
94. **His fruity dessert?**
96. Middle East title
98. Fencer's lunges?
99. Alternative to a blvd.
100. Shogun's capital
101. Blood protein
103. Avalon Peninsula city: Mount _____
104. Hunts (with "on")
106. **His best-loved movie?**
108. Humourless
110. Jasper National _____
114. Ontario motto start: "_____ she began . . ."
115. Actress Dunaway
117. Architectural column style
118. Nerve cell thread
119. Play it broadly
120. Flin _____ MB
121. Prima _____
122. '84 Juno single of the year: "_____ Up"
123. Portfolio item
124. Way too complacent
125. Belfry sound
126. Latin 101 verb

DOWN

1. Blubbers
2. Vera's salve?
3. Fibber
4. Native art, say
5. **His favourite silent film actor?**
6. Boise resident
7. Sign after Pisces
8. Fast food order words
9. *Much _____ About Nothing*
10. Rats and roaches
11. Sprightly, perhaps?
12. Arena whistler-blowers
13. Stable worker
14. Ma or pa
15. Bring good cheer
16. Plant again
17. Tennis great Arthur
20. Share in a meal
29. Eastwood's *Rawhide* role
31. Fox or turkey follower
33. Local _____ network
35. Kraków country (abbr.)
37. Underdog's victory
38. Sweetener, in 67-D
39. Full speed ahead, to the captain
41. Skedaddle
42. Pub purchase
44. Opposite of post-
45. Hairy *Addams Family* character
46. Shearwater and Suffield, for example
47. Thespians Celeste or Ian
48. Furniture company since '43
49. Bird that makes a right?
52. Gun an engine
53. Juno winner Ofra Harnoy plays this
54. _____ Worlde
57. Born as (Fr.)
58. Alpha follower
59. **His preferred fish dish?**
61. Major artery

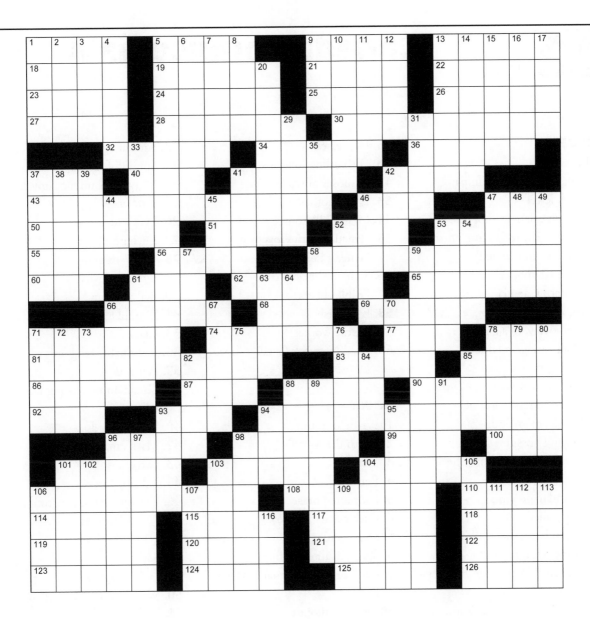

63. Pend
64. Wrath
66. Third down CFL option
67. _____-Eustache QC
70. Airport level (abbr.)
71. Islamabad language
72. Poet's adverb
73. In one _____ swoop
75. Compass point (abbr.)
76. Glasses, for short
78. Shakespeare contemporary George
79. Skinned spuds
80. Houston MLB player

82. Sound of the surf
84. Kenya neighbour (abbr.)
85. Consumer protection org.
88. Cooks in a hot pan
89. *National Enquirer*, for example
91. Do as directed
93. "I Just Wanna Stop" Montrealer Vanelli
94. Class-conscious grp.?
95. _____ *Burana*
96. CBC show since '75: *The Fifth* _____
97. Cereal grain
98. "Bye-bye"

101. Weaving machines
102. Kids' toys
103. Hymn
104. Tubular pasta
105. Fifth wheel?
106. Pooches' pest
107. Gangster's euphemism for "murders"
109. Snowbird's manouevre
111. Graph line
112. *As For Me and My House* scribe Sinclair
113. Leg joint that bends
116. An official language (abbr.)

12 Canada Cornucopia 4

ACROSS

1. Jiffies
5. Canadian mining company
9. Greek letter
14. Jewish calendar month
15. Sitcom Jethro Bodine portrayer
16. Tune from *Carousel*: "_____ Nice Clambake"
17. Eastern Canada
19. *SCTV* star Harold
20. Copiously, to a gardener?
21. Data storage medium
22. _____-in-a-bag
23. QC-born *Sabrina the Teenage Witch* actress Caroline
24. Jerusalem greeting
28. Playing possum, say
32. Céline Dion smash: "The _____ of Love"
33. Birthday presents
34. Hightailed it
35. Beach barbecue, in Waikiki
36. Some restaurants
37. Montréal-born singer/musician Aldo
38. "_____ me no questions . . ."
39. Precept
40. Tendon
41. Casual attire item
43. Ancient oracles
44. Calgary park: _____ Hill
45. Depressed
46. Forbidding folklorist?
48. Disposes of stocks, say
53. Hens' homes
54. Manzanilla source
55. Canada's 25th Governor General LeBlanc
56. State of shock
57. Edible tubers
58. Embellish
59. Textile worker
60. Food Network Canada show: *Dinner Party _____*

DOWN

1. Pre-final round
2. Joy to the world?
3. Mutts
4. Berth place?
5. Footnote phrase
6. Cash classic: "A Boy _____ Sue"
7. So-so grades
8. Surgical suites (abbr.)
9. Old Toronto landmark: Maple Leaf _____
10. Biblical mount
11. Exec's note
12. Injure
13. Canadians Waxman and Purdy
18. Calfskin drum
21. Poker markers
23. Kit out again
24. Sound of falling, in cartoons
25. Margaret Laurence novel: *A Bird in the _____*
26. Eyes wide open
27. Bucharest buck
28. _____ mignon
29. Literary device
30. Belly button
31. Bites like a beaver
33. Class
36. Reasonable religion?
37. Pen end
39. Canadian newspaper family name
40. Edge towards
42. Mark's man?
43. Large tray
45. Take by force
46. Canadian country group: The _____ Brothers
47. NFL QB Tony
48. Kill
49. Lade away?
50. West Coast water tour sight
51. Dread
52. Small-screen *Daniel Boone* star Parker
53. Canadian "taxman" (abbr.)
54. Kooky

13 Into the Water

Canadian peninsulas

ACROSS

1. Monastery manager
6. *Coup d'_____*
10. Canadian music industry magazine (1964–2000)
13. Confront one's fears
17. Canadian specialty channel
18. _____ Scotia
19. Phoenix resident, say
21. Sovereign
22. Small amount
23. Carbon _____
24. Genus of a maple
25. Provincial and territorial office name: _____ Statistics
26. Curling rock
27. Netting
28. Tied the score
30. Before, to the Bard
31. CRTC counterpart, in the US
34. Green land?
36. Resistance units, in physics
38. Place to dock
39. **Hudson Bay peninsula**
42. Sheep's skin disorder
45. Wee
46. Molson and Labatt
47. South American monkey
48. **Sunshine Coast peninsula**
51. 1893 J.D. Edgar poem: "This Canada of _____"
52. Caulk again
54. Pilgrimage place, in France
56. RBC foyer machine
57. Scolding
59. US gov. property org.
60. Neptune's spear
62. Saskatchewan CFL fans: Rider _____
63. Cobra's shape
64. **Gulf of St. Lawrence peninsula**
66. Landlord's due

67. San Antonio tourist attraction
68. "Sweet Dreams" singer Patsy
69. Reproductive organ
71. **Newfoundland peninsula**
72. Ransom's mobile?
73. Queue
75. Historical periods
76. "See ya!"
77. Exclude
78. Prince _____ BC
82. Long story
86. Sew with big stitches
88. States with conviction
89. Palindromic title for a lady
90. 2010 Olympics snowboarding gold medallist Jasey-Jay
93. Scrabble rack item
94. Foot bones
95. Prisoner's release document
96. 1958 film: *The Defiant _____*
97. Quits
98. First name in motorcycle feats
99. French pronoun
100. Takes home fish?
101. *Seinfeld* character: Elaine _____

DOWN

1. The "A" in James A. Garfield
2. **Georgian Bay peninsula**
3. Makes hay?
4. Eavesdrops
5. CN Tower city (abbr.)
6. Salad leaf
7. Rich dessert
8. For the birds?
9. Furniture piece
10. Ewes' mates
11. For the time being (Lat.)
12. Those not of legal age
13. **Baffin Island peninsula**
14. DiFranco's pet bird?
15. Blackguard

16. Toronto-to-Ottawa direction (abbr.)
20. Region
25. Lynn or Wang
29. Labrador retriever
31. CFL score
32. Panama coin
33. 1999 Terri Clark hit: "Everytime I _____"
35. ER drips
37. The Pointer Sisters song: "_____ So Shy"
38. Equal of an aristocrat?
39. WWII vessel
40. Without bias
41. Strep slayer?
42. Whisky brewed in Collingwood: Canadian _____
43. Stayed home for supper
44. **Peninsula near the US border**
45. Hoodlum
47. Seed shell
49. Famed US federal agent Ness
50. *Grease* actress Didi
52. Sari-wearing royal
53. Not now
55. Hairdresser's milieu
57. Yield
58. Long-running Hamilton TV show: _____ *Talent Time*
61. Ottawa-born NHLer Boyle, et al.
63. School acquaintance
65. Word of refusal, in Repentigny
67. Gardner of *Mogambo*
68. Corn serving
70. Relax, colloquially
71. Son of Hera
73. Rodeo ropes
74. Chant
75. Exit
77. Canadian pairs skater Underhill

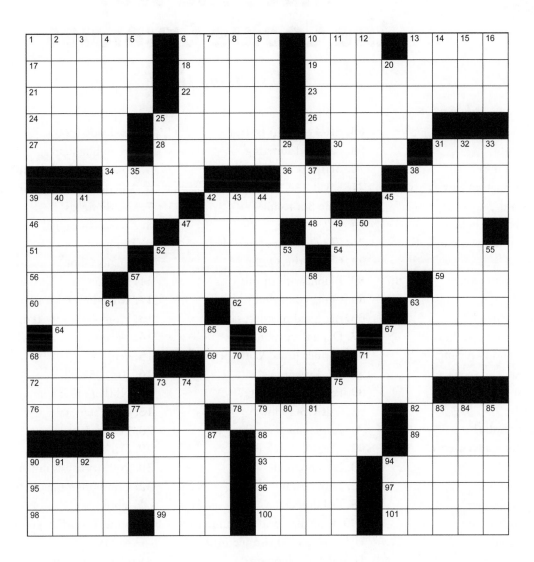

79. Long-time Canadian retail name
80. Sheep related
81. Find a new tenant
83. Baseball great Hank

84. **Peninsula opposite 64-A**
85. Out of whack
86. **Southampton Island peninsula**
87. *All's Well That _____ Well*

90. *Fish* star Vigoda
91. Internet browsing helper: _____ bar
92. Casino cube
94. Cdn. accident investigation org.

14 That's the Way the Cookie Crumbles

It's rhyme time!

ACROSS

1. Tennis shot
6. Rustic lodgings
11. Canadian "Tom Sawyer" trio
15. Bed board
19. WWI French fighter
20. One of nine mythological Muses
21. '85 Madonna song: "_____ the Groove"
22. Hourly stipend
23. Latin year
24. Simcoe and Nipissing, in Ontario
25. Goulash, say
26. Pinnacle
27. Clumsy hobo?
29. Andersen's adventurer?
31. Defeat on the field
32. Horse's pace
33. Coughs up, say
34. Check out a crime?
38. Holiday, say
40. Toledo's state
42. Old Prudential slogan: "_____ the Rock"
44. See 32-A
45. Winnipeg radio station: _____-FM
49. "Myself, also" comparative phrase
50. Pillowcase
51. Throat-clearer's noise
52. Tim Hortons offering
53. Long-time CBC drama: _____ *Legal*
55. Fit _____ fiddle
56. Paint and paper, say
58. Some batteries
60. Parasite eggs
62. Went long, as a meeting

63. Ali–Foreman fracas?
68. Pain and suffering
70. Active person
71. Small insect
72. One-pot recipes
74. BYOB word
76. *The Dark Angel* star Merle
82. Out of this world
83. Bloom with thorns
84. Quiet coop cluck
86. Accepted practice, say
87. Depilatory brand
88. Former Royal Winnipeg Ballet star Evelyn
89. Perfects a marriage?
91. '70s CBC show: _____ *of Kensington*
92. Crazy Canuck Brooker
93. Picture puzzles
94. Drove away
98. Dal dipper
100. Canadian waters mammal
101. Elton's '70 connection?
103. White elephant?
109. Jai _____
110. Granola ingredient
111. Bravery (var.)
112. Nobleman
113. Shoppers Drug _____
114. Golden Rule preposition
115. Not perfectly round
116. Obliterate
117. Public interest announcements (abbr.)
118. Stairway increment
119. Died down
120. Some bridge seats

DOWN

1. Relaxing spots
2. _____-Tremblant QC

3. Hokkaido group
4. Urban blight area
5. Abashed British band?
6. American actress Holm, et al.
7. Speedy steeds
8. Azerbaijan capital
9. Thing
10. Digits (abbr.)
11. Hindu seer
12. Not educated
13. From _____ to stern
14. Nevertheless, old style
15. Fen
16. _____ lazuli
17. NHLer's representative
18. Lone Star State
28. Venues (Lat.)
29. Dance style
30. Psychoanalysis milieu
32. Computing image format (abbr.)
34. Some Canadian grocery store names
35. Hatchling's home
36. Luminary
37. Hidalgo tribe in Mexico
38. English Breakfast, et al.
39. Caesar's schnozz?
41. Big play at the ballpark
43. Pursue a lead
44. Sinatra song: "_____ Boots Are Made for Walkin'"
45. Long-time TV star Burnett
46. "_____ at the office"
47. Head, in Rimouski
48. *The Sopranos* actor Robert
51. Crustacean or arachnid
52. Big bell sound
54. Alberta town known for its corn
57. Epic poem section

59. Penultimate speaker on election night?

61. Samson's suffix?

63. TV personality O'Donnell

64. Like loose diamonds

65. Air about one

66. That is (Lat.)

67. Canadian author Urquhart, et al.

68. Open ____ of worms

69. Forceful storm?

73. Spectacles on a stick

75. Make one's way

77. Honey of a product?

78. Bible brother

79. Landfill scavengers

80. Moulding type

81. Capone's nemesis

85. Pedigreed pups, say

88. Extremely ugly

89. Pro's opposite

90. Lunch or dinner

91. *Survivor: The Australian Outback* contestant Gleason

92. Smidgen

94. Canada Post product

95. Hawaiian dances

96. *Terra Nova* star Jason

97. Parting words?

99. Famed fable writer

100. Clobbered, old style

102. Covet

103. Programming language invented by Albertan Gosling

104. ____ Bator

105. "Nobody doesn't like ____ Lee"

106. *Survivor: Panama* champ Baskauskas

107. Blue Rodeo hit: "____ Together"

108. Chemical suffixes

111. "I do," for example

ACROSS

1. Vancouver exercise centres for women: _____ Fit
5. Grape or tomato, for example
10. Residential abbr.
14. Big book of short stories?
15. Looks at lustfully
16. Hockey player Paul Henderson, in 1972
17. Stir the sediment
18. Fingerprint pattern
19. Once more, to a Scot
20. Exhorted
22. Political system of 37-D
24. Drug enforcement agents, colloquially
26. Canadian moving company: _____-Richardson
27. Slums
29. Dined sumptuously
32. St. Lawrence _____
34. Not wild
35. 1994 Blue Rodeo single: "_____ Timing"
38. Whistler ride
41. Canadian sandwich shop: Mr. _____
42. Sweeping story
44. Term of office
46. Lego line
49. Older relative
53. Firm facts
55. Goa guitars
56. Place for a newel
59. Abate
60. Toques and tams
61. "See you later," in Seville
63. Big BTO hit: "Let It _____"
64. Many
65. Urban dwelling unit
66. With, in Québec City
67. Cautious
68. Canadian concert pianist Kuerti
69. Dry run

DOWN

1. Put up the Xmas lights, say
2. Cheer word (var.)
3. French exile?
4. Chooses
5. Calgary river
6. Ottoman Empire rank (var.)
7. Influence
8. Guaranteeing
9. Not level
10. Long-time Québec premier Jean
11. Yacht races
12. Canadian equestrian star Lamaze
13. Big name in electronics
21. Showers with love (with "on")
23. Accounting pro (abbr.)
25. Enjoy a spa tub
28. Lit the lamp, say
30. Aussie bird
31. Reform Party's first MP Grey
33. Labatt 50 _____
35. Track stake
36. Jungle animal
37. Tyrant
39. Minks and ermines
40. Edmonton roadway: Calgary _____
43. BC Liberal premier Clark
45. _____ your own risk
47. Turkish mountain range
48. New York city
50. Indirect objective noun type
51. Fuddy-duddies
52. Facet
54. NB city: _____ John
56. Canadian telecommunications company
57. Samoan monetary unit
58. Dumb old bird?
62. Edgar Bronfman Sr., to Samuel

Solution on page 211

O Canada Crosswords Book 13   ■   *37*

16 Eponymous Edibles

Foods for thought

ACROSS

1. Poets
6. Undisturbed: In _____
10. Axle
15. "Skedaddle!"
18. Run-of-the-mill
19. Lift
21. Place for placemats
22. Alas, to a German
23. **New Brunswick fish**
26. Doo-wop group: _____ Na Na
27. Knocking sound
28. More wise
29. Mark on Helios?
31. Pornography
33. Supreme Court group
35. Spuds
36. Deplete a maple?
39. Bad places to be during earthquakes
42. Fifteen and 132 (abbr.)
43. Make less dense
45. Chic, in the '60s
46. Accounting statement line
50. Perfect
51. Canadian ballet star Harrington
52. Ignobly
55. Northern Canada Natives
56. SW Nova Scotia community
57. Dessert menu words
59. Settle a dispute
61. Excessive emotion
63. Plutarch's plaza
65. Archie or Edith, on TV
66. **Alberta cocktail**
69. Bicycle built for two
73. *Ghostbusters* goo
74. Mythological labyrinth builder
79. Funereal vehicles
81. Burdensome
83. *South Pacific* song: "There Is Nothing Like _____"
84. Top-notch number?

85. *Sense and Sensibility* scribe Jane
87. Appear on stage
88. *Lost* actress Raymonde
89. Considering that, old style
91. 22nd Greek letter
92. Sea east of Greece
93. Ex-dictator Amin
94. Basset's candies?
99. Edmonton CFLer, for short
100. *Plus ça change, plus c'est _____ chose*
103. '71 Stampeders song: "Sweet City _____"
104. '07 Diana Krall cover: "You _____ My Head"
106. Mineral source
108. Boondocks
110. Birch bark dwellings
115. Scientist's milieu
116. **Prairie dessert**
119. Aspirin, for short
120. Guilty _____
121. Slow-moving gastropod
122. Grand River gorge in Ontario
123. Calgary Health Region (abbr.)
124. Appears like
125. Baking ingredients
126. Passover meal

DOWN

1. BC-born *Perry Mason* portrayer Raymond
2. In the Red?
3. Neil Young and Crazy Horse album: _____ *Never Sleeps*
4. Numbers to crunch, say
5. Opens an envelope
6. Grew quickly
7. Promissory note (abbr.)
8. Facial twitches
9. Like a horseshoe
10. Rude looker

11. '50s Canadian labour union leader Banks
12. Money machines (abbr.)
13. Ignore at a convention?
14. '70s National Ballet of Canada star Veronica
15. **Québec fry-up**
16. Immortals' golden fluid, in mythology
17. 1974 film: _____ *Entertainment!*
20. Canadian indie duo: _____ and Sara
24. High on hunting? (var.)
25. Faxed, say
30. What the locum did
32. Waiting periods
34. _____-*majesté*
36. With a heavy heart
37. Regions
38. Rush drummer/lyricist Neil
40. Hip bone
41. River name in Austria and Germany
43. Canada's "Man of a Thousand Voices" Little
44. Polar attire?
47. '89 Canadian film: _____ *Blues*
48. _____ *meridiem*
49. Look of lust
51. Train track
52. Marsh monsters? (var.)
53. One who admires
54. Lacking moisture
58. United States _____ Corps
60. Estimated time of delivery
62. French baroque composer Jean-Philippe
64. Citing references
67. Many parking stalls?
68. Sunrise direction
69. Spicy cuisine type

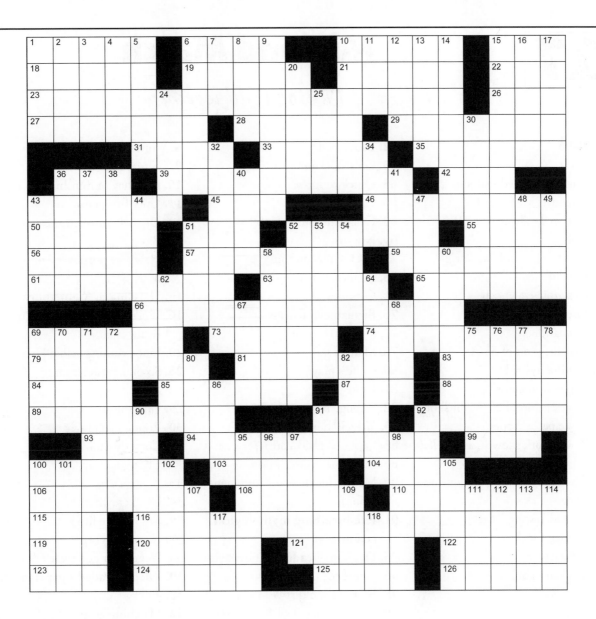

70. Geological time measurement (var.)
71. **BC treat**
72. German porcelain
75. "Haste makes waste," e.g.
76. Road divisions
77. Inuit boat
78. Genie- and Emmy-nominated Ontarian McCann
80. 1999 Coldplay song: "_____ a Rush"
82. Island of Obama's birth

86. '70s CTV fare: *The Alan Hamel* _____
90. Champagne/orange juice drinks
91. Overlook an offence
92. Up and about
95. Atkinson's shrubs?
96. Discharge
97. Angels' circlets
98. Furniture pegs
100. Lighter shade of purple
101. _____ of bad luck
102. Rub out

105. Grimm beasts
107. Existing: In _____
109. Minor setback
111. *ER* star Noah
112. Like two peas in _____
113. Bog down
114. Lightly burn
117. 1993 prime minister Campbell
118. _____ Hill NS

17 Mix and Match

Putting it all together

ACROSS

1. Spill it
5. Canadian canned seafood company: _____ Leaf
11. National railway since 1881 (abbr.)
14. Annual shareholders' mtg.
17. Ebb off
18. Cenozoic era epoch
19. Insect wing spaces
21. Basmati, i.e.
22. Classification of 58-A
23. **Canine hybrid**
24. **Eagle–lion cross**
26. Relationship of 29-A, for short
27. Some pasta shapes
28. W Network show: *Candice Tells* _____
29. US boxing siblings Buddy and Max
31. '87 Judds song: "Isn't _____ Strange One"
32. Sufficiently
35. Weekend abbr.
36. *To Catch a* _____
38. Third degree?
41. Stepson of Claudius
42. Sedate
44. In-Circuit Test (abbr.)
45. Plodding plum?
46. Former federal politician Stockwell
47. Poet's contraction
48. He made famous a Winnipeg bear
50. Make butter, old style
51. Early Mexican empire name
53. Near, poetically
54. Asian flower
55. 1836 Texas battle site
58. **Hybrid fruit**
60. Unevenly notched
61. Mason–_____ Line

62. Baby's bed
63. Great acclaim, in Abitibi
65. Quick to move
66. Group of six
68. Canadian artist Danby
69. Not to
72. Rock star Simmons
73. Formerly, by name
74. Cassettes
76. Big name in faucets
77. .0000001 joule
78. Manger gift
80. Child's play?
81. Unite
82. Scrooge portrayer Alastair
83. *Take 30* host Paul
85. _____ Wilfrid Laurier
86. Monument inscription
90. Metric thickness measurement (abbr.)
91. **Fire-breathing mythological creature**
95. **Elephant-headed Hindu deity**
96. Home for the birds
98. By and by, old style
99. Drapery ring
100. Nice and friendly
101. Canadian film producer/director Reitman
102. Hankering
103. Sat down to lunch
104. Major Canadian business sector
105. Unit of force, in physics

DOWN

1. Ice mass
2. Place to hibernate
3. Spore sacs
4. **Lean meat source**
5. Mr. B. DeMille
6. Pork cut, say
7. Sept.–Nov. link

8. Word for word
9. Get used to (var.)
10. Norquay or Sunshine
11. Cries from crows
12. Divinely inspired speaker
13. Bas-_____
14. Hawkeye portrayer on *M*A*S*H*
15. The clink, in Canterbury
16. *When Harry Met Sally* star Ryan, et al.
20. Juno-winning cellist Harnoy
25. Second Rush album: _____ *By Night*
29. Flock bleat
30. Roofing rectangle
32. Comedy duo: Cheech _____ Chong
33. _____ *culpa*
34. Use a crowbar
35. Ambulance litter
37. Canada's sport
38. Planet that got dwarfed?
39. **Falcon-headed Egyptian deity**
40. Thick
42. Matching group
43. Archie's moniker for Edith
45. 1986 Canadian *SNL* star Martin
47. Atmosphere gas
49. '89 Colin James hit: "Why'd You _____"
50. Neat and tidy
51. Agave plant, say
52. Callings
55. Maxim
56. **Big cat cross**
57. Job dismissal of a logger?
59. Kibosh
64. _____ *Misérables*
67. NBC show featuring Saskatchewan's Keith Morrison
69. Pro

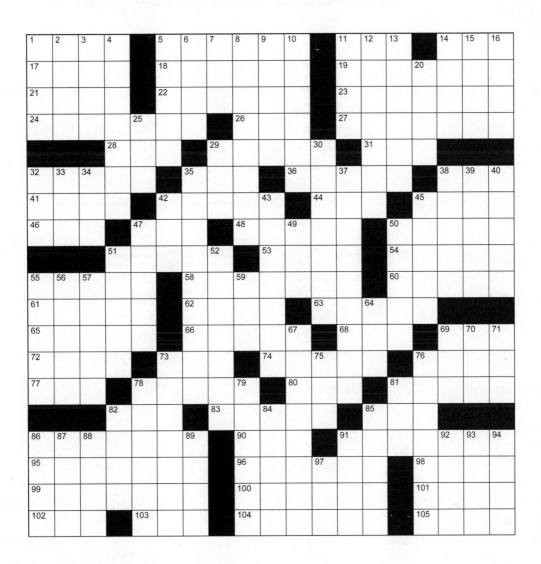

70. CBC C&W music star Gibson
71. "We're number _____!"
73. Sweet young thing?
75. Not neg.
76. **Mythological aquatic maiden**
78. Unhealthy atmosphere
79. Respect

81. 1002, in Rome of old
82. Part of a pipe
84. Pep up
85. With reticence
86. Like nog, say
87. Long-time Canadian cookbook
    author Jean

88. Wise to the plan
89. Really dislike
91. Rocky spot
92. Green-eyed attitude
93. Sheepskin leather
94. Beheaded Boleyn
97. _____ Canada

Solution on page 212

18 Canada Cornucopia 6

ACROSS

1. Iraqi city
6. 2004 *Closer* star Owen
11. Completed
14. Some voices
15. "Old _____ Bucket"
16. Marital vow
17. Saskatchewan CFL team
19. Canadian's gov. ID no.
20. Canary Islands island
21. Calgarian Duff who won Turin skeleton gold
23. '50s movie star Hunter
24. Soil, old style
25. BC provincial park: _____ La Hache
28. Intro to economics?
31. Forty winks
32. Tooth trouble
34. Gallows knot
36. 20th-C. NL wireless station: _____ Race
39. '84 Olympics golden Canadian Larry
40. *Global National* anchor Friesen
41. Latin list ender
42. Tartan garment
43. One small step for man?
44. Nintendo rival
45. Women's _____

47. Just plain silly
49. CBC program: *Dragons'* _____
50. Gatineau galas?
53. Chapter in history
55. BC Garibaldi range peak
56. Sociologist's undertaking
61. Canadian air, rail and marine regulator (abbr.)
62. Aboriginal transport
64. _____ room
65. "If it looks like _____ . . ."
66. Duke or duchess
67. *Raiders of the Lost* _____
68. Office correspondence
69. SK-born NHLer Jarret

DOWN

1. Homer Simpson's son
2. _____ vera
3. Flabbergast
4. Man of many words?
5. Yoga retreat, say
6. Hairdo
7. Stow cargo
8. '50s political slogan:"I Like _____"
9. Brink
10. Coast Guard rank
11. Faded away
12. Manner of speaking?

13. John who finished many poems?
18. Accolades, in some sports
22. Teen's silver linings?
24. 1990s Canadian peacekeeping locale
25. Dearth of
26. Berry type
27. Shared name of BC city and a band
29. Omnivorous mammals
30. Dick Martin's '70s co-host Dan
33. Whole
35. Sincerely heartfelt
37. *Front* _____ *Challenge*
38. Zest
46. Hag
48. Raises the roof?
50. Bones in the pelvis
51. Canadian plane: Twin _____
52. Avoid capture
54. Anticipate
56. Canadian fashion model Rocha
57. Seabirds
58. Able to see through a ruse
59. Throw the dice
60. Boat bottom
63. Excel, in Canada

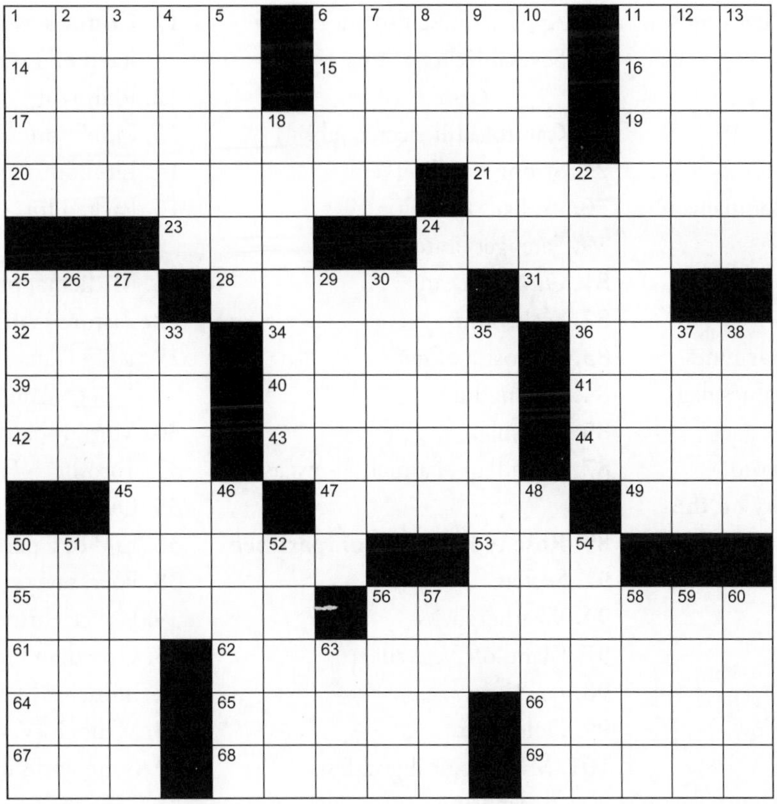

Solution on page 212

19 Words and Images

From Canada's coat of arms

ACROSS

1. US Department of Justice bureau (abbr.)
4. Ontario-born ex-NHLer Lindsay
7. Jalapeno's kin
12. Rapunzel's ladder
17. *Mal de* _____
18. _____ Lanka
19. Cowboy movie, colloquially
20. Directions, say
21. Obtain
23. Feudal title
24. Canadian country star Lines
25. Canada's London Games flag-bearer Whitfield
26. Winter underwear word
28. **Symbol of monarchy on the crest**
29. Elite police team (abbr.)
31. Slalom turn
32. Author's anecdote
34. Green soup type
35. History Television show: _____ *Road Truckers*
37. *This Hour Has 22 Minutes* star Walsh
39. Zero
40. Kings and queens
41. Like a helot??
43. Hot springs
45. One of baby's first words
47. 19th-C. French novelist Pierre
48. Organized processes
51. Waded across a river
55. " . . . _____ 'til he takes a wife . . ."
56. Selects a jury
58. Thin pancake
59. Greek letters
60. **Repeated French floral emblem (var.)**
62. Pose for a painter
63. Dismal, poetically

65. CPP recipients, say
66. They're spotted in Vegas?
67. Preserves jar
69. Applies oneself to adoration?
70. Several Keats poems
71. _____ *Geste*
73. Capitol Hill electee (abbr.)
74. Strong smelling
76. "What's the big _____?"
79. Serengeti antelopes
81. On the ocean
82. Scale notes
83. Opposite of *oui*
84. Fishing lure
85. "Hush!"
87. Canadian channel: Showcase _____
89. **Rose type in the compartment**
91. Secrete
94. Weathercocks
97. Island off Venezuela
98. *La Bohème*, e.g.
99. Doldrums
101. Mythological goddess of agriculture
102. Kitchen device
103. Got together
104. Energy measuring unit
105. Deuce toppers
106. Unadorned
107. Spelling _____
108. Observe

DOWN

1. Stage equipment
2. *Desperate Housewives* actress Hatcher
3. **Motto translation: *A Mari usque ad Mare***
4. Destructive wave
5. Slip up
6. Losing proposition?
7. Canadian bookstore

8. Villi
9. Big-ticket _____
10. Smoothly, musically
11. **Country represented by the harp of Tara**
12. Remnant
13. Lion's sound
14. Liechtenstein locale
15. Packed for a ski trip to Vermont?
16. Medicinal plants
22. Pasture mama
27. 1975 Canadian #1 single: "_____ You"
30. Mortarboard attachment
33. Toronto NHLer, for short
35. Queen Charlotte _____
36. End of a parliamentary debate
38. Poet, say
39. Use celebrity to impress
40. Canadian Golf Hall of Fame inductee Dave
42. Wine, in Verdun
43. Soup and salad, say
44. Moody
46. Holliday and Severinsen
49. Ejected (var.)
50. Driving hazard
52. **Ribbon motto: _____ *Meliorem Patriam***
53. Asexual
54. Abhors
57. Gets some REM
60. NAFTA word
61. Published a magazine?
64. *Dark Angel* star Jessica
66. Poodle or Pomeranian
68. Indian music style
72. **One-horned beast that holds a lance**
75. Innocence
76. National insurance company
77. More humourless

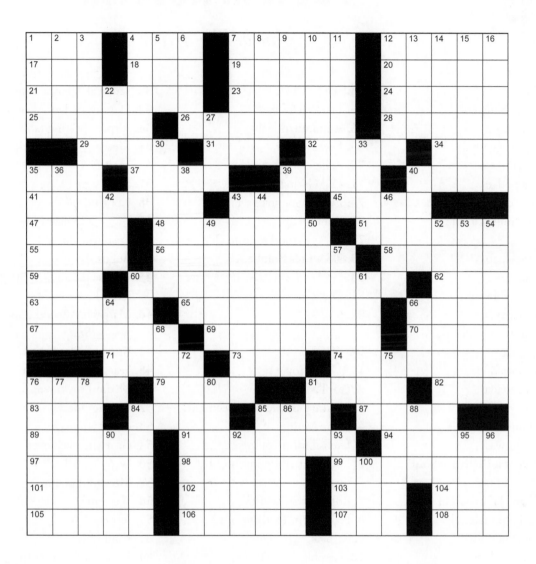

78. Withstand
80. Ideal place
81. Cry of triumph
84. Quintet since 1970: Canadian
    _____

85. Rock pile
86. Listened to
88. Occasional crossword abbr.
90. Follow the rules
92. Head–torso connector

93. Leg, for example
95. Land of the leprechauns
96. Wise
100. Hillary Clinton, _____
     Rodham

Put it in Reverse

You be the driver

ACROSS

1. Louisville Sluggers
5. King or queen
9. Strongly suggested
16. Colourful fish
17. Hodgepodge
18. Largest city in Sri Lanka
19. French military hat
20. Pay
22. Paddock papas
24. Dazzle
25. Blasting substance
26. Irish coat?
28. Antiquity, in olden days
29. _____-Cola
31. Transported via the TransCanada
32. Link
33. Sped on two wheels
36. Place for waste
38. **Memo at a British school?**
39. Bit for a horse?
40. "O Canada" pronoun
41. Gene pool material
42. Notable periods
43. Painters' helpers
47. Alberta-based retailer: Value Drug _____
50. Not 'neath
51. Prefix with propyl
52. Not quite a failing mark
55. **Unique decorating project?**
58. Juicy fruit tree
60. Besets
61. Run along?
62. Nonchalant
63. _____-A personality

64. See 5-A
65. Like ducks' feet
66. Amniotic pouch
68. Lewd looker
70. Ache
71. Old German colour?
74. Dog-loving jokesters?
77. Bubbles up?
78. "_____ Too Proud to Beg"
79. US writer Bombeck
80. '33 *She Done Him Wrong* star
81. Dregs
82. 6/6/44

DOWN

1. _____ choy
2. Gorilla
3. **Military music disagreement?**
4. Some Muslims
5. Utensil for prepping apples
6. Long-time Edmonton Oiler Hemsky
7. Edge of the Pacific?
8. Half a Tim Hortons order
9. Sorbets, say
10. Casablanca country
11. 1986 Oscar best picture
12. Fate
13. Parrot, for example
14. Jet black, to Blake
15. 2005 Shania Twain single
21. Canadian rowing great Hanlan
23. 1993 Paul Haggis film
26. _____ the minute
27. Euros replaced this currency
28. "Ich bin _____ Berliner"
30. Ice cream holders

32. Tropical Atlantic catch
33. Hamilton's Ivor Wynne _____
34. Airport posting (abbr.)
35. Musée _____ beaux-arts de Montréal
37. Stage signal
38. Conclude
41. _____ es Salaam
43. Lost little dogie
44. August-born sign
45. Course for a new Canadian (abbr.)
46. Margaret Atwood book: *The _____ Bride*
47. Bird of bygone days
48. Years, to a Quebecer
49. Medical treatment for stress
52. **Boring poet?**
53. Celtic language
54. Gave the once-over
56. Witty comeback
57. Mournful poems
58. Wet earth
59. Jostled
61. Kind of tea
64. Ian Millar's horse: Big _____
65. Sharpens on a stone
66. Canned meat brand
67. Specialty
69. Wear well
70. Whistler's melody
72. Tool with teeth
73. Prevaricate
75. ABC morning show since '75
76. Two cents' worth

ACROSS

1. Indian mystic
6. Suppresses
12. "Let's go!"
16. Keith who duetted with Victoria's Nelly Furtado
17. Open an envelope
18. Bloodsucking bugs
19. Manhandles
20. New York state prison
21. Add to the poker pot
22. Horseshoe Falls attraction: *Maid of the _____*
23. Relative, for short
24. Sold to a retail broker
26. Suffix with social
27. Alberta city: Medicine _____
28. See 23-A
31. Devoutness
32. Forwards/backwards/forwards driving movements
36. 1942 drama: _____ *Miniver*
37. Petawawa and Gagetown, for example
38. *Royal Canadian Air Farce* star Luba
40. LP
43. _____ Van Winkle
44. Acid trip drug
46. Haul
48. Early auto name?
52. Astonishment
53. Popular vehicle style, for short
54. Clod chopper
55. "Tomorrow" musical
56. Deplete
58. Yellow fruit
60. Not one
61. UN organization on which Canada served six terms
67. Scheduled, at the pub?
69. Robertson's OLN show: _____ *Up*
70. Cleo's snake
71. Vein find
72. Native Israelis
74. Federal electees (abbr.)
75. "When You Wish _____ a Star"
76. Old Testament prophet
77. Western Canada rock formation
81. "It's _____ Way to Tipperary"
82. Gambling game
83. Canny
84. Indigenous Canadian
85. Yemen city
86. Shake like a snake?
87. Door locking device

DOWN

1. BC provincial park: _____ Lake
2. Spectre
3. One who employs power for nefarious means
4. Grain for a brewery
5. _____ and outs
6. Elizabethan-era book style
7. Bible preposition
8. French direction
9. Hula dancer's accessory
10. Ontario, to a Quebecer
11. High-five, e.g.
12. Scratching the surface?
13. Manitoban's US neighbour
14. Square dance group, for example
15. Indigent
23. Scottish rolls
25. Mo. for showers
27. Greek messenger god
28. Photos
29. Third-person pronoun
30. Carved cemetery monuments
33. Ostriches' kin
34. Long-legged wader
35. Brezhnev's country (abbr.)
39. Jellystone Park bear
40. "I knew it!"
41. Down times
42. Ribs adjunct
43. Idolize
45. Make a will, say
47. Lilliputian
49. '60s British songstress
50. a.k.a. rabbit
51. Involved with
57. Former prime minister Lester
59. Prefix with day
60. Pitch
62. Accounting firm employee (abbr.)
63. American author Truman
64. Quit the force?
65. Mocking
66. Not width
67. Honshu port city
68. Titled
73. Chinese pooch: _____ Pei
74. Work hard
75. Elbow–wrist connector
78. Former Harper cabinet minister Bev
79. Scrap of food
80. '90s Canadian kids' show: *Polka _____ Shorts*
81. Feel awful

22 Recipe for Good TV

Canadian culinary shows

ACROSS

1. Gilligan's fish?
8. Honoured playwright at Niagara-on-the-Lake
12. Roman earth goddess
15. Plants' bristly bits
19. Grande _____ AB
20. Sarcastic farmer?
22. Bit of a sweet, in Britain
23. **Show with Canada's first TV chef Fread**
25. None, in Navarre
26. Ovum
27. Like newspaper columnists' columns
28. Long-distance data transmission device
30. Child of cuisine
33. Main meal, in Montréal
35. Puerto _____
36. Holder of 26-A
37. Shopkeeper on *The Simpsons*
38. Parcel out
40. Schuss at Whistler
42. Big event on 34th Street?
44. **'80s series featuring Asian chef Stephen**
48. *77 Sunset Strip* star Byrnes
50. Not deceived by
51. Battle of the blades: Snick and _____
52. Greeting word
53. Bryan Adams' "It's Only Love," for example
55. Exchanges (var.)
58. They specialize in bouquets
61. Québec party once led by Duceppe
63. Family related?
64. Savage
67. Australian marsupial
69. One of *Charlie's Angels*
71. Paddle

72. Morley Callaghan novel: _____ *Joy in Heaven*
74. Tic–toe connector
75. Sonny's ex
76. Finland neighbour (abbr.)
77. Chest protector
79. With an _____ the future
81. Well-groomed
83. Them, too (Lat.)
84. Non-metric CFL measurement
87. Hoagy Carmichael classic
89. Incurred debts, say
91. Speaker's platform
93. Not outer
94. At home, in Abitibi
98. Chick's chirp
100. Short flight, say
101. **Michael Smith's long-time Food Network series**
103. Electra's brother
106. Screwball
108. Blush wine
109. Canadian restaurant: Pizza _____
110. Long scarf type
111. Plenty
113. Ontario-born country music star Prophet
116. One of South Africa's official languages
118. NM Manhattan Project test site
121. April shower
122. School org.
123. Approve
124. **Graham Kerr show taped in Ottawa (with "The")**
130. One less than ten
131. Ancient Balkans language
132. Sun's surround
133. '97 Shania hit: "Love _____ Me Every Time"

134. Union of former Soviet republics (abbr.)
135. '40s movie star Nelson
136. Vend before a release date

DOWN

1. Imperial speed unit (abbr.)
2. A Gershwin brother
3. A Bobbsey twin
4. Japanese–Canadian
5. Art of paper folding
6. On a _____ and a prayer
7. Ready
8. Cleaned up, at curling?
9. Rockies' walker
10. Comments to an audience
11. Not dry
12. Yellowish pigment (var.)
13. Early round, for short
14. Daisy family genus
15. Teen's blemishes
16. **'80s CTV show with food specialist Ruth Frames**
17. End of a transaction, to Howie Mandel
18. Not plentiful
21. Work in films
24. Similar to sweet talk?
29. Sunrise times, for short
30. Scary '75 Spielberg film
31. '84 film: *Once _____ a Time in America*
32. *Star Wars* Skywalker
33. Firmament, old style
34. Got by on little
39. Study of animal behaviour
41. Queen to a new knight: "_____ thee sir . . ."
43. NFB documentary: *Canada _____*
45. It's drawn through a warp
46. Further
47. Comment in the margin

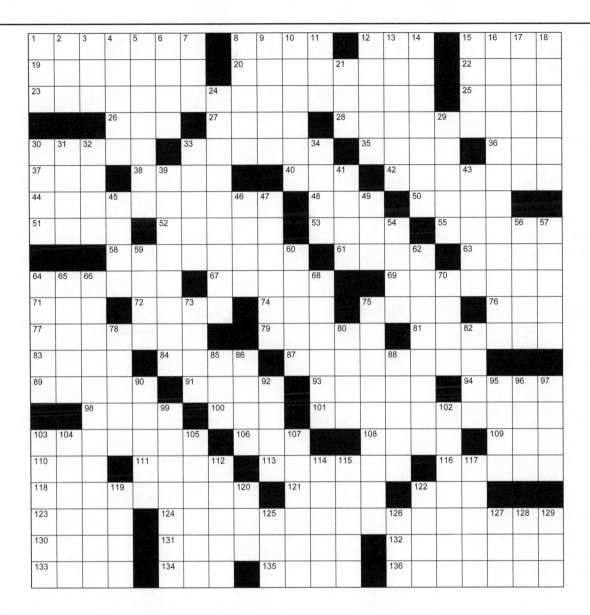

49. Marc Jordan song: "Marina _____ Rey"
54. Reggae star Peter
56. Affix a donkey's tail?
57. Entrap
59. Dalai follower
60. Kills the dragon
62. Pauses, in poetry
64. Woodworm, for example
65. Indian side dish
66. James Barber's 10-year CBC series (with "*The*")
68. Vinegary
70. Ian and Dave Thomas, for short
73. Crazy Canuck Ken
75. Monopolizing the market?

78. What a crossword compiler writes
80. Trig function
82. Urge to scratch?
85. "Go team!" word
86. Céline of Charlemagne QC
88. *Robinson Crusoe* scribe
90. Colourful flower part
92. Cowboy boot attachment
95. Part of Santa's laugh
96. Aussie birds
97. Actress Catherine_____-Jones
99. Seabird description
102. Tactile characteristic
103. Like a rounded rectangle
104. Global TV police drama: _____ *Blue*

105. Mogadishu citizen
107. Sluggish
112. Fees for travelling on Ontario Highway 407
114. Lake nymph, in mythology
115. Simpleton
117. Runs after a rabbit?
119. "The _____ have it"
120. Canny
122. Serve tea, say
125. Prospector's goal
126. Space between teeth
127. Canadian golf great Norman
128. Building extension
129. _____ Aviv

Solution on page 213

23 Armed and Musical

Musicians and their songs shoot for the top

ACROSS

1. Open a crack
5. Clean the floor, say
10. Yodeller's terrain
13. To write, in Trois-Rivières
19. Fake out move by 39-D
20. '81 Loverboy hit: "Turn Me _____"
21. Expire
22. Glows
23. **1993 Rod Stewart song**
26. Strategic move
27. Just fine, after an accident
28. Animal fat
29. _____ magnesia
30. Not planned
33. Nickelled and _____
34. *Chocolat* star (with 111-D)
37. Not sweet (var.)
38. Software users' trial runs
42. Screwdriver alcohol
44. Harlem Globetrotters founder Saperstein
45. *Full House* star Bob
46. Brawl
47. Suffix for lemon or lime
48. Laser guided weapon (abbr.)
51. Popular Internet search engine
53. Stock up on supplies
55. Flex one's muscles?
58. Thomas' uncertainties?
60. Cringe
61. Cold first aid item
63. Romanov title
64. Dido's love
65. Berton CPR history book: *The _____ Spike*
68. **1999 Imajin song**
71. Cheats
72. Leftovers
74. Crippled
75. Husband or wife
77. Reluctant
78. Brazilian ballroom dances
80. Hold sacred
84. Close to land
86. Bulls and rams
88. Lake Muskoka concert venue: The _____ to Bala
89. Steppenwolf singer John
90. London art gallery
91. Collision type: Rear-_____
93. Tuck's partner
95. Firewood delivery
97. Pale complected
99. Suspense?
102. Beams of sunlight
103. Buffy Sainte-Marie song: "_____ It's Time for You to Go"
104. Get rid of
106. Adriatic peninsula
108. Swindle
109. National TV network
112. Northern hemisphere tree
113. **'00s Slash rock group**
117. Prince _____ SK
118. Ottoman Empire title
119. Bang or boom
120. Years and years
121. Long-time NBC sportscaster Bob
122. "_____ so fast!"
123. Horses' paces
124. Exchange

DOWN

1. Spam pop-ups
2. Ancient Israeli king
3. US R&B artist
4. Ponder again
5. Impolite imbibing sounds
6. Reagan era scandal: Iran–_____ affair
7. Column's counterpart
8. Purpose
9. Covering for a queen?
10. French farewell
11. Canadian fantasy genre scribe: Charles de _____
12. 1977 Steely Dan hit
13. Autobody ballpark
14. Canadian restaurant chain: Swiss _____
15. **"Rock and Roll, Hoochie Koo" singer**
16. "What's gotten _____ you?"
17. Niagara region winery name
18. PC key
24. Chewing _____
25. Obligation
29. Joins corners, in woodworking (var.)
31. What fertility clinics store
32. _____ *Dick*
33. U of W grad's achievement
34. White House office shape
35. '69 Creedence Clearwater Revival song
36. The same, to Octavius
38. a.k.a. monkey bread trees
39. Nova Scotia-born hockey great Crosby
40. Workboot feature
41. Pressure symptom
43. *Star Wars* star Guinness
45. "The Stars and Stripes Forever" composer
49. Sandra Oh show: _____ *Anatomy*
50. Lymph node swelling
52. Summertime retail promotion?
54. Have payments to make
56. **1980 Motörhead song**
57. US news personality Zahn
59. Metaphor, for example
62. *Frasier* star Kelsey
64. Mistreat
65. Nabokov novel

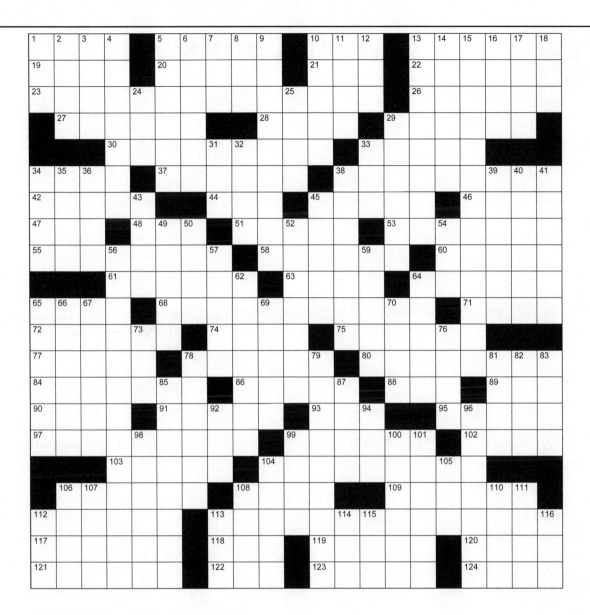

66. Discordant
67. Daisy type
69. Lock up, old style
70. Abbey brother
73. 17th Greek letter
76. Mares and ewes
78. Remitted
79. Nostalgic notion
81. Swedish retailer with 12 Canadian stores
82. None, in Aberdeen
83. Storm centres

85. Begins anew
87. Setting of *The King and I*
92. Wilmington state (abbr.)
94. 23rd Greek letter
96. Increases by three
98. Turkish capital
99. Czech or Serb
100. Swallow
101. Healing ointments
104. Public approval
105. Additionally
106. Western tie

107. Police dept. alerts
108. Lily type
110. Make a promise
111. See 34-A
112. Arcade fave: _____-Man
113. Singer Morrison's transport?
114. Queen's Park city (abbr.)
115. Amazon feeder: _____ Negro
116. Canadian retirement savings option (abbr.)

ACROSS

1. Thin wood strip
5. *Entourage* character Gold
8. Burnaby BC campus: _____ Fraser
13. Canadian TV classic: *The Littlest* _____
14. Winnipeg-born *Blue Bloods* star Cariou
15. William and Catherine's first official tour country
16. Not "fer"
17. Got around (var.)?
19. PEI floral symbol
21. WSW's reverse
22. Casual pants
23. Laryngitis sound
27. Highway 401 bridge in Toronto: _____ Hollow
28. Macaroni or ziti
29. US gov. agency
32. Women with good habits?
33. More runty
34. Old salt's sword
36. Grand gateways
37. Input again
38. Schwartz's in Montréal, for example
39. Mila Mulroney, _____ Pivnicki
40. BC-born singer Bryan
41. Old-style carts
42. Criminal, colloquially
43. Battled
44. Alberta women's gym company: _____ Lady
47. Salon pros
50. Cheered on
53. Home of Jazz?
54. *Mr. Dressup* host Ernie
55. Always, in vintage verse
56. Speechless
57. Arm bones
58. Some forensic evidence
59. PGA event: RBC Canadian _____

DOWN

1. Oil source
2. Preeminent peak in the Yukon
3. "_____ With Me"
4. Ontario-born ex-NHL goalie Esposito
5. Dickensian lodgings
6. Straightens
7. Baseball game segments
8. Rescue
9. Not fallible
10. Alberta's former Washington envoy Gary
11. Poet's due?
12. Cell coenzyme
15. Stanley and Grey
18. Poetry saga
20. Peppermint spirits, say (var.)
24. Oriental
25. Stone marker (var.)
26. Mince words?
28. Pedagogues
29. Discard metal?
30. Elvis hit: "Blue _____ Shoes"
31. Oil of rose
33. Three-dimensional star shapes, for example
35. Malignant tissue
36. Colour of some veggies?
38. Toiled
41. Toronto theatrical award: _____ Mavor Moore
43. Douglas' trees?
44. Arrangements, say
45. Go on . . . and on . . . and on
46. Not rosy
48. River to the Seine
49. Japanese wrestling style
50. Euro forerunner, in France
51. Former Cambodian prime minister Lon
52. Scam a crook?

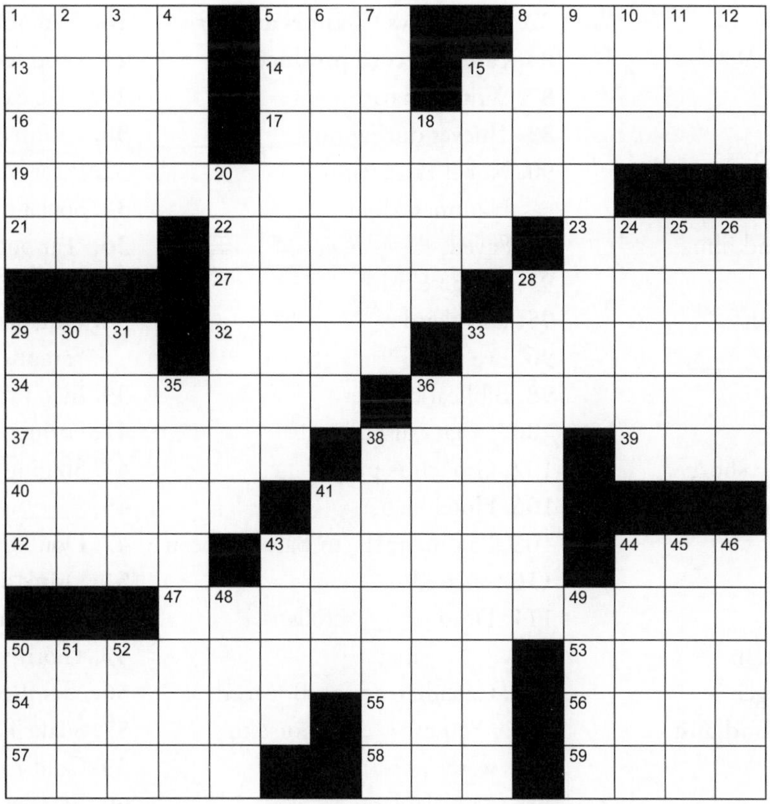

Solution on page 213

25

Oh Danny Boys

Famous Canadian Daniels

ACROSS

1. Clothes line?
5. Lies
9. Light touch
12. '52 film: _____ *Devil*
17. Tropical flu
18. Matinee star?
19. Actress MacGraw
20. Fraser or Ottawa
21. 1995 James Bond film
23. Untruthful
25. Sonar predecessor
26. Sleeman Cream _____
27. Hawaiian island
28. Scraps of food
29. Police officer, for short
31. UFO crew members
33. Ilk
35. Tofu source
36. Horrifies
40. Big brat, in Britain
42. **"Bad Day" singer**
44. **Former Newfoundland premier**
46. Yuletide drink
48. _____ Brunswick
49. Baseball stats
50. Bluish-green
52. Greyhound, e.g.
54. Lets up
58. Declare
59. Ring around the _____
61. Quad or quint
63. Single attempt at the rifle range?
65. Gymnast's cushion
67. Smaller than an adult?
68. Strict disciplinarian
70. Fast cat
72. Quick kip
73. Industrial area in Germany
74. Former Rideau Hall resident Hnatyshyn
76. Sew socks

77. Cornbread
78. Old Saturn car
80. *etalk* host Mulroney
82. **CTV News Channel anchor**
84. **Famed record producer**
87. Writer Anaïs
89. Thieves during riots
90. Nobel Prize winner Hammarskjöld
91. Saved
93. Japanese fish
95. Drunkard
96. Eye part
98. Biblical brother
100. "That's disgusting!"
102. Groucho's prop
106. Hotel helper
108. Bad manners, in Baie-Comeau
110. Abetted
111. Dead _____ scrolls
112. _____ mater
113. Canadian actress Botsford
114. "You can _____ horse to water …"
115. Miscalculate
116. Stadium seating section
117. Recipe abbr.

DOWN

1. 1982 Juno-winning group
2. Freudian explorations
3. "_____Lang Syne"
4. Annual exams
5. Mascot name at Rogers Arena
6. Concept
7. **2004 Stanley Cup team member**
8. Like icy precipitation
9. Decorative wall board
10. Pseudonym
11. Canadian WWI flying ace Billy
12. Dude
13. One who overimbibes

14. Opposed to
15. **Tennis grand slam doubles champion**
16. Pretentious
22. Food recall bacteria
24. Lake east of Michigan
30. Group of troops
32. Peter MacKay, to Elmer
34. Social network user
36. "Far out!"
37. Fish with sharp teeth (var.)
38. Canadian cinema chain: Famous _____
39. Inco processing place
41. Former Ontario premier Rae
43. Singing star Shania
45. _____ volatile
47. Doublemint, e.g.
51. Drink like a dog
53. Like a surgeon's stitches
55. Thorny
56. Mrs. Roosevelt
57. Snakelike constellation
59. Cold-to-warm event in Calgary
60. Former Alberta NDP leader Pannu
62. Shacks
64. Glass raised at Oktoberfest
66. Mom's mate
69. Keyboard key
71. Betty Grable limb
75. Desire to travel to Japan?
77. Most narrow-minded
79. Female family member
81. Long-time Calgary Stampeders receiver Lewis
83. Moonshine
84. ***Nirvana bleu* singer/ songwriter**
85. Board's order of business
86. Scanty
88. Big Turk filling
90. Of Cambridge or Kent

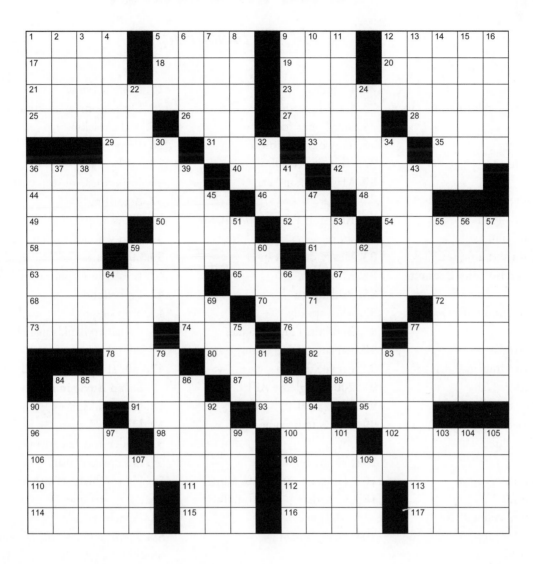

92. 2004 Giller Prize finalist: *The _____ Claw*

94. Golden Olympic wrestler

97. Passed with flying colours

99. At hand

101. Ontario-born *Cocoon* star Cronyn

103. Snatch

104. Broadcasts

105. Gather grains, say

107. Gilbert and Sullivan opera: *Princess _____*

109. Elevator cage

Solution on page 214

Ode to Vivaldi

Music to your ears

ACROSS

1. The Mamas & the Papas member Elliot
5. Sick as a dog?
10. Small songbird
18. Stuck in _____
19. Draw out
20. Like some income
21. Shells and bullets
22. **1956 movie theme song performed by Tony Bennett**
24. Skinflint
26. Shunts to another track, say
27. Mai _____
28. Hotel arrivals
31. Car service franchise that came to Canada in '61
32. Maritime character in *Goin' Down the Road*
33. Bobby's paddle?
34. Viny
36. Provocative, in a way
37. Apple drink
38. First claim, colloquially
40. Signs up for service
42. Gangster film gun
43. Trial's partner
45. Happy German place?
46. Great _____
50. Jug with a big mouth
52. And so on, for short
53. Flightless flock
54. _____ corda
55. Dined
57. **Theme of this puzzle**
60. Golfer's shirt?
61. European alp: _____ Bernina
62. Former CFL stars Stewart and Lancaster
63. Mo. to celebrate Kwanzaa
64. Vegetarian protein source
66. Overhead transparency
68. Subatomic particle

70. Deadens
73. Casual greetings
74. Fixed one's footwear
76. Tiny buzzing insect
77. Church periodical?
80. Maglie's moniker: _____ the Barber
81. Kingston *Whig-Standard*, for short
83. Heavy-duty cleanser
84. Mint bit
85. Bridal path
87. Most speedy
89. Buddhist prayer plaques
90. LaFlamme and Mansbridge
92. Female demon
93. **2006 single by AFI**
96. Hertz rival
99. Allows to become trite
100. West _____
101. Home for a bird
102. Housing projects building
103. Canadian political trailblazer Macphail
104. Genesis name

DOWN

1. Cdn. auto club
2. Chair part
3. **1972 Seals and Crofts song**
4. Emotionless
5. Get
6. Beautifying
7. Nogoodnik
8. _____ tea
9. Jeans fabric
10. Formal suits
11. Desktop mailbox
12. Examines
13. Atlas contents
14. *Catch-22* bomber pilot
15. _____ Empire Loyalists
16. Red Chamber

17. More nervous
23. Ousts from an apartment
25. Make tracks?
28. Postal _____
29. Locks
30. Inspector Clouseau portrayer
32. Actor Brad
35. Slims, hopefully
37. Two-wheeled military cart
39. Sty parent
41. Breaks away, politically
42. Pig's sound
44. Stop singing?
46. Canadian bank since in 1817 (abbr.)
47. **'50s standard covered by Susan Boyle in 2011**
48. Chemical suffix
49. Dundee denial
51. Underground network?
53. Deep waters fish
55. US psychiatrists' org.
56. _____-tac-toe
58. French article
59. *The Tortoise and the Hare* scribe
65. Stuffy atmosphere, in Sussex
67. 1959 Hugh MacLennan book: *The Watch _____ Ends the Night*
68. Easygoing
69. Like many Sherpas
71. Hudson and James
72. Editorial note
74. Least prudent
75. Goes
77. Wildcat with spots
78. Delete
79. _____ image
80. Make ill
82. Lip
85. Licorice flavour
86. Toronto-born actress Luttrell
88. '70s Canadian pentathlete Jones Konihowski

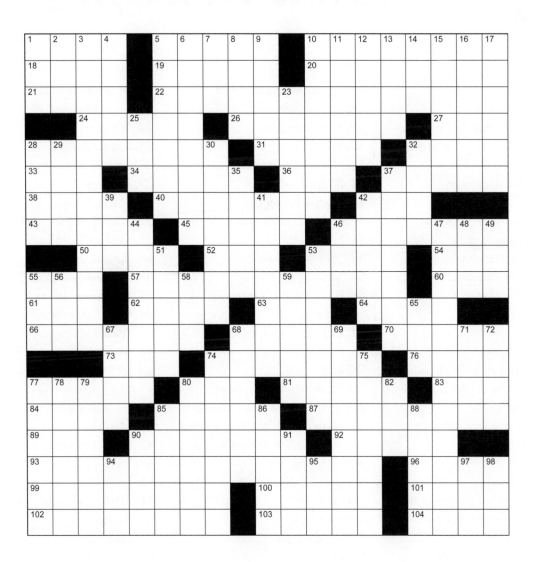

90. Reunion attendee, for short
91. Nuzzle, in Nottingham
94. Before, to Burns

95. *The Joy Luck Club* scribe Amy
97. '91 Tom Cochrane hit: "Life _____ Highway"

98. Hart wrestling family patriarch

Canada Cornucopia 9

ACROSS

1. Easter hunt find
4. Male family member, for short
7. Number Shania had a party for, in 2004
10. Neckline shape
13. Use AC, say
15. Montréal-born actor Shatner
17. Pop-O-Matic game
18. Support a candidate
19. Old-style Canadian beer bottle
20. Temporary craze
21. Hallowed suffix?
22. Wages
23. Canuck spud
25. LPGA pro from BC Coe-Jones
27. *Canada's Worst Driver* panellist Woolley
28. Hardship
29. Oklahoma town
30. A bit
31. Made eyes at
35. Some Newfoundland mammals
37. "_____ I plight thee my troth"
38. Gets gussied up
39. _____ Network Canada
40. CIBC machine, for short
41. "_____ was saying"
42. Music genre of Toronto's Drake
43. Clement Clark Moore poem opener

44. Spoke to a postal clerk?
48. _____ soup
49. Snorkelling site
50. JFK sibling, for short
51. Northern Canada animal
54. Steeped, say
56. High-schooler's test
57. Old-style calling, in Chicago
58. Silk fabric
59. *"C'_____ la vie!"*
60. Sault _____ Marie
61. Cordoba or Cadboro, off Victoria
62. CQD successor

DOWN

1. Old show on 39-A: *Good _____*
2. Prepare for combat, old style
3. Collaborative computer program
4. '60s Canadian singer Curtola
5. _____-poly
6. Cheer for Nadal?
7. Fine-tune
8. Browse only
9. Cheddar type
10. Passerine
11. Art gallery display item
12. Blue-pencil
14. Fidel's cigar?
16. Hill climbing option with a stick shift

20. Be smoking mad?
23. Sweet potatoes' kin
24. Wrote down
25. A little wet
26. Last Jewish month
27. Uniform
30. Have a hunch
32. Stirs up interest again
33. "At Last" icon James
34. Benedictine titles
36. Sobbing
37. Amphibian in the hole?
39. Canadian singers Eaglesmith or Penner
43. Seed's protective shell
44. 1970 Top 40 hit: "Hitchin' _____"
45. Canadian talk-show host Marilyn
46. Skim the gravy
47. Wetlands plant
48. See 5-D
51. *Mighty Aphrodite* Oscar winner Sorvino
52. Rice-like pasta
53. Dec. event
55. 4-A's relative
56. Unruly group

28 Country Gentlemen

Canadian C&W stars

ACROSS

1. CBC drama: _____ *Erica*
6. Genesis name
10. Top of Canada description
15. Muscat's land
19. Hawaiian veranda
20. *Decree* _____
21. Moulding type
22. Piece of glass
23. Like a root of eight
24. Some snakes
25. **"Canadian Man" Juno Award winner**
27. Beach shoes
29. Large African animal, for short
31. Indefatigable
32. Greek letter
34. Santa _____
36. Grass
37. Picturesque Alberta lake
41. Encouraging word to a lad?
43. Monopolizes a motorcycle?
47. **2001 CCMA male artist winner**
49. Vietnam Veterans Memorial designer Maya
50. Pulitzer-Prize-for-Fiction winner Shields
51. Not married
52. Added part, in architecture
53. Quaker _____
55. American singer/actress Demi
56. Crime tech's target
57. Vestal
59. Work in a darkroom
60. Conger
61. Kilt-wearing musician's instrument
62. Washes
63. Total up
64. Rubber
65. Tarzan's kin?
67. Long-running sitcom: _____ *and a Half Men*
70. Olympic golden pairs partner Salé
71. Riles
73. "Star-Spangled Banner" preposition
74. Alexander's empire (var.)
77. Friendly international pacts
78. Brian, to Ben Mulroney
79. Lucky charm
80. Best of _____ worlds
81. Zero
82. Lift
84. Triangular sign
85. ABBA's call for help?
86. **"Father" of Canadian country music**
88. Around
89. More desirable, say
92. Chef who makes hash?
93. Confucian principle
94. Torso indent
96. Chatty animal?
97. Try, in Tennessee
102. Empire
104. US version of Canada's Genies
109. **CBC *Country Hoedown* host**
111. Hard work
113. Water wheel
114. In awe
115. Perch on the cliff
116. Jekyll's favourite park?
117. Theatre chain: Cineplex _____
118. Yep's opposite
119. River east of Peterborough
120. Rework words
121. Refuse

DOWN

1. Ink _____ test
2. A head
3. Captivated by
4. Indian bread
5. **"Famous First Words" fellow**
6. Female tennis player Ivanovic
7. Former Food Network Canada show: *Party* _____
8. Savoury jelly
9. Get an error on the diamond
10. Come loose
11. Eggs
12. Galoot
13. Sackville university: Mount _____
14. 1995 film about a Scotsman
15. October's gem
16. Horse's tresses
17. No ifs, _____ or buts
18. Fishing gear
26. Merlot, say
28. Thin wood strip
30. Long-time Winnipeg MP Martin
33. Over
35. Like a sailor's dirty joke?
37. Staffed with guys?
38. Kennedy assassin
39. Seafood bit
40. Solar or lunar event
42. Sue Grafton book: _____ *for Burglar*
43. Those with
44. Viva voce
45. Monopoly instruction: _____ jail
46. Spill swill?
47. Old Israel area
48. 1950s hit, today
50. Witches' groups
53. "The loneliest number"
54. Region in NE France
55. River embankments
57. Jasper National Park ski area: _____ Basin
58. Digital document

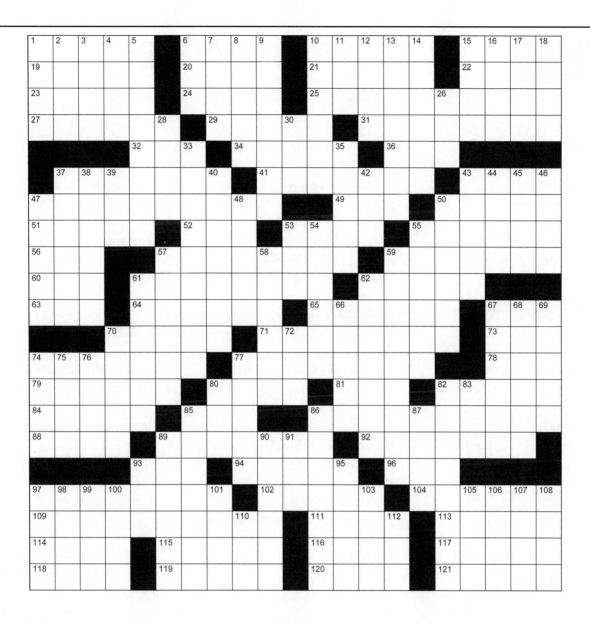

59. Insect that distresses a lady?
61. Like some evening bags
62. High protein beans
66. Old currency in Finland
67. Thus far
68. Basket maker, say
69. National honour: _____ of Canada
70. Jiggly dessert
72. Mathematician's ordinal
74. Hellmann's product, for short
75. Middle East ruler
76. Billiards sticks
77. Red dye

80. Greeting to Casper?
82. **He charted 70 singles on Billboard**
83. Work unit
85. Quick drink for a sniper?
86. Encircle
87. Goodbye, in Guadalajara
89. _____ emptor
90. Berber decor item
91. *Brady Bunch* star Plumb
93. US figure skater Babilonia
95. Long-time Canadian news anchor Robertson
97. Elvis co-star Richard

98. Scrubbed mission, say
99. Bit in the bucket?
100. Verge
101. Like a blue moon
103. Noon, in Saguenay
105. End of a piece
106. Greek god
107. Mob scene
108. Rational
110. RBC no., say
112. 1995 Amanda Marshall hit: "_____ It Rain"

Solution on page 214

29

Orienteering

Find your way with this puzzle

ACROSS

1. Maritime fisheries catch
5. 0 degrees
10. Breaks a statue?
15. Golf-course units
17. Condition to
18. Hijinks
19. Cay, say
20. a.k.a. mucus
21. C-D-E-F-G-A-B-C
22. One-time Canadian ladies figure skating champion Kim
23. Decorative display jar
24. 1954 Robertson Davies novel: _____ of Malice
25. Cashmere or angora
26. Old WTN Mag Ruffman show: *Anything I _____ Do*
27. Annual Calgary rodeo event
29. Courtly German dance
32. Clinches a hockey victory?
33. Flit about
34. Women's undergarment
35. Eucharistic plate
37. Annual Alberta C&W celebration: _____ Valley Jamboree
40. Chinese revolutionary
41. Former BC premier Vander Zalm
42. More than that?
44. 270 degrees
47. Children's illness
50. 90 degrees
51. Weapon of mass destruction
53. Helen's hometown
54. Five Ws question
56. Blood typing system
57. Bar order
59. _____ Paulo

60. Three letters that precede CP in an acronym
63. Canada Savings _____
64. *The Sound of Music* ballad
67. Goethe contemporary
71. Alice Munro ana: *Something _____ Been Meaning to Tell You*
72. They help you find your sense of direction
73. Without vitality
74. "Present!"
76. Bacall's mate
77. Like non-mainstream music
78. Up and about
79. Luminary of the Fab Four?
80. _____ Plain AB
81. Lay down the law?
82. Rate a raise, say
83. Expresses through music
84. 180 degrees
85. Newsmen Matheson and Rather

DOWN

1. Informal chat
2. Skin rash
3. In sum
4. Volkswagen vehicle
5. Blissful place for a Buddhist
6. Readily available
7. Streets, in Saguenay
8. Sets straight
9. Haw's partner
10. Where a man cave is often located
11. Opens a Labatt Blue
12. Barrel slat
13. Not carpeted, say
14. Public spat
16. Hog haven
24. Shoestring

26. Bank off of
28. Name
30. Grad student's achievement (abbr.)
31. Show piece?
36. Partner in politics, say
37. _____ constrictor
38. Skylab successor (abbr.)
39. Acquire
40. Company that produced *The Mary Tyler Moore Show*
41. Hockey arena, colloquially
43. Farmer's call to attention?
44. NHL alternative in the '70s
45. Diminish
46. Ontario city nickname: The _____
48. Study piece for a pianist
49. Marshy hollow
52. Plymouth parasols?
55. In what way?
58. Sole
59. _____-day Adventist Church
60. It precedes Falls and Peninsula in Ontario
61. Headache reliever
62. Postulates
63. Cycling
65. Canadian power provider: _____ Energy
66. Hammed it up
67. Cheese choice
68. Prefix with grade
69. Wore
70. Horned beast in Africa, for short
75. Isaac's oldest son
76. Toronto tourist attraction, for short
78. Thing, to an attorney

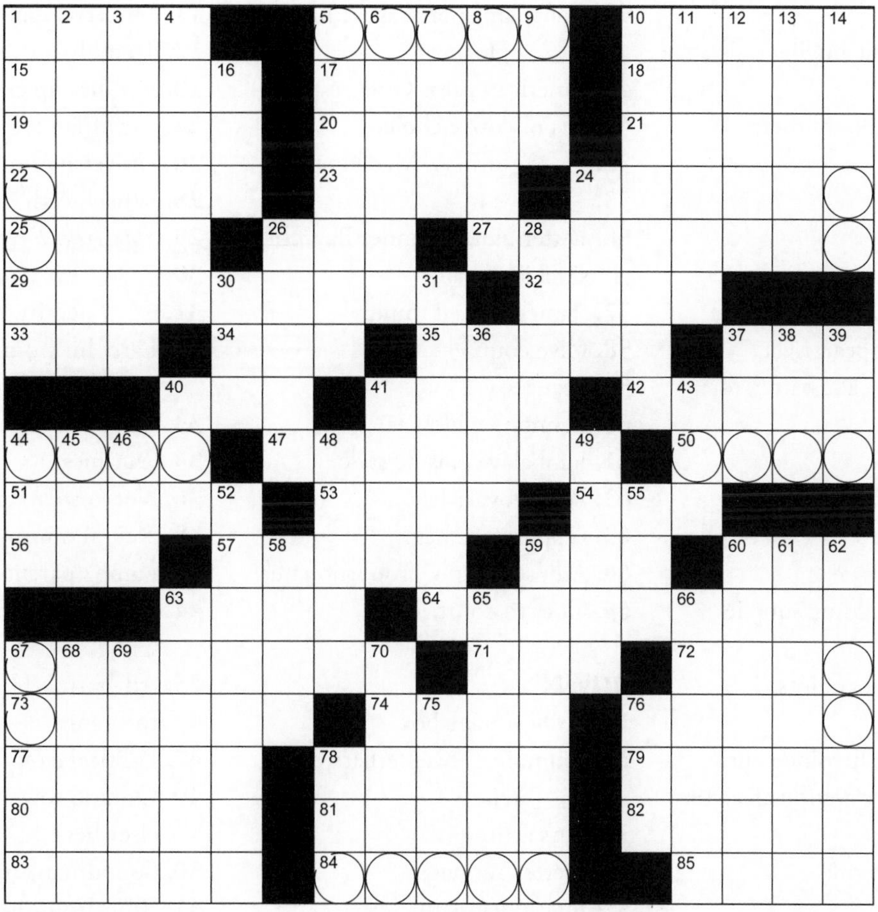

Solution on page 215

30

Canada Cornucopia 10

ACROSS

1. Canadian home buying assistance org.
5. Toronto-based publisher: _____-Hill Ryerson
11. Big primate
14. Get wind of
15. Pet food company since 1894
16. Computing network (abbr.)
17. Central European river
18. Commercial cake batter, for example
19. Not so young
20. Error on ice?
21. In good taste
22. Not downs
23. Canadian building supplies retailer
25. Some compass points
26. Agnus _____
27. War of 1812 heroine Laura
30. Ontario conservation area: Terra _____
32. *Survivor* network
35. Went by bus
36. Sauce with fish
37. City council, say
40. A *Dynasty* Carrington
41. Saw red?
42. Pigs' enclosure
43. North American conifer
44. Hydrocarbon type
46. Canadian sportscaster: Jim _____ Horne
47. American actor Gulager
48. Tea or coffee choice
52. _____ John A. Macdonald
53. _____ vain
56. Letterman's Thunder Bay-born sidekick Shaffer
57. James Clavell tome: _____-Pan
58. Give counsel
59. Secrete
60. Lennon's widow
61. Jambalaya cuisine style
62. Port Dover's lake
63. Opposite of neg.
64. Adjusted type, proportionately
65. Goes to court?

DOWN

1. Sturdy storage box
2. Mountain Dew alternative: _____ Yello
3. Nun's attire
4. Suzette's servings?
5. Ontario legislature electees (abbr.)
6. Heal
7. Environmentalists' uprising?
8. Like a salted margarita glass
9. Michael Ondaatje Giller winner: _____ *Ghost*
10. Like some Dutch cheeses
11. Montréal Grey Cup winners
12. Trembly
13. Finishes up curling?
24. Arthurian legends wizard
26. University housing, for short
28. Wheel teeth
29. *Star Trek: Deep Space Nine* name
30. _____ *Camera*
31. _____-crafty
32. Early hit from Canada's Beau-Marks: "_____ Your Hands"
33. La Paz monetary unit
34. Outlines
36. Not kosher (var.)
38. Neural transmitter
39. Lamb's parent
44. Long-time CTV journalist Craig
45. AB-born NHLer Brett Sutter, to Brent
47. Political gang
49. Ontario town that's a capital elsewhere
50. Soundman's milieu
51. Runs from the law
52. *Arrêt, en Anglais*
53. Strange, in slang
54. _____ of Capri
55. Penury

31 Made It Good

Well-known names in Canadian manufacturing

ACROSS

1. Can-Am comedian Fink
5. Rip off (var.)
8. Prov. near Sask.
12. Beasts of burden
17. Half a Britcom title (1982–92)
18. *Kidnapped* scribe's monogram
19. Onion relative
20. Five-pin frame score
21. Virtuously
23. Toronto landmark: _____ Loma
24. #1 men's tennis player (1964–70)
25. **Winnipeg cabinetry company since 1972**
27. Musical gourd
28. London-to-Toronto direction (abbr.)
29. Some
30. "Dog Lover's Mysteries" author Susan
31. Circular shape
34. "The Boy Who Cried Wolf" writer
36. Plump up poultry?
37. Respond
39. Where she sells shells?
42. Knocks aggressively
45. Big projector?
47. Gutters
48. US speed skating star Apolo Anton
49. Stingy ones
50. Slept like a logger?
51. SW Ontario town and county name
52. Top card player?
53. **Canadian auto parts company since 1957**
54. Ottawa, say (abbr.)
55. SWAT operations
58. Teems
59. *The Women of Brewster Place* character
63. Humerus neighbour
64. "I _____ fortune for it!"
65. Holiday send off?
66. Pant
67. Not supple
69. Green fence?
70. Affixes with glue
72. Comes to rest
74. Over there, old style
75. Shotgun spring back
76. 1,101 to a Roman
78. Make a wager
79. '58 hit: "_____ Robin"
80. **Long-time sporting goods manufacturer**
86. Keyboard key
87. Noisy Norse god?
88. Empress Hotel flowers?
89. Feel passionate about
90. Created
91. Dissenting vote
92. Trig abbr.
93. _____ code
94. Tranquil scene (var.)
95. Internet income generators
96. 1969 Fonda film: _____ *Rider*

DOWN

1. NL folk song: "_____ Was Every Inch a Sailor"
2. K–12 school, for short
3. Horn sound
4. Pear variety
5. Ottawa-born *Bonanza* star Lorne
6. Maladies
7. Canadian university arts course abbr.
8. **Long-time aluminum manufacturer**
9. Verdant
10. Mid-term or final, say
11. Wanted poster info
12. Not on the level
13. **Canadarm maker**
14. Tropical grasslands
15. Build
16. Red Cross fluids
22. Melodrama at the Met?
26. _____ Nui
27. Dust particles
30. Showed concern
31. Utah city
32. Ex-premier Lévesque
33. Muskoka town
35. Done, to Donne
36. Macula centre
38. **Long-time national meat processor**
40. **Alcohol producer founded in 1857**
41. Goldie, et al.
43. Yearly Vancouver fair (abbr.)
44. Boston Red _____
46. "Gosh!"
50. Middle East resident
51. Mushroom that's out of this world?
53. Slaves away
54. See 92-A
55. Carpet piece
56. Pie _____ mode
57. RCMP rank
58. Jury
59. Pone
60. '98 Juno group of the year: Our _____ Peace
61. *Cogito–sum* connector
62. Hagman's '60s TV co-star
64. Russian prime minister Vladimir
65. Shooter pellet
68. Radar screen image
71. Party in Plessisville
73. Rots

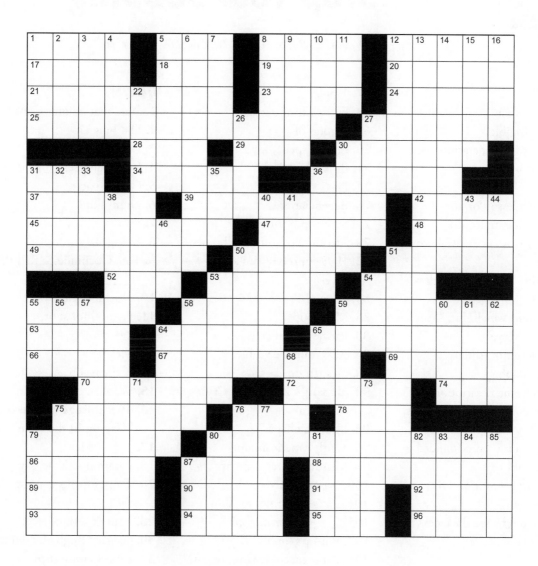

75. Piece of classical music

76. Burnaby BC neighbour: Port
_____

**77. Ottawa software company
since 1985**

79. Paper purchase

80. Country in Africa

81. Italian peak

82. Facial protuberance

83. Marco Polo crossed it

84. Retreat rooms

85. Pasty-faced

87. 1979 PA nuclear plant accident
site (abbr.)

32 Stop Your Sobbing

Musicians who need to get happy

ACROSS

1. UK New Wave star Adam
4. Huge dirigible?
9. Content Confederation poet Carman?
14. Stairs
19. Church lesson orator
21. Like some molecules
22. Gypsy Rose Lee's BC-born sister June
23. **Halifax "Weeping Widow" band**
24. '74 Gino Vanelli hit: "People _____ Move"
25. Last letter in Athens
26. Bang a door
27. Lymphoma description
29. **He recorded "When Doves Cry"**
31. Toronto museum founded in 1912 (abbr.)
32. Former Edmonton Oiler Linseman
33. Time to change the clocks (abbr.)
34. Ear
36. Like a defendant, say
38. Michaelmas daisy, say
40. *American Psycho* actress Sevigny
42. Not artificially coloured
45. **Canadian who covered "Cry Me a River"**
51. Rhett Butler portrayer
52. Literary orchestral works
55. Wild animals' abodes
57. Smash-and-_____
58. _____ vera
59. Tumultuous tide
60. Temporary parliamentary breaks
63. Holy brats?
65. Catherine of _____
66. Past the point?

67. Tippler
68. Furrow in the road
69. Shroud of _____
70. Engine speed, for short
71. Bit of shade
74. Pile
76. Beneficiaries
77. Stovetop burner
79. Attribute of some US bombers?
82. 1999 Juno best single: "_____ Week"
83. Piece of Price?
84. Messes up
85. Pacific coast berry
86. ADT nuisance causers?
88. Freshen up
90. **He sang "Blues Eyes Crying in the Rain"**
93. Learned chap?
95. South American range
96. Missouri River tributary
100. Nazareth native
104. *Platoon* setting, for short
105. _____ *Constitution*
107. Pin-up's limb
108. Large machine component?
110. **Albertan who duetted with Orbison on "Crying"**
112. Campaign slogan
114. Canadian golden Olympic cyclist: _____-Ann Muenzer
115. Spirit of a people
117. Repressive Russian place
119. **Canadian who sang "Cry Cry, Cry" in '83**
121. Roadside gully
122. Ridge in the Rockies
123. Meet
124. Try to write?
125. Gave five stars, say
126. Reeked
127. Adherent, for short

DOWN

1. State that adjoins Canada
2. SW Italy city
3. Dictator
4. Italian cheese: _____ Paese
5. Green spaces
6. Numbskull
7. Fix
8. Evangelizes
9. Tom Cochrane & Red Rider hit: "_____ League"
10. Thread circlet
11. Preface, for short
12. '60s protest
13. Meagre
14. Farrier's job
15. Woollen cap
16. **The siblings who recorded "Crying in the Rain"**
17. _____ stick
18. Pyramid scheme, say
20. Tim Hortons contest: Roll Up the _____ to Win
28. Lounge around
30. Calgary Rugby Union (abbr.)
33. Faucet annoyance
35. *The Friendly Giant* host Homme
37. Leisurely piece of music
39. Mideast VIP (var.)
40. Order of Canada officer Dalton
41. Funeral speeches
43. Zip
44. Cotillion ladies
46. Subverts
47. Burglary
48. Some royals
49. BC CFLer
50. Fraction of a joule
52. Body art, for short
53. Old bread spread
54. **Canadian music industry "Tears Are Not Enough" group**

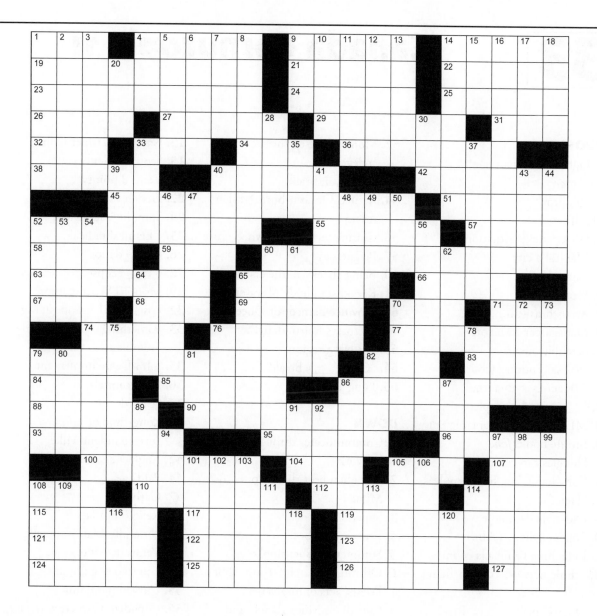

56. Needlework pieces

60. *Fawlty Towers* actress Scales

61. Some steak orders

62. Hefty volume

64. Not written

65. Hard to hear?

70. Kidney related

72. Condo, say

73. Some Greek vowels

75. Garrett tripods

76. East Timor capital

78. Water pipes

79. Medieval servant

80. Oak or elm

81. TV classic: *Hee* _____

82. Madrid cheers

86. Flowering plants

87. Lows, in the lea

89. Lazy

91. Place for a keeper?

92. Dutch cheese

94. Roll of dough

97. West Indies animal

98. January birthstone

99. Refugee from Rouen?

101. British composer Edward

102. Food Network Canada *French Food at Home* host Calder

103. Rankin _____ NT

105. New York city

106. Athenian wise one

108. Give it up

109. Last name in elevators

111. Lions _____ Bridge

113. Pup's shelter?

114. Contemporary of Bela

116. Mozart's "L'_____ del Cairo"

118. Scholastic assessment test (abbr.)

120. Loud laugh

33 Canada Cornucopia 11

ACROSS

1. Hugh MacLennan book: _____ *Solitudes*
4. Cdn. prov.
7. Pacify
14. Sticky cricket situations?
16. Manitoba city
17. Curtain calls
18. Woes
19. Accustoms (var.)
20. Madagascar carnivore
21. Scrabble pieces
22. Walesa's country (abbr.)
23. '70s actress Samantha
27. _____ good example
28. MD's temporary replacement
30. Brontë book: *Jane _____*
31. Shingles can cause this
34. Canadian Club, for example
35. "Here!"
38. Old-style desk hole
40. Tolkien trilogy (abbr.)
41. Indochina Peninsula country
43. Ethnic network on Canadian TV
45. Ontario place: _____ River
46. 1998 Canadian film: _____ *Night*
50. Irish Rovers hit: "_____ That a Party"
52. Montréal-based theatre arts college (abbr.)
53. Even if, in brief
54. Retired Ontario-born NHLer Adam
56. Cuisine term for browned crust
57. Plague, say
60. Being cheeky to the chef?
61. Kazakhstan body of water
62. Province named for Queen Victoria's fourth daughter
63. Outlying region
64. "Give _____ break!"
65. Long age

DOWN

1. Communicates through a social network
2. Canadian bear that inspired A.A. Milne
3. Supernatural
4. Dads in Québec
5. Summers in Sherbrooke
6. Orbiting research facility (abbr.)
7. Priests' acts of forgiveness
8. Canadians Milos Rancic and Mike Weir, say
9. Break down syntax
10. Make mad
11. Big bother
12. Plant on behalf of a pig?
13. Navy one-striper (abbr.)
15. Seoul residents
20. Central points
22. French traveller's bag
24. Spin, in "Jabberwocky"
25. Chemical radical
26. Group dance
28. _____ eclipse
29. Mork's TV companion
32. Post-WWII European org.
33. Something to do at Mont-Tremblant
35. John Deere implement
36. Italia capital
37. Seabirds
39. Long-time *60 Minutes* correspondent Mike
42. Angler's snack?
44. Paid _____
47. Garb
48. Religion in Japan
49. "Friendly Islands" people
51. Venus de Milo, et al.
53. Curacao neighbour
55. Curved moulding
56. Canadian Garnett who sang "We'll Sing in the Sunshine"
57. Québec commerce liquid
58. Loire Valley vineyard
59. Silken Laumann implement
60. Canadian singing star Roberts

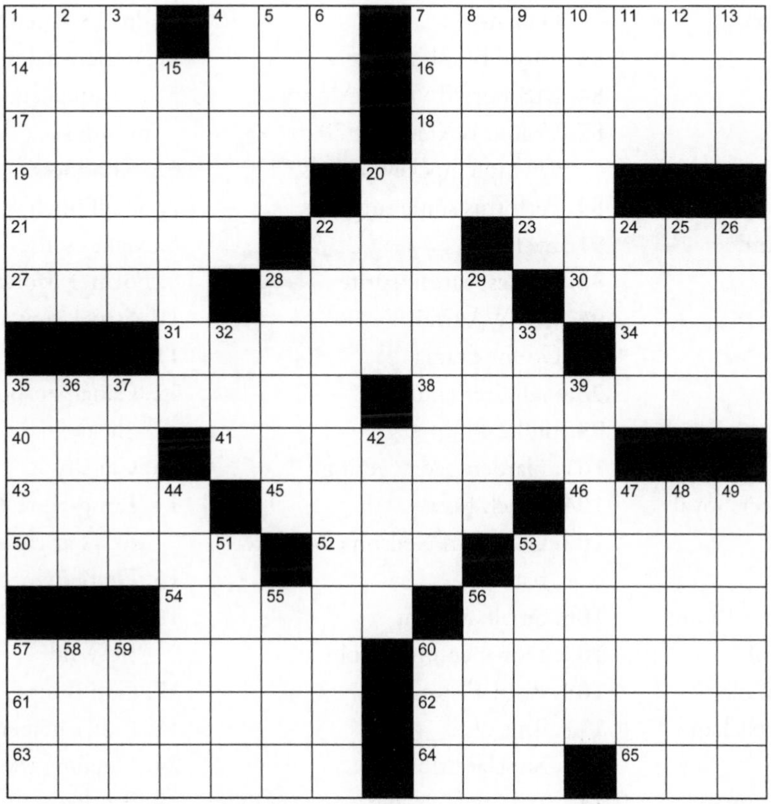

Solution on page 216

34 For Pete's Sake

Name these famous Canadian Peters

ACROSS

1. Ticket remnant
5. Phoenix suburb
9. Coastal African country
14. Decorative collar
19. Vatican personage
20. Ripened
21. Numbers meaning nothing?
22. _____ *Gay*
23. **Jazz vibraphonist and percussionist**
25. Debtors
26. Nostrils
27. Get ready to drive
28. Renounce a relative
30. Rise and shine time
32. Well-known Quebecers Joyal and Savard
34. Wimple wearers
35. Parti Québécois leader Pauline
36. Long, long time (var.)
38. First-rate, in India of old
40. Canadian cable sports channel (abbr.)
41. Canadian flautist Koffman
44. Tastes a drink
47. Captain's diary
49. Long-term blockade
51. Self-aggrandizement
53. Commercials
54. Those with vision
56. Unfeeling?
58. Tarnish a reputation
59. Former NL premier Wells
61. *Persona non grata*, say
64. National restaurant chain: White _____
66. Rona purchase
67. Summaries
69. Appointed
71. Owl sounds
73. Trash can, in Tottenham
74. Blinds and curtains
76. 1984 Cyndi Lauper hit
80. Computing speed units
82. Canadian short story writer Gallant
83. '60s CBC show: *Chez* _____
84. MB-born TV host Monty
87. Colour of Canada's 2010 Olympic hockey medals
89. Performs some surgeries
91. Eyeholes
92. Shakespearean sprite
94. BC–WA strait
96. Go for drama
98. Gangster's gun
99. Biblical hunter
101. Garden bed covering
104. Much fuss
105. Canadian Neilson chocolate bars
106. Small amount
107. Dubai country (abbr.)
109. Bottled spirits?
111. The War _____
113. Shoelace tips
115. Jarl's wife, in Norse mythology
117. Marine species
121. Not any particular place
123. Cheap
125. Breathing
126. Luminous stars
127. Muslim religion
129. **Screwdriver inventor**
131. Goldie Hawn film: *Bird on* _____
132. *Paint Your Wagon* song: "I Still See _____"
133. Airline in Israel
134. Redo words
135. Waited out
136. Black bird
137. Wee dagger
138. Fishing poles

DOWN

1. Fights over footwear?
2. Pith helmet (var.)
3. Pre-1841 name: _____ Canada
4. Arctic whales
5. Canadian statutory holiday month
6. "Goodness!"
7. Small finch
8. Makes sense
9. **Former *Morningside* host**
10. Struck down?
11. You _____ here
12. Canadian-born '30s actress Shearer
13. Classify
14. **Long-time Toronto-born ABC news anchor**
15. Diarist/writer Nin
16. Steppenwolf smash: "_____ to Be Wild"
17. Couturier Cassini
18. Prof.'s helpers
24. Duelling tool
29. Burden
31. Alberta's "wild" provincial flower
33. Shoe bottom
35. Ancient sorcerer
37. Speaker of Canada's senate Kinsella
39. Former Canadian ambassador to Iran Taylor
41. Venus de _____
42. 1952 Olympics city
43. US mystery author Jenkins
44. Bones that connect hips
45. Runs in neutral
46. Intimidate, with "out"
48. Big baseball play
50. Lung disease
52. Vend more
54. Old photo finish

55. *Toronto* _____
57. Halloween greeting
60. Dilettante
62. Mosque prayer leader
63. Mount Everest country
65. "Baloney!" to a Brit
68. Cozy
70. Hindu divine being
72. Guess Who classic: "_____ Eyes"
75. Rankin Family hit: "_____ Again"
77. Bland shade
78. Like draft beer
79. Bothersome people
81. Homer Simpson expression

84. Lend a _____
85. "Nessun Dorma," for example
86. Arm or leg
88. National pharmacy: London _____
90. Pop
93. Alberta's tenth premier
95. Flamenco cheer
97. Male turkeys
100. Chip's cartoon partner
102. *The Canadian Establishment* **scribe**
103. *Heroes* character Nakamura
105. Liturgical book
108. More creepy
110. Deep-seated from birth

112. Green fruit
113. On the ball
114. Magnetic flux density unit
116. Spicy mayo
118. Bungle
119. Keep clear of
120. Campers' shelters
121. "_____ lay me down to sleep"
122. Old Roman poet
123. Shoot with a stun gun
124. Sun Peaks transport
126. Arrest
128. *Scenes from a Marriage* star Ullmann
130. Antlered animal

35 Tops-y-turvy

Start with anagrams

ACROSS

1. Deadly snakes
5. _____ de boeuf
9. Police, to gangsters
16. Fired a rifle
17. Not locked
18. Pilots
19. Crosby hit: "_____ Smile Be Your Umbrella"
20. Buck's party?
21. '30s Canadian prime minister
22. Oft-used French verb
23. Canadian gas station name
24. Tolkien creatures
25. Lahore language
26. Ills
27. Vineyard in Savoie
28. Greek "h"
31. Baden-Powell group regatta participant
33. Marker pens
35. NL town: Joe Batt's _____
36. Trendy in the summer?
37. **Where an actor shines?**
38. Young fellow
39. Avro Arrow, say
40. Shortened name of ex-Flame Fleury
41. Seethed with anger
44. Birds that inspired a coin nickname
45. Citizen, at election time
46. Singer Fitzgerald
47. Drops suggestions
48. Waste bin
49. **How a track official tells time?**
51. Mas' mates
52. Plaid hat
55. Hodgepodge
56. Mining shaft
58. Some high-schoolers (abbr.)
59. Falsehood
60. Subterfuge
61. Milky or fiery gemstone
62. AB-born NY Rangers GM Sather
63. They go with crafts
64. Suffix with ideal
65. Slogan
68. Necklaces for a luau
69. Nickname for Hamilton's newspaper
71. Teems
72. Glass square
73. Bliss Carman poetry opus: *Low _____ on Grand Pré*
74. Latino community convenience stores
75. Embraces
76. Coat fastener

DOWN

1. Communication without sound (abbr.)
2. More transparent
3. **Where German chefs train?**
4. Rona Ambrose federal ministry: _____ of Women
5. It could be used in lieu of walnut
6. **How an umpire throws in the towel?**
7. Afternoon service?
8. Composer Molnár and skater Steuer
9. Rounded jewellery stones
10. Estimate too highly
11. Twirled tress
12. Skillets and double boilers
13. Summer in Sherbrooke
14. Soak hemp
15. The Concorde, for example
25. Below the 49th (abbr.)
28. Ovechkin's jersey number
29. Titter (var.)
30. *Titanic* character John Jacob
32. Nickelback singer Kroeger
33. Bridges
34. Rock climber's spike
37. It accompanies lust and envy, et al.
38. Jumped
39. _____ de Leon
41. Canadian education savings plans (abbr.)
42. Church table
43. Lip _____
44. Flexibility
45. Bouquet holder
47. Estate in Alicante
48. Strokes a Siamese
50. Ready to inherit?
51. **What a mailman might apply to?**
52. **How to describe a tennis pro's publicity?**
53. Saskatchewan dam and town name
54. Former mayor of Toronto Lastman
56. J. Edgar Hoover's dresser?
57. Raises
60. Former Alberta premier Klein
62. Sticky stuff
65. File folder adjunct
66. Blood-typing letters
67. '85 Meg Tilly film: *Agnes of _____*
70. Mushroom with a big top

36

Canada Cornucopia 12

ACROSS

1. PEI product, colloquially
5. Mimic
8. European perennial
13. Canadian prairies city
15. Calgary's Kyle Shewfelt won Commonwealth gold in this
16. Intertwining
17. Street fight
18. First-rate pilot's nickname
19. Jabber
20. Street person, colloquially
21. Flock member
22. 2004 Wayson Choy Giller nominee: *All _____ Matters*
24. Ornate button material
26. Like a sassy gymnast?
27. Decorative flourish, in script
29. Indochinese language
30. Tennis and golf equipment
31. Show contempt
33. Like current events
35. Apply a bit
37. Alberta-born skating star Browning
38. 2003 Pink album
41. US chewing tobacco brand
44. First astrological sign
45. Schwarzenegger, previously (abbr.)
47. Stable dads
49. Pot toppers
50. Financial services holding company: _____ Corporation of Canada
52. Dire destiny
53. Supped
54. Winery tank
55. Canadian retirement income option (abbr.)
57. Beehive State Native
58. Lethal loops
60. Massive
62. Northern Canadian people
63. Not professional
64. See 17-A
65. Doug and the Slugs smash: "Too _____"
66. Combines

DOWN

1. Workout wear
2. Nips in
3. Forget about it?
4. Common forensic substance
5. Like some swarms
6. Friend via the mail
7. 1983 Margaret Atwood collection: *Bluebeard's _____*
8. Source of conception
9. Animal symbol of 44-A
10. German measles
11. Hostility
12. Makes a cuppa
14. Cool, attitudinally
17. JoÚ Candy *SCTV* character: JoÚny La_____
20. Newfoundland city: Corner _____
23. Colours, '60s-style
25. Persian or Siamese
26. Newsy bit
28. Stunts
30. Canadian jeweller since 1879
32. Swiss skating star Lucinda
34. Cyst contents
36. Prejudiced person
38. Musical step of three
39. Short-term '89 NL premier Tom
40. Mama pig
42. Caught one's interest
43. National Ballet of Canada attire
44. Ottawa-born Grammy winner Morissette
46. *The Two Gentlemen of _____*
48. Refines ore, say
50. The _____ MB
51. Annoyed
54. Reject a request
56. Canadian actor Michael J.
59. Rest a bit
60. First three letters of a Canadian bank acronym
61. Place where you want to get steamed up

37

The Party Line

Past and present federal groups

ACROSS

1. Come to pass
6. Life source
9. Asian language
12. Old CBC show: *Mr.* _____
19. Slang for funds (var.)
20. TV show type
22. Bring back to life, say
23. **Party from *La Belle Province***
25. Siren, say
26. Devoured
27. Toronto singer/actress Salome
28. a.k.a. ermine
30. Legal decree
31. Keep
33. Pretentious one
34. In the manner of, in Montréal
35. Royal wedding broadcaster, for short
38. Give the slip to
39. Supreme _____ of Canada
40. Resides
43. Middle East nation
45. **Party linked with 115-A**
48. Pair
49. Wavy
52. Young beaver
53. Be inclined
54. Sandwich type
55. Stage star
57. No longer working (abbr.)
58. Halley's cleanser?
59. Endurance test
60. Opposite of rosy
63. Idealization, in psychology
65. Greek letter
66. Work over?
68. *The Fountainhead* author Rand
69. Bodily blood carrier
70. National drs. grp.
73. Make smile
75. Afternoon snooze
77. *Canada's Worst Driver* host Younghusband
79. 2011 drama that took flight on CTV?
81. Canadian railway pioneer Donald
83. Girlfriend
85. Show the way
86. Home Depot rival in Canada
87. Chance
89. Shipbuilder's wood preservative
90. www.cbc.ca, for example
91. **Party founded in 1975**
94. '72 Stampeders single: "_____ Eyes"
95. Like lava
97. Screen queen Oberon
98. US anthropologist and author Margaret
101. Civil War ship name component (abbr.)
102. Sundial number
103. Wave or pool preceder
104. Closer
106. *Romper Room* host: Miss _____
108. Lamb Chop's puppeteer Lewis
109. Tonic's partner
110. Practice piece
113. "It's a _____ to Tipperary"
115. **'30s agricultural-based party**
119. Éclat
120. Thug, say
121. Sultanate citizen
122. Cajole
123. _____ Lanka
124. Exchange of info via computer (abbr.)
125. Measuring cup glass

DOWN

1. Ontario planning act arbiter (abbr.)
2. RC or Tab
3. Codger
4. Gastric woe
5. Hollywood bombshell Welch
6. Bette Davis classic: *All About* _____
7. More chatty
8. *Anne of* _____ *Gables*
9. DiCaprio, to fans
10. *The National*'s news panel segment
11. Seafood dish
12. Fear
13. Lease a car, say
14. *Humanum* _____ *errare*
15. Suppress
16. **Early labour party (1911–20)**
17. It precedes formaldehyde
18. Sprightly
21. Slick like a sidewalk
24. _____ no good
29. Beginning
32. Colorado skiing mecca
33. Channel-_____ aux Basques NL
34. Amazement
35. High-ranking cleric
36. Prickly patches
37. **Party that elected 66 MPs in 2000**
39. Computer-Generated Imagery (abbr.)
40. Data collection device
41. See 25-A
42. Chimney grime
44. In the raw
46. Mucilaginous vegetable
47. Not mainstream
50. Old-fashioned warning
51. Ceramic blocks
54. Big fat pig
56. Early Anka hit: "_____ Beso"
57. Reagan, et al.

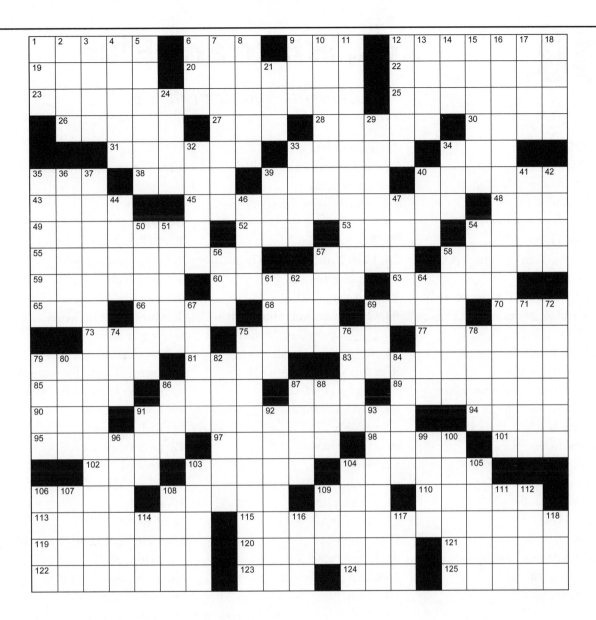

58. Former federal Tory Lawrence
61. Reposed
62. Stronger cleanser
64. '80s TV drama: _____ Vice
67. Muster out of the military
69. Family vehicle
71. Iron and zinc
72. Geminis and Genies
74. Ticked off
75. Percussion instruments
76. Native abode (var.)
78. Sketched
79. Juicy fruit
80. Bubbly chocolate bar
82. Red blood cell deficiency

84. Sleep disorder
86. _____-Tin-Tin
87. Canadian comedy troupe: The Kids in the _____
88. '81 top ten hit: "Our Lips _____ Sealed"
91. Hula hoop?
92. Obedience school staffer
93. Edited
96. Prickling sensation
99. _____ 51
100. Excessive, in Drummondville
103. Spice rack herb
104. One of the family
105. Card game

106. Diamond imperfection
107. *The Hockey Sweater* scribe Carrier
108. Go by boat
109. Biggest metropolis in Canada (abbr.)
111. Salutation for Abby?
112. Bird seen from the shore
114. Gum plug
116. Chris Cagle #1: "I Breathe _____ Breathe Out"
117. TGIF day
118. Half a dozen

Solution on page 217

38 Red, White and Blue

Colourful American movies

ACROSS

1. Seashore cookout
9. *Little Women* character
13. Unkindly
20. British river workers
21. Like a loft
22. Person taken from the eye of the storm
23. 1984 Wilder/Radner comedy
25. Mythical stories
26. Elton's john?
27. Made love?
29. Tolkien creature
30. Like washed out blue jeans
33. Lion's crowning glory?
34. Piece of info
36. New newts
39. Filled with amazement
40. Contemporary
42. Skinny candle
44. a.k.a. aha
45. See 26-A
46. Weekday abbr., in Wakefield
47. Ups the stakes
49. Categories
51. Scan the milk?
54. Radium Hot Springs, for example
55. Italy seaport
56. *Canadian Idol* viewer, say
58. 1933 Betty Boop animated short
61. Absinthe flavouring
62. Now-defunct apple orchard spray
64. Onomatopoeic
65. Performed
68. Wetland areas
69. It cometh before a fall
70. Henley or polo
71. Tibia or femur
72. US Department of Health agency (abbr.)
73. Medical office location
74. Care for
75. Russian retreat
76. 1946 Crosby/Astaire musical
79. Began again
81. Canadian catch
83. QC convention centre: Palais _____ congrès de Montréal
85. As _____ as a mule
86. More severe
87. Engage in art, say
90. Elvis ultimatum: "_____ Now or Never"
91. Honey maker
92. Hurry along
93. Southernmost point in Nova Scotia: Cape _____
95. Tunes' text
97. Composes
98. Uses an abacus
100. Like a crazy bird?
102. Spindly
103. Saskatchewan and Macleod, in Alberta
104. Major Montréal road: _____ Saint-Denis
106. Conceptual thinker
108. 2002 Avril Lavigne song: "Sk8er _____"
109. Wave optics pioneer Augustin-Jean
112. 2002 Michelle Pfeiffer drama
117. George or George W. political supporter
118. Primo
119. Poe story: *The _____ Heart*
120. Whistle-blower, often
121. Plenty
122. Wins producer of the month, say

DOWN

1. 100 lbs., American style
2. _____-di-dah (var.)
3. Chowed down
4. Cried like a kitten
5. Worry about the clan?
6. Shotgun shells, say
7. New Zealand parrot
8. Supreme Court, for example
9. *The Skin I Live In* star Antonio
10. Hibernia a.k.a.
11. Radial pattern
12. Give an IV, say
13. Robbed
14. "_____ Maria"
15. Road _____
16. Play part
17. 1990 Sean Connery thriller (with "*The*")
18. Marshalled the troops
19. Survey answer word
24. Empress Hotel environs: _____ Harbour
28. Airport arrival times (abbr.)
30. Sir John who appears in three Shakespeare plays
31. Roused
32. 1995 Denzil Washington film noir
33. French painter concerned with cash supply?
35. 46-D or 110-D, e.g.
37. Mordecai Richler novel: *Joshua _____ and Now*
38. Mediocre
40. Digital audio player trade name

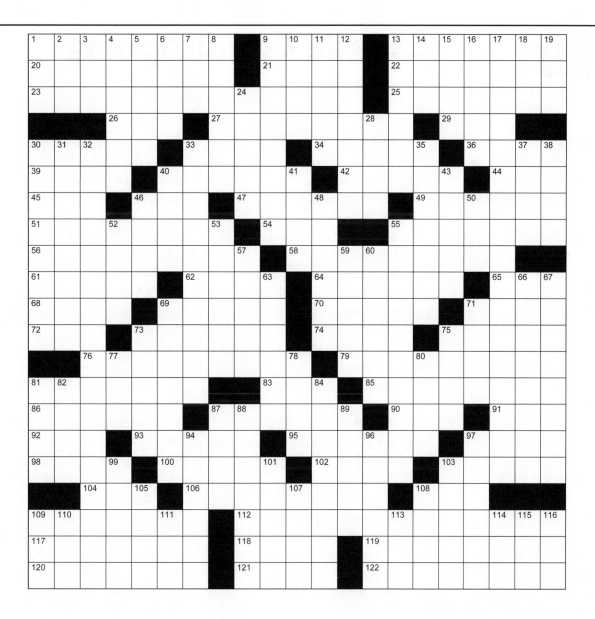

41. Sharp bites
43. *The Beachcombers* character
46. '97 Shania Twain single: "_____ Gets Me Every Time"
48. Most compos mentis
50. Snood
52. Something to clean up
53. Join up again
55. Cane that conceals a weapon
57. Spokes, for example
59. Earthy pigment (var.)
60. Complains about Cabernet?
63. Move back from
66. Innate
67. Loss of elasticity
69. Of lung membranes

71. 1960 golden Canadian pairs skater Wagner, for short
73. Ice and dice
75. Fingerprints, in Britspeak
77. Ignited
78. Gulf of St. Lawrence mammal: Harp _____
80. Scolds the boy king?
81. Double the laughter?
82. Battery fluid
84. Byzantine pillar-saints
87. Dolt
88. Urban reclamation, say
89. Clear the chalkboard
94. Water heating vessel
96. Altogether, to Augustus

97. Ballerina's shoe style
99. Japanese roll ingredient
101. Hick's search engine?
103. Horse farm newborns
105. *National Velvet* novelist Bagnold
107. Fuzz
108. Waist cincher
109. US investigative org.
110. 1984 Bryan Adams single: "_____ to You"
111. Hot time in Huberdeau?
113. Romanian money
114. Sri Lankan serving
115. Hades, in Cockney?
116. They follow dos

ACROSS

1. Lucy _____ Montgomery
5. "Too bad," old style
9. '85 Juno-winning band: Parachute _____
13. *East of Eden* character
14. 1869 novel: _____ *Doone*
16. Assess
17. Campus bigwig
18. Put a cap on?
19. Egyptian goddess
20. Carefully consider
22. Annual spring event in much of Canada
23. Guessed wrong
24. Organic compounds
26. Not digital
29. Jordan's capital
31. Stitch
32. Petro-Canada rival
34. Rope at a rodeo
38. Pain reliever
41. Canal city, in Ontario
43. Lake Erie island
44. Tousle
46. Spring time in Saint-Sauveur
47. Take _____ down memory lane
49. Endorse with another
52. CTV anchor Rinaldo
55. Sailing vessel
57. Chemical compound
58. It follows *Hockey Night in Canada*
63. Not in favour
64. Factory
65. Paying attention, colloquially
66. Big cat
67. French composer Erik
68. Genial place on the French Riviera?
69. Samoan money
70. Southern Ontario community: Grand _____
71. Tuck away

DOWN

1. Org. that crusades against drunk driving
2. Busy as _____
3. Russian river
4. Gilles Duceppe's successor Paillé
5. It may cause itching and scratching
6. Long river in France
7. Naval forces
8. Huff
9. Felon
10. Operated on a eye, say
11. Serviceable
12. Outdoes
15. Elite group, colloquially
21. Sis's sib
25. West Edmonton _____
26. PDQ
27. Hawaiian goose
28. Missing from roll call, say
30. Cuts the lawn
33. Part of a truck?
35. Ex-Vancouver Canucks D-man Salo
36. Glitch
37. Valhalla VIP
39. Crunch time in the newsroom
40. Abominable Snowman a.k.a.
42. Accompanied
45. Toward northern New York?
48. Harvests
50. Delighted interjection
51. '80s Canadian "Nova Heart" band: The _____
52. Marine mammals
53. Canadian speed skating double gold Olympian Perreault
54. "_____ your life!"
56. Bolsheviks' Vladimir
59. Spare tire?
60. Apartment
61. Puerto _____
62. Crock-Pot meal

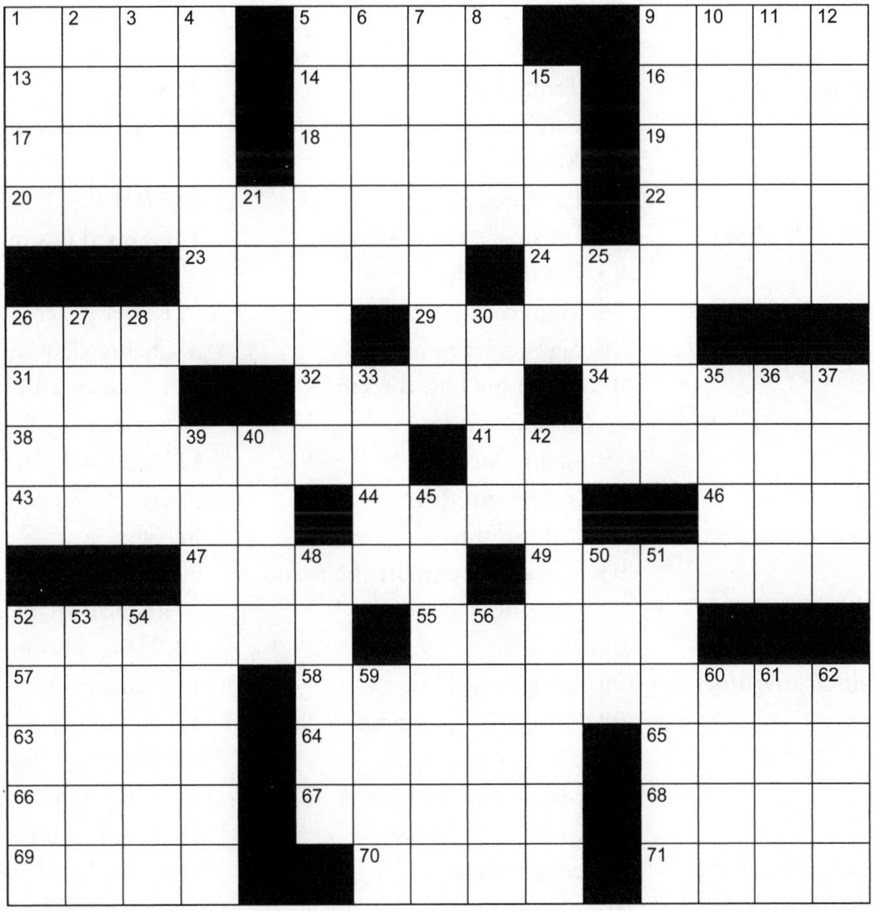

Solution on page 217

Natives make good

ACROSS

1. Study stuff?
5. Moisture in the air (var.)
10. Military music
14. Piles of fish?
19. Humdinger
20. '80s film starring ON-born Kate Nelligan
21. Gumbo veggie
22. Lowest deck on ship
23. Biblical brother
24. Gin and _____
25. Watch face
26. CBC _____ 2
27. Canadian military journalist Gwynne
28. Standard tithing amount
29. Cuckoo
30. **Trivial Pursuit co-inventor Scott**
31. Poetic tributes
33. Not clerical
35. Raspy gasps
37. Hit on the head, colloquially
40. Backyard building
42. Catlike mammal
43. _____ Saint-Jean QC
46. TV comedy classic: *Green _____*
47. Jewelled headpiece
48. Mound
49. Popular Japanese sport
50. Like Santa's cheeks
51. Brassy
52. *Sextette* star West
54. ***Star Trek* icon William**
56. "Telephone Line" rock grp.
57. Infectious proteins
59. Blood mass
61. Former NL premier Grimes
62. Lush
64. Protective foot covering
66. Romeos, say

67. Salad oil dispenser
69. Misery
70. Traffic snarl
72. Cobbler's victory?
75. Modifies
78. Parfait or pie
82. US singer/actor Billy Ray
83. Put in stitches?
84. Train conductor?
86. Sign of peace
87. **Two-time best director Oscar nominee Jason**
89. Actor DeLuise
91. Sailor's greeting
92. Prima donna
93. Canadian composer Southam and singer Mortifee
94. "Drat!"
96. Long-legged bird
98. Soft palate membrane
99. Choke on a joke?
100. Master of ceremonies
101. *Let's _____ a Deal*
102. Ships' bow parts
103. Similar to
104. Canadian military rank (abbr.)
105. Geometry or algebra
106. **Most-winning NHL coach Scotty**
109. Paternity identifier
111. Shoestrings
114. Stratford-_____-Avon
118. Not suitable
119. 1993 Reese Witherspoon film: *_____ Off Place*
120. Wonky
121. Rock climbing aid
122. Fashion
123. Litigator's attire?
124. August NS/PEI celebration: _____ Day
125. Zagreb resident, say
126. Fleeced a fireman?

127. Feminine pronoun, in Frontenac
128. Heart #1: "_____ Dreams"
129. Lacquered metalware

DOWN

1. Covered in siding, say
2. Halifax-born *42nd Street* star Keeler
3. Sheltered, at sea
4. **TV entertainment host Ben**
5. Examined a dog thoroughly?
6. Medicinal plants
7. Oscar winner Sean
8. "Step _____!"
9. ***The Apprenticeship of Duddy Kravitz* scribe Mordecai**
10. NBC morning show
11. See 103-A
12. Alberta or Saskatchewan terrain
13. *Dog Day Afternoon* character
14. Fruit-based frozen treat
15. Grumpy crustaceans?
16. Canadian-based shoe retailer since 1972
17. Nike slogan: Just _____
18. Dalmatian's dilemma?
30. First Hebrew letter
32. Montréal venue: Place _____ Arts
34. Canadian country singer Gregory
36. "Halt!" to a salt
37. Denudes
38. Where *élèves* go
39. Property crime
40. Farm storage space
41. Dusty Springfield song: "If It _____ Been For You"
42. Scorpion's claw
43. Fencing thrust
44. African chieftain (var.)
45. Irish "Breathless" band

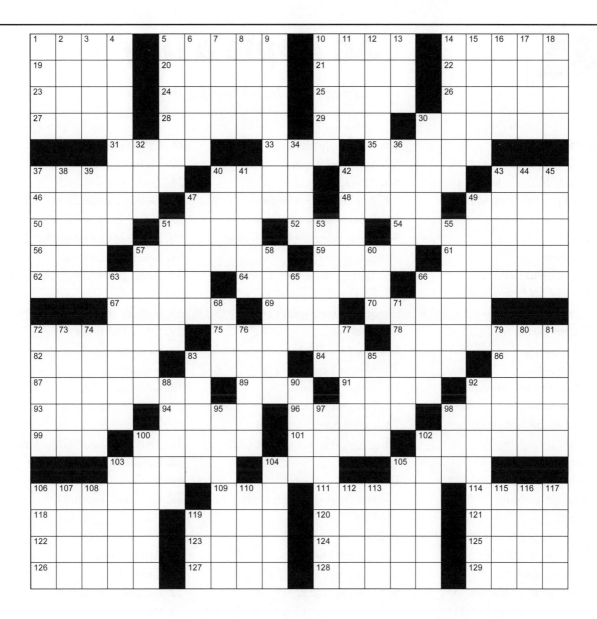

47. Patterned fabric

49. Hunches over

51. Canadian baritone Russell

53. Submit to

55. Kindle suspicion

57. Excessive attention to correctness

58. Johannesburg townships site

60. Elect

63. National youth organization: _____ Canada

65. Centuries on end

66. Tiny

68. Victoria landmark: Fan _____ Alley

71. Dummkopf

72. Mutton cut

73. Doglike scavenger

74. Space shuttle gasket

76. Skeeter's cousin

77. Critical Lewis Carroll creature?

79. Iniquities

80. Show variety?

81. Canucks and Senators

83. Special talent

85. Indian cooking ingredient

88. Office work, for short

90. Note to staff

92. **Four-time Emmy winner Colleen**

95. Indispensible

97. **Mavis who wrote *Home Truths: Selected Canadian Stories***

98. Winery tank

100. Happy

102. Annoy

103. More than enough

104. À la _____

105. Elevated land formations

106. Rose or rhododendron

107. Not duped by

108. Methods

110. Carpentry fastener

112. Eastern nurse

113. Quote

115. Pony's pastime?

116. Like some milk glass

117. Guelph-born *Scream* star Campbell

119. Peer Gynt's mother

41 An Apple a Day

Healthy food for thought

ACROSS

1. The _____ Four
4. William Shatner, for example
9. Like a persistent poodle?
15. Gladly, old style
17. Dull
18. Infuriate
19. Movers and shakers?
21. Former *SNL* cast member Kevin
22. Teapot part
23. Turn type
24. Explosive talk?
25. **Apple for BC coastal residents?**
27. Sandwiches with a pocket
28. Spew
29. Rouse again
31. Dracula, sometimes
34. Massage parlour?
35. Club _____
36. Rainbow goddess, in mythology
37. Papa, in Plessisville
38. Summer cooler
39. Soon, to an unknown poet?
40. Annual Canadian horse race: Queen's _____
41. **Apple beloved in BC?**
45. Voyageur's craft
46. Convenience
47. Thanksgiving mo., in Canada
48. Gawk at
49. Tale that takes time to tell
50. Battery size
51. Gift of the _____
54. *The Partridge Family* actress Susan

55. Fence adjunct
57. Turn about (var.)
58. Attacks
59. **Apple for a rainy day?**
61. Biblical contradictions
64. Genie-winning best picture: *Away from* _____
65. Take to the soapbox
66. CBC talk-show host Stroumboulopoulos
67. Improves
69. More reminiscent of venison?
70. Marine organism (var.)
71. Sassy
72. Fast and slow, say
73. Ceremonies
74. _____ Moines

DOWN

1. Does what the dentist tells you to do
2. Bike tire filler
3. Colourful flower
4. Tuna type
5. Deceived, old style
6. '89 Oscar-winning song: "Under _____"
7. Pronoun for two
8. _____ *Titanic*
9. Signifies
10. Multi-tasking musician: _____ band
11. Gets the brass ring?
12. **Party apple?**
13. MuchMusic program: _____ *and Icons*
14. Fender ding

16. 1859 opera
20. To the _____ degree
24. Two-piece swimsuit
26. Goddess of peace
27. _____ Board of Canada
30. **Apple for an oenophile?**
31. Lovely, in Lachine
32. Royal Canadian Academy of _____
33. Golfer's starting point
35. Old CBC sitcom: _____ *in Canada*
37. Conspiracy
38. Ice in the water
39. Memorable sayings
40. Type size
41. Hamilton park with a bandshell
42. Canadian eatery: Joey's _____
43. With precision
44. Raccoon's relation
45. Cape _____ MA
49. Aliens' dishes?
50. Attribute to
51. Crowed
52. Lacking fun and flair
53. Commands
55. Bullied: _____ up on
56. Frittata (var.)
57. Guitar adjunct
58. Sault Ste. _____
60. Land in Scandinavia (abbr.)
61. Ingredient for 56-D
62. Bring home the barley?
63. **Italian style apple?**
64. Sporty engine type
67. Desecrate
68. 65+ federal program (abbr.)

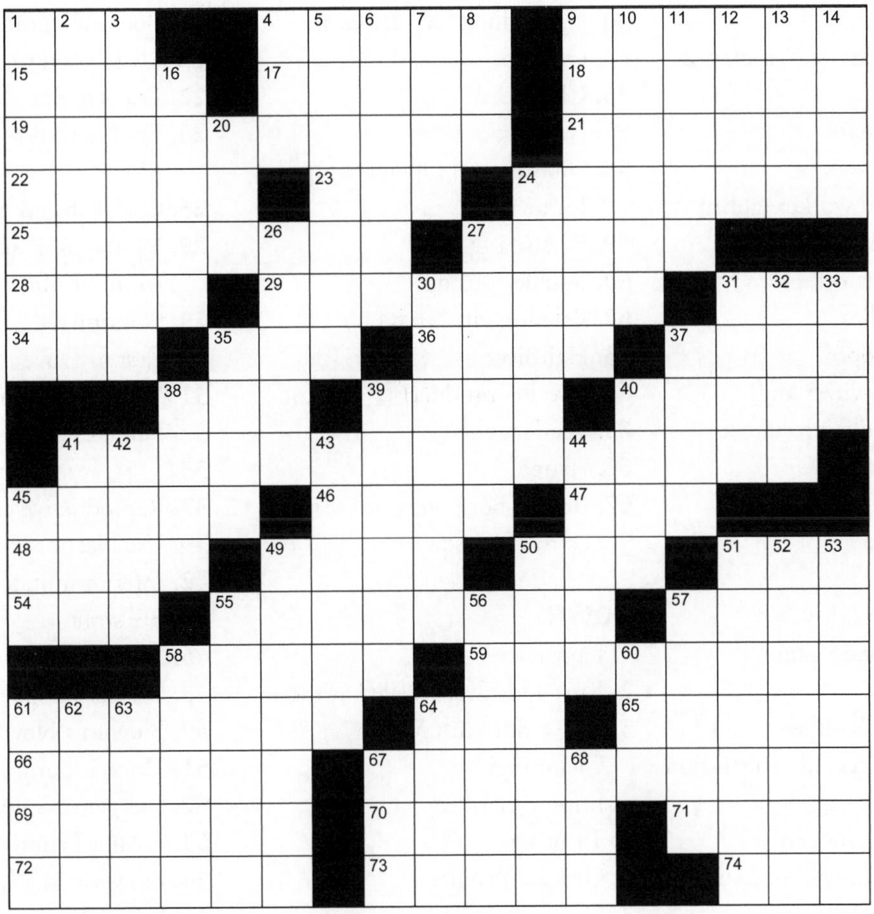

Solution on page 218

ACROSS

1. Capital southeast of Casablanca
6. Pull
9. Dog on *The Jetsons*
14. Give off
15. Hospital ward worker (abbr.)
16. Cut down on potatoes, say?
17. Colonial India titles for European ladies
19. African antelope
20. Top spot in Switzerland?
21. Natural Canadian resource?
22. Characteristics
23. Like mental illnesses
26. Order to Fido
27. British _____
30. Little bird
33. Trick-taking card game
34. Songs for one
35. Conquistador's target
36. General Services Administration (abbr.)
38. Hippie's hallucinogen
40. Title for Macdonald or Laurier
41. NL national park site: L'_____ aux Meadows
43. Some lap dogs
45. English exam part
47. Lens in a door
49. Massage milieu
50. Groundhog Day critter in Ontario
55. CFL word
57. Not fake
58. 2008 French Open champ Ivanovic
59. Pursue a tip, say
60. Rabble-rousing
62. Belgium city
63. Hairpiece
64. Ore-Ida product: _____ Tots
65. Tender spots
66. "Nope"
67. Regina-born *Stargate Universe* actress Levesque

DOWN

1. Update an atlas?
2. Kurt and Elvis excelled at these
3. Like a ride with Margo Channing?
4. Infomercials, e.g.
5. Tutoring
6. Ordeal in court?
7. Clear a drain, say
8. See 21-A
9. Quick look, in Québec?
10. Bows for a Muslim
11. Cattle herding honcho
12. '96 Tony-winning musical
13. Bookies' numbers
18. Owl's good time?
22. Leans to one side
24. TV drama set in NV, NY and FL
25. Oilers objectives?
28. '98 Olympic skating gold winner Kulik
29. Gossamer
30. Zest or Dove
31. White-tailed eagle
32. Floral eau de toilette
33. _____ Ste. Marie
37. Reproductive cell in plants
39. Use Neet or Nair
42. Inferior imitator
44. BC strait
46. '50s movie star Mineo
48. Ghosts' hangouts?
49. Blow to a blowfly?
51. Horse's sound
52. Clergyman's flock
53. *ER* star Laura
54. Big wave in a small place
55. Falls behind
56. Reverberation
60. Grass bristle
61. "She's So High" Canadian singer Bachman

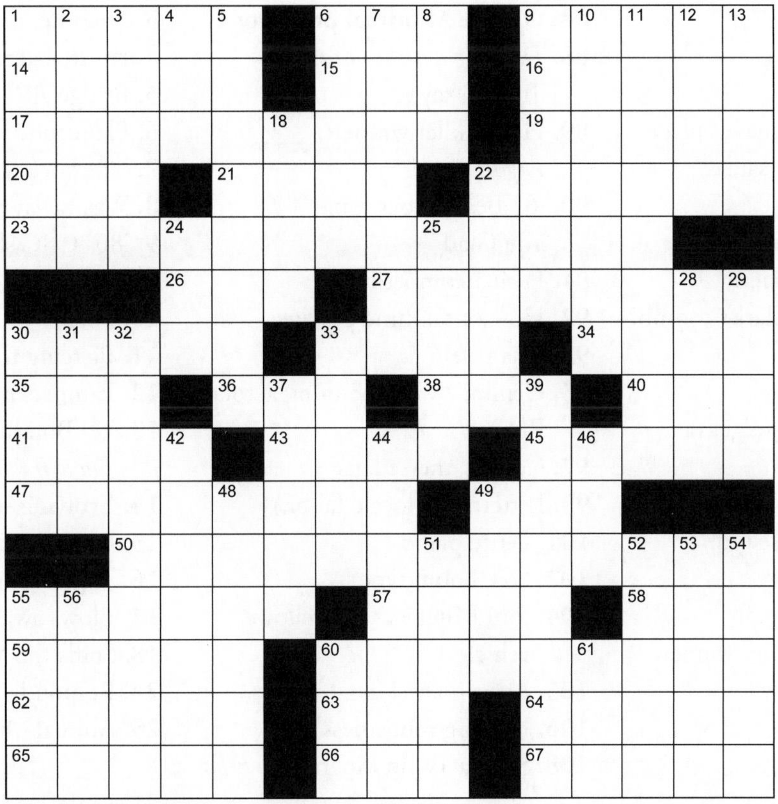

Solution on page 218

43 | Are You Game

. . . for Canadian Monopoly (first edition)?

ACROSS

1. Son, in Saguenay
5. Gadabout gardeners?
10. Low point
15. Unwanted email
19. Secular
20. Northernmost Nunavut place
21. "_____ man once said . . ."
22. Des Moines state
23. Trillium province B&O Railroad replacement
26. Former premier Clark's coomb?
27. Tenant's payment
28. _____ ex machina
29. Passion fruit/orange/guava drink
30. Famed Scottish loch
31. Factory-built house type
34. Fruit rind
35. Optic membrane
37. Canadian-born Tony winner Cariou
38. _____ fan tutte
40. River in Rome
42. Ready to roll
46. Bluto's target: Olive _____
47. Double delivery?
49. Family dog, say
50. Not at sea
51. Bites
53. Bad habit
55. Not prone
57. Early spring bloomer
58. Comme ci, comme ça
59. Water Works substitute
61. Freezing rain
62. _____ projection
64. Crossword box
65. Sri Lankan language
67. Bypass surgery type
69. Green Eggs and Ham author
72. Go from A to B?
76. False name
78. Lesotho money
80. Bath alternative
81. Pasta sauce brand
84. Orange Montréal property
88. Dancing with the Stars pro Trebunskaya
89. Hay's Giller winner: _____ Nights on Air
90. '67 Beach Boys song: "_____ You Glad"
91. Purina competitor
92. Horizontal mine passage
93. As a rule
95. Gemini Award-winning actor Rubes
97. Coupes and sedans
99. Letterman's locale (abbr.)
101. Petite piano
102. SST boom type
104. Joni Mitchell's big yellow vehicle
105. African antelope
106. Lacking robustness
108. Shania Twain biography: From _____ Moment On
110. Regaled
112. Not panicky
115. "Wizard of Menlo Park" monogram
116. Hay for the heifers, say
117. Sound of a hoof
118. Space
119. Blue Halifax property
125. O. Henry story: The Gift of the _____
126. Beneficiary
127. Breakfast slice
128. Zero, in Glasgow
129. Bard's word for black
130. Slalom turns
131. Strike down, old style
132. Northern First Nations group

DOWN

1. US rapper: _____ Rida
2. CBC journalist Hanomansing
3. Fired up
4. Knitted accessory
5. Bridge at Niagara Falls
6. Plentitude
7. '70s hockey star Dryden
8. Wear away
9. '80s CBC show: The Kids of Degrassi _____
10. Nopes
11. Piercing tool
12. Pampers product
13. '99 Bond film: The World _____ Enough
14. Evolving star
15. Purple St. JoÚ's property
16. Top of Canada, say
17. Blows away
18. Staffs the YMCA?
24. Responds
25. Annual Ottawa event: Canadian _____ Festival
31. Arafat's org.
32. Mexico city
33. Joins the Royal Canadian Air Force
34. Yearning for yews?
35. "Blast from the past" style description
36. Canadian lifeguarding org.
39. Slavic goddess (var.)
41. Horn sound
43. Aching
44. Point Pelee National Park lake
45. Juno-winning band: Crash _____ Dummies
48. Leaves a mark
50. Group of eight
52. Yellow Winnipeg property
54. The Sopranos star Falco
56. Is, in Île-Dupas

58. Settle down?

59. 152, to a Roman

60. Grown-up

61. Expel a deep breath

63. Folk singer Guthrie

66. Military dining hall

68. '69 Stampeders hit: "_____ Me"

70. Canada Dry ginger ale, to an American

71. Old-style grave marker

73. Shade providers

74. Gum brand name

75. Notable period

77. Litigate for libel, say

79. Some signals

81. Math sign

82. Woodworking tool

83. Case to take to Saint-Tropez?

85. Take delight in

86. Musial of baseball

87. Greek letter

90. Height, to a pilot

92. American sci-fi writer Isaac

94. *Glee* star's meadow?

96. Fertilizer component (var.)

98. Rhubarb acid

100. Ruminant's mouthful

102. Molson mugs?

103. Trunks

107. Canadian polling firm

109. Dialect

111. Turn topsy-turvy

112. Showed up

113. Man of Oman, say

114. Toy company since '32

116. Legal charges?

117. Bodily sac

120. Neckline type

121. Sea bream, in Japan

122. Highlander's "no"

123. Buffet appliance

124. Watch a hurricane?

44 Cross-eyed?

Theme clues will help you see straight

ACROSS

1. Hockey "helpers"?
8. Mixed nuts component
15. Hammer holder
16. Super sniper
17. Vote counter
18. Pungent
19. Fleur-de-lys
20. Don's valley, in Toronto?
22. Cheerleader's data type?
23. **International humanitarian organization**
24. **Combative exchange**
25. Diamond or ruby
26. Pare down
28. _____ Lake AB
29. Genius, colloquially
31. Amazing
33. 1998 Sony PlayStation video game
34. Extend
37. Much praised
38. People in dire straits
39. French Impressionist Édouard
40. Modify
41. Equal
42. Not hard
46. Dwelling abbr.
47. **Dirt bike sport**

48. **Archer's implement**
49. *Wheel of Fortune* contestant's purchase
50. Milk container
52. _____ gin
53. Repeating
55. Hit the spot
57. Authorize a trademark
58. Booted out
59. Royal mace (var.)
60. Not hiders

DOWN

1. Wardrobe
2. Flew high
3. Punctuation slashes
4. Woes
5. **Ashleigh McIvor's golden Olympic sport**
6. Level
7. Firing from above
8. Respect
9. Sierra _____
10. Foal's mother
11. Weird
12. Ottoman Empire, old style
13. It blows up real good
14. BC-born *Knocked Up* star Rogen

21. American actor Rhames
25. Ex-goalie Fuhr and ex-premier Devine
27. Juno-winning band: Billy _____
28. Brooches
29. **Non-profit health-care provider**
30. Bob one's head
32. **Current activity**
33. *Bête noire*
34. Stephen Ames org.
35. Like a candlelit dinner
36. Swimsuit style
37. Scrams
39. TSN CFL analyst Dunigan
41. Canada Post worker
43. Religious person
44. Ibid. location
45. Jacket fabrics
47. Parsonage
49. Garlic bulbs
50. Isn't able to
51. Pew area
52. Toronto hospital moniker: _____Kids
54. MP, say
56. **Railroad track timber**

45 Canada Cornucopia 15

ACROSS

1. Whitehorse territory
6. Some male singers (var.)
11. Calendar abbr.
14. Do penance
15. Dedication to detail, say
17. Canadian-born NHLers Duchene and Cooke
18. Former federal cabinet minister Day
19. Play at a casino table
21. Not in the wind
22. Untruthful ones
23. Biblical second-person verb
24. British term of endearment
28. Long time, geologically
29. Nabisco cookie
30. Moved artwork, say
34. Tirana currency
37. 18-A or 65-A, for example
40. Alberta's _____ Island National Park
41. Daze
42. Big hairstyle
43. Exercise program: _____ Bo
44. Critical
46. Old Iranian titles
49. _____ Jaw SK
52. Veil trim
53. Not likely
58. Italian meal course
60. Indian ethnic group
61. Classic Québec dish
62. Fend off
63. Imbibe
64. Some hook shapes
65. Mulroney minister of communications Marcel

DOWN

1. Orange tubers
2. State where Canada won 17 Olympic medals
3. Stringed Japanese instrument
4. '75 Ambrosia hit: "Holdin' _____ Yesterday"
5. Company that makes Coffee Crisp
6. Iraq oil port
7. Henry Hudson's oil?
8. Prevents
9. Parts of minutes, for short
10. Bic fluid
11. Yoho National Park town
12. Functions
13. Burrard _____ BC
16. Mark or Shania
20. Chemical salt
23. ". . . paddywhack, give a _____ bone . . ."
24. Rough Trade singer Carole
25. Spoken
26. Staff member's reward
27. Slovakia border country (abbr.)
28. Assign responsibility to
31. Big bird
32. Like a cool cat?
33. Crazy Eights cousin
34. Biography topic
35. Take home pay
36. Granny or slip
38. A nod _____ good . . .
39. Scott Joplin's tabloid?
43. Possessive pronoun
45. Preston Manning founded this party
46. Venetian blind boards
47. Capital in Asia
48. Misbehave
49. Canadian playwright/poet Daniel David
50. Unconventional
51. Orchestral reeds
53. Throne's riser
54. _____ formaldehyde
55. Places for kisses
56. Strong soaps
57. Harvard rival
59. Canadian military rank (abbr.)

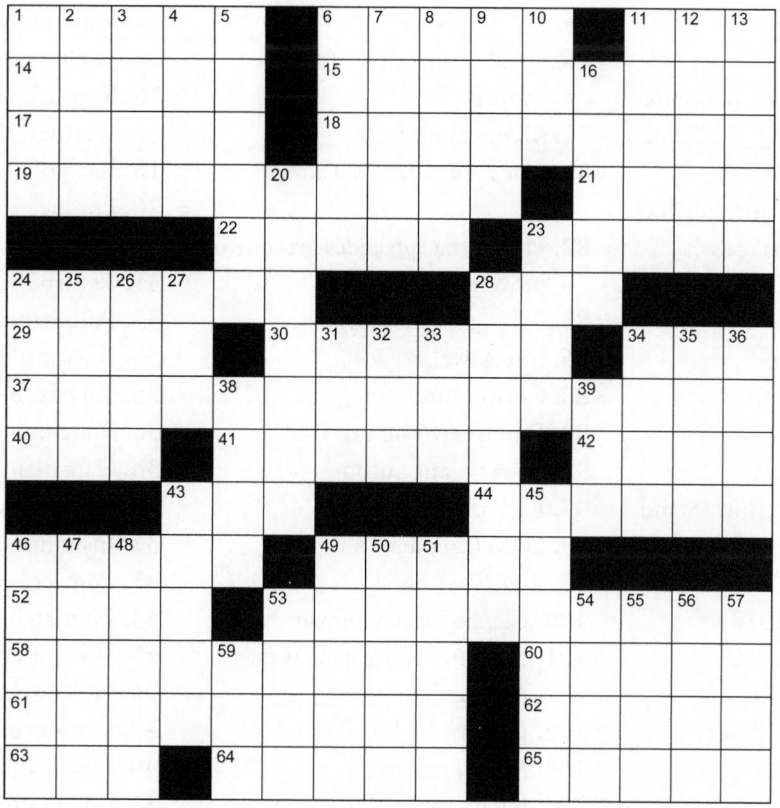

Solution on page 219

46 Big Mac Attack

In Canada and beyond

ACROSS

1. _____ *Here to Eternity*
5. Canadian C&W channel
8. German "alas"
11. Exploited Elsie?
17. Canada's first female Aboriginal senator: Sandra _____ Nicholas
19. Timid
20. *Mon oncle Antoine* director Jutra
21. Rosary component
22. Tree liquid
23. Hang _____
24. Rundown residence
25. Mayo with a kick
27. Mausoleum
28. Commit treason
30. Burton Cummings hit: "Stand _____"
32. Utter
33. Monarch before 1917
37. See 2-D
38. Sri Lanka, pre 1972
40. Reindeer group without Rudolph?
42. Transfer liquid using a tube (var.)
44. 1899–1902 war combatants
48. Hostile mood for a hiker?
50. Just about
52. Microwave, colloquially
53. *A Streetcar Named Desire* character
54. Pentameter poems
57. Ship's front
58. **Expanse for a proposed NWT pipeline**
61. Infant
63. Moderately slow, in music
64. Three-foot stein: _____ ale
67. Indonesian holiday spot
68. Place to get pastrami
69. Country music star Jo Dee
70. Canadian concert pianist Angela
72. Humphrey Bogart hat style
75. _____-pocus
76. Smallest mainland Africa country
79. Mythical birds
81. *One Flew Over the Cuckoo's _____*
82. Phrase that precedes grecque or provençale
85. "_____ See Clearly Now"
86. Impassive
88. Cotton unit
90. Rub the wrong way?
92. Power plant output
97. Lack of oxygen
99. 2006 Canadian film: _____ *Cop Bad Cop*
100. Classic Disney movie
101. Hamilton-area attraction: African Lion _____
102. Jack-in-the-box cover
103. More anxious
104. Nickname of 107-A
105. 2012 British Open champion Ernie
106. '60s drug
107. Canadian wrestler Bret

DOWN

1. One-dimensional
2. Wander around
3. Gas appliance
4. The same, in Shawinigan
5. Vocation
6. **Apple with a big bite of market share**
7. It holds cups, saucers and a pot
8. Appraise a mine
9. Hot, spicy beverage
10. Suffering from low blood pressure
11. **Large Montréal campus**
12. Unhealthy
13. Café au _____
14. High praise
15. Swelling source
16. Kentucky race won by Northern Dancer
18. Rack of _____
26. Produce an egg?
29. Band aid?
31. Return shot, in tennis
33. Pulls behind
34. "Get lost!"
35. Shivery, old style
36. Watching a video again
38. Canadian Christian Cardell who painted the Queen Mother
39. Insignificant one?
41. Powder
43. Human or ape man
45. Wife of Orpheus
46. Golden Age "pictures" studio
47. Use a needle pulling thread
49. Dhaka money
51. ON chiropractic grp.
54. Not easily categorized
55. Rhododendron kin
56. Roy Rogers' real surname
59. *Pirates of the Caribbean: At World's _____*
60. Tie down a sail
61. Network in Britain and beyond (abbr.)
62. Sound at a spa
65. Load to bear
66. Quick
69. **National magazine with wide circulation**
71. Moo goo _____ pan
73. Dehydration treatment (abbr.)
74. Several guests for dinner?
77. **Worldwide Canadian food conglomerate**

78. "Pfui!"
80. "_____, Sealed, Delivered"
82. Embarrass
83. It's south of Molokai
84. Up in the air

86. Remits
87. Facts and figures
89. Test
91. Aluminum _____
93. Cleanse

94. China's continent
95. Stadium section
96. Bakery buy
98. *Deathtrap* playwright Levin

47 Games People Play

Memory lane for adults

ACROSS

1. Court officials, for short
5. Defeat decisively
9. Attention-getting sound
13. Mimicked
17. Off-ramp, say
18. Give a review
19. Billy Ray Cyrus smash: "_____ Breaky Heart"
20. Filmmaker Wertmüller
21. Fencer's tool
22. Seaweed-sourced gel
23. Most like an Ivy Leaguer?
25. **Politician's pastime?**
28. Billiards stick
29. Put off
30. Plastic sheets
31. Curved mouldings
33. Baby amphibian
35. Monk's title
36. Maiden name indicator
37. Mount Fidelity BC gets this 144 days a year
38. Former Canadian astronaut Garneau
40. **Hunter's game?**
46. Dunce
48. Baseball stat.
49. South Pacific dish
50. Shoppers _____ Mart
51. Mend
53. Stocking shade
56. Kilkenny country (abbr.)
58. Place to get a steak: The _____
59. Diffusely
63. European peak
66. I, to Augustus
67. Recognize
68. Quagmire
72. 2009 Neil Young album: *Fork in the* _____
74. PEI's 26th premier James
76. Grazing ground

78. 2002–03 Ontario premier Eves
79. **Composer's contest?**
83. European volcano
84. Ocean bird
85. Western omelette ingredient
86. Work on a doily
89. Common verb in Charlemagne
90. Space ciné genre
92. Underwater explorer
94. Japanese or Korean
96. Annex
97. **Detective's diversion?**
102. Veronica Tennant, in the '70s
104. Colorado skiers' resort
105. Woodwind section reed
106. _____ formaldehyde
107. Smelting detritus
108. Slave to crosswordese?
109. Builder's blueprint
110. Priest's milieu
111. Likewise
112. Third-person pronoun, for some
113. Campers' covering

DOWN

1. Underwater rock ridge
2. 1967 Montréal event
3. Students' outing
4. Plant part
5. Cabinetry component
6. Fashion industry, in slang
7. Salt Lake City locale
8. Flat hat
9. Decorated a wall
10. Gather together
11. Farmyards buildings
12. Sort of font?
13. "The Greatest"
14. Bit of sewing?
15. Come to pass
16. Saturday night outings, say
24. Fork part

26. Not on
27. Like flat hair
32. Burnard's Giller Prize winner: *A* _____ *House*
33. Mideast potentate
34. Lose colour
37. Avoids kilts and minis?
39. Joseph's jacket?
41. Large vases
42. Seal the cracks
43. Loonie, say
44. Canadian TV/radio sex educator Johanson
45. Iconic Fabergé item
47. Goodyear product
52. Sleeve type
54. Greyish-brown
55. Harmful bacteria
57. Magazine for her, in Montréal?
60. Actor Coward
61. Water jug
62. Days of old
63. Salmon _____ BC
64. National sports award: _____ Marsh Trophy
65. Lozenges
69. Indefensible, in logic
70. Cotton production machines
71. Warmth
73. Ex-PM's nickname
75. Australian termite eaters
77. Unstable radioactive element
80. Arson or burglary
81. Try
82. Part of AARP
87. Cape Breton fiddling star MacIsaac
88. Windsor's knot?
90. Waxy skin secretion
91. Speed skating and cycling Canadian Olympian Hughes
92. Power tool
93. Disk on denims

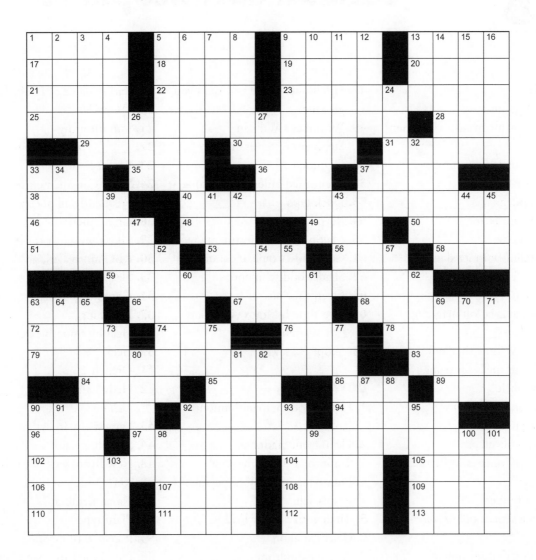

95. Get a pet, say

98. Minor or Major preceder

99. Knowlton who read the news

100. Mottled mare

101. Canadian "Scud Stud" Arthur

103. "Deck the Halls" syllables

ACROSS

1. Pago Pago place
6. Former prime minister Chrétien
10. Tins
14. Like artistic innovators
16. Canadian kayaker van Koeverden
17. Mild approach
18. Small horse
19. Chatham-born ice dancer: _____-Lynn Bourne
20. Severe fear
22. National aviation magazine: *Canadian* _____
24. How a Winnie the Pooh character spells his name
27. Silky fabric
28. Very long time (var.)
29. Occur in autumn?
31. Cousin of calypso
32. Racy roommates in Rivière-Rouge?
35. Stores fodder
36. Narnia series book: *Prince* _____
40. Murderer's punishment
42. Posed
45. Canadian a cappella group (with "The")
46. Burn a bit
47. Hitchhiker's query: "Could you give me _____?"
49. Winnipeg's William Stephenson, for example
50. Dignified
51. She turned onlookers to stone
53. Duck type
54. Revolve
55. Making more adjustments
61. Columnist's type of column
62. Shades of discontent?
63. Overly curious
64. Five-time Eskimos Grey Cup QB Warren
65. Shoptalk, say

DOWN

1. Hollywood thespians' union (abbr.)
2. Hello from Hadrian
3. Toronto's Casa Loma, et al.
4. Phrase for "immediate payment," in Ipswich
5. Titan with a heavy load
6. Calendar abbr.
7. Poetry palindrome
8. Public notices
9. Birds' abode
10. Tyrrhenian Sea isle
11. Decorates
12. Inuit polar bear
13. Earlier name of Izmir, Turkey
15. "Wow!"
21. Join the army
22. _____ *Time Next Year*
23. Enthusiastic
24. Some Canadian critters
25. Frequently, in poetry
26. Grand theft?
29. Like a muscular cattle rancher?
30. RBC mortgages, say
33. Flashes of light
34. Hamilton's newspaper
37. Breathing
38. Healthy smoothie berry
39. Geek
41. Drench
42. Hedy Lamarr film: _____ *and Delilah*
43. Largest city in Syria
44. Straightens up
48. New Brunswick bay with the world's highest tides
50. Nasal membranes
52. Plant type
53. It goes with nicotine
56. One-time Roxy Music member Brian
57. Flurry
58. Cubs' home
59. Famed Keanu Reeves role
60. National tax since 1991

ACROSS

1. Woman's shirt
7. Cut short?
11. Groupie
14. Wood sorrels
18. Paycheque recipient
19. Cat's meow?
20. Go _____ length
22. Round in the ring
23. **1971 album and single**
26. _____-European
27. Use a Kindle
28. High card
29. North and South states
31. Juan's uncle
32. Mountain lake
33. Yahtzee cube
34. Aaron's oak? (var.)
35. Chatted
37. Any time now
39. Peameal _____
41. Veggie for a princess?
42. Chimney sweep's illness?
45. Natural gas component
47. Organic compound
51. Semis
54. Hang around
56. Canadian entertainers: Wayne _____ Shuster
57. Lebanon capital
59. Negative adverb
60. *M*A*S*H* star: David _____ Stiers
61. Obedience school command
62. Vertical mark on a staff
63. Not wet
64. Diana Krall Grammy winner: _____ *I Look in Your Eyes*
65. Edicts from Peter I
67. Nautical current
69. Gait
71. Pertaining to 1 or 100
74. Some computers
75. Scared, in *A Study in Scarlet*
77. Rings on a mushroom
78. Fury
80. Title, in Trois-Rivières
81. _____ Company of Canada
84. *Michael Collins* star Stephen
85. Helicopter blade
86. Food Network show: _____ *Chef Canada*
87. Lawn cutters
88. Sealer
89. Château Laurier and King Edward, say
90. Battle of Normandy locale, for short
92. Caste conscious one
93. Ma's pots?
95. Prohibited pesticide, in *Silent Spring*
96. Sean _____ Lennon
98. National sports organization: _____ Canada
100. '50s singers: The _____ Brothers
102. Canned pasta brand: Chef _____
107. Alien beings, for short
108. BlackBerry download
109. Hairstylist's wave?
113. Scotiabank money dispenser (abbr.)
114. One who murders merriment?
116. '70s US urban militant grp.
117. Toronto hospital: Mount _____
118. Cyndi Lauper debut LP: _____ *So Unusual*
120. **Ship he immortalized in song**
123. Some bills
124. '85 Michael J. Fox film: _____ *Wolf*
125. Whit
126. Talks like a windbag
127. Fine pastimes?
128. Parliamentary rules of conduct (abbr.)
129. Does and roes
130. Most ashen

DOWN

1. Assail
2. 1812 heroine Secord
3. Channel Islands abalone
4. Emasculates
5. Ovum
6. Miss the mark
7. Thyme or tarragon
8. Unclothed
9. See 78-A
10. Make vegetables?
11. **His music genre**
12. It's attracted to an anode
13. Continental trade pact since 1994 (abbr.)
14. Kimono sash
15. Not advised, medically
16. Soldier-turned-movie star Murphy
17. Endured
21. Udder adjunct
24. Winnipeg electoral district: _____ Boniface
25. Yukon town named for a card game
30. Automotive oil co.
33. 20th Manitoba premier Gary
34. '70s Canadian group: Five Man Electrical _____
36. Bard's "forever"
38. Sign
39. Small fowl
40. _____-do-well
42. Ebb's counterpart
43. **His surname**
44. Opposite of overqualification

46. Japanese poetry style
48. Squat
49. His Ontario birthplace
50. Crescent moon
52. 1975 greatest hits album
53. Eye irritant
55. Italy city
57. Bathroom fixture
58. Pour
61. 1974 Billboard #1 hit
62. Swiss city
66. Toronto Eaton Centre chain store
68. Divination deck
70. Use clippers
72. Priest's stand-in
73. Siren

75. Termites
76. February 14 figure
79. Once, old style
82. _____-Georgian
83. Royal symbols
85. Thorny flower
88. Winnipeg NHL team
89. Cannabis plant
91. "Put _____ Happy Face"
93. Grasshopper
94. Bolivia capital
97. '70s sitcom planet
99. '60s Maple Leaf Dave
101. Kicking Horse Pass tunnel type
102. "Enough!" in Italy
103. None of the above

104. Japanese legislature
105. Esteemed First Nations member
106. Looney Tunes' Fudd
108. Union station?
110. Related maternally
111. Gasping breaths
112. Centre of things
115. Music award he's won 16 times
116. Place
117. Doris Day song word
119. Snake's sound
121. Antagonist
122. US Republican Party, colloquially

Let's Pretend

Fee-fi-faux-clues

ACROSS

1. Some parents
7. Got 100 percent at tennis?
11. Diplomat's skill
15. Kitchen commotion?
19. Crush
20. Mosey
21. Beyoncé hit: "If I Were _____"
22. Trudeau-era cabinet minister Campagnolo
23. Antibacterial drug type
24. **Deceptive children's game?**
27. Story
28. Postgrad deg.
30. _____ on a rope
31. Hoof infection
32. Mystery writer Paretsky
34. Nocturnal insect
35. Engagement gift
36. Banking machine (abbr.)
39. Prohibited
41. Lather
42. Actress Gardner, et al.
46. Irish, say
48. Mythological discord goddess
49. Article in *Le Devoir*?
50. Clark-era cabinet minister MacDonald
51. On the job
52. Ocasek of the Cars
53. JFK predecessor
54. Bakes in the sun?
55. Canadian hardware chain: True _____
56. Harper Valley grp.
57. Zoology and botany, for example
59. Once, once upon a time
60. AFL-___
61. Mountaintop
62. Geological process to form 61-A

63. **Sleight of hand from rockers Styx?**
66. Oboe's orchestra neighbour
70. Seals' meals?
71. Raggedy _____
72. Nationwide convenience store name
76. Pipe up
78. *Antiques Roadshow* network
79. Time for sleep
80. Sparkly stones
81. Canada _____ ginger ale
82. Necklace of orchids
83. _____ than thou
84. Artisans' pots
85. Roman sun god
86. Singe
87. '40s UK PM Clement
88. Typical Justin Bieber fan
89. Reproduction
90. Embraces a nomination
92. Mulroney-era cabinet minister Jake
93. The Who classic: "_____ O'Riley"
94. Jet black
95. Nuclear bomb bit
97. Text correction, on paper
101. Palm tree type
102. Big name for the Bruins
103. At a distance
107. **Counterfeit garment?**
110. Folklore demons
112. Canadian music station: Much_____
113. Clothing line?
114. Gobi Desert continent
115. Competed at the Brier, say
116. '92 film: _____ *Good Men*
117. Strange numbers?
118. Postponement, in court
119. Small hills

DOWN

1. "Hey you!"
2. _____ Velva
3. Tow
4. Drains
5. Volcano residue
6. **Phony clover?**
7. Actress Jessica
8. Military rank (abbr.)
9. Like TV serials
10. Indicates
11. Press down
12. Former league for the Montréal Matrix (abbr.)
13. Share a secret
14. Ian and Sylvia
15. Bank deposit?
16. See the sights
17. The skinny
18. Actor George's lifesaver?
25. Morse Code word
26. Wetland
29. Meet market?
33. John Ritter sitcom: *Hearts _____*
34. Louis Hémon's CanLit classic: _____ *Chapdelaine*
35. Old Germanic letters
36. Desert plant
37. Early Europe marauders (var.)
38. Kitten's whimpers
40. Canadian author Pierre
41. Numbers puzzle
42. ". . . _____ came a spider"
43. Speak about one's concerns?
44. "Over the Rainbow" composer Harold
45. Smart-mouthed
47. Big oaf
50. Outlawed refrigerant
53. Old-style phone features
54. QC-born NHL goalie Martin
56. Diana Krall's instrument

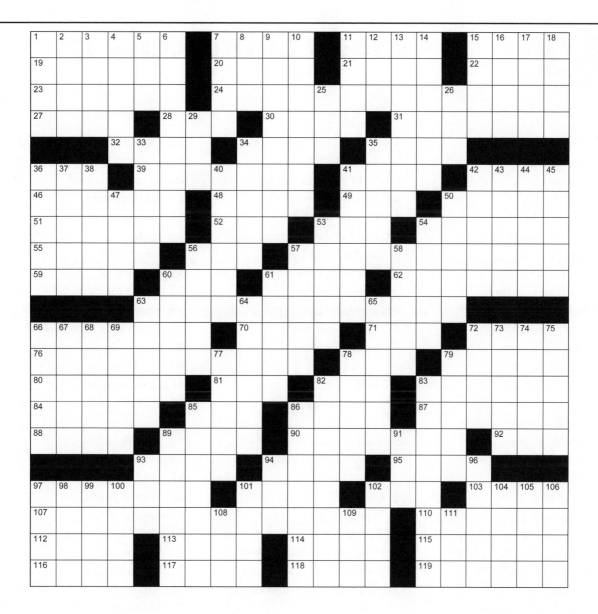

57. Strait in Newfoundland: _____ Isle
58. Loonies and toonies
60. Canola and wheat
61. Religious devotion
63. Pierces
64. "_____ beloved . . ."
65. Nunavut peninsula
66. Racist
67. Anoint, old style
68. Fur garment
69. Family vehicle
72. 14-year Blue Bombers star Stegall

73. Nimble like Jack
74. Tweet
75. Infection type
77. Parkinson's drug
78. 1928 Canadian Olympics sprinting hero Williams
79. "_____ fast!"
82. Most fortunate
83. **NHLer's legerdemain?**
85. Got serious about rehab?
86. Apes' treats
89. Opera great Enrico
91. Links average
93. Except

94. Freezer build-up
96. Computer shortcut word
97. *Harry Potter* films star Watson
98. *Cat on a Hot Tin* _____
99. Farm field measurement
100. Warp
101. Dickensian donations
102. Fine
104. Up to the brim
105. Genesis name
106. Purges
108. Touch
109. American espionage org.
111. Sister

Solution on page 220

51 Canada Cornucopia 17

ACROSS

1. Johnson of *Rowan & Martin's Laugh-In*
5. Stranger
10. Not straight
14. Lose, in Laval-Ouest
15. Innocent
16. Islam group
17. French needle case
18. West Kootenays BC city
19. _____ Level AB
20. Makes *une erreur*?
23. Stamen section
24. Mud bath place
25. Foot part
28. Parliament vote
29. Aries or Taurus
32. Lurks
34. Merchants
36. Bit of food
38. Grass bristle
39. Mouths, anatomically speaking
40. Famous Canadian septet
45. Sauerkraut sandwich
46. Vintage
47. Canadian Healthcare Association (abbr.)
50. Sprog
51. Sleep type
53. Threads
55. Faux pas

59. "Big Yellow Taxi" singer Mitchell
61. Yellow bread spreads, old style
62. Pine for
63. Caesar's *bête noire*
64. She won six Grammy Awards in 2012
65. First Shania Twain hit: "What Made You Say _____"
66. Cluttered dining hall?
67. Water barriers (var.)
68. Pieces together

DOWN

1. Sasquatch, say
2. Eye part
3. Tried and true
4. Jasper National Park mountain: _____ Cavell
5. Great Lake
6. Repair a rip
7. *Buenos* _____
8. Contents of Pandora's box
9. Backslide
10. '68 US Open tennis champ Arthur
11. BC ski resort
12. Oilfield equipment
13. "Kum Ba _____"
21. Forty winks, say

22. Old CBC current affairs show: _____ 30
26. Gumbo thickener
27. Ski slope turn
30. Multiple grand slam winner Steffi
31. Informative
33. Over top of
34. Bang a toe
35. Body part that bends
36. This cookie turned 100 in 2012
37. Gymnasts' performances
40. '70s Canadian record company
41. Defendant, for short
42. '93 Céline Dion song: "Only _____"
43. Overnight bags
44. See 5-D
47. Trite thing
48. Minnie Pearl show
49. Strong suits
52. Like rotten cream cheese, in Philadelphia?
54. ERA and RBI
56. Strike out
57. Mountaintop view?
58. Function
59. Harper government finance minister Flaherty
60. Beethoven's 9th Symphony theme: "_____ to Joy"

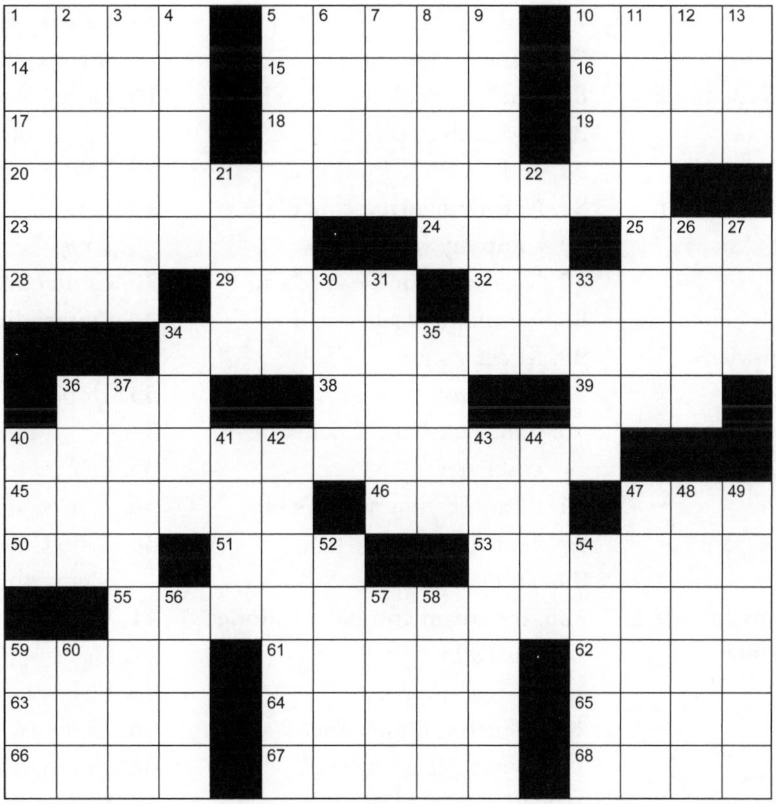

Solution on page 220

How Sweet It Is

Enjoy a taste of Canada

ACROSS

1. Into the swing of things?
6. Ceiling treatment
13. Ghana city
18. Collision
19. Small South American monkey
20. Tartan, say
21. Explorer Polo
22. **His food empire debuted in 1882**
23. Volley
24. Glowing coal
25. Toronto musical grp.
26. Half a Cuban dance
27. 18th-C. Swiss mathematician
28. English *Revolver* actress Francesca
30. Canadian furniture giant
32. Very dry
33. **Chocolate company founded in Vancouver in 1907**
35. Out of town
37. Short stars?
39. US singer India._____
40. Goodbye, in Gatineau
42. It comes after *nota*
43. Give a helping hand
45. Grasp a concept
47. Materialize
49. Trick
51. Post-Expo 67 exhibit: _____ and His World
52. Long fish
54. Asian nursemaids
56. Thing
57. Personal control?
61. Colloquial greeting
64. Serviceable
65. Health-care worker (abbr.)
66. Winnipeg river
69. Wore one's heart on one's sleeve, say
71. Get loose

74. Become indistinct
76. Fuel-efficiency measurement (abbr.)
77. Little bottle
79. President born in Hawaii
81. Stocking shade
82. Succumb to pressure
84. Today's name for Persia
85. **New Brunswick chocolate company since 1873**
87. Nickname for Dean Martin
88. Hormone organ
90. Kitchen style
91. Frivolously
93. Canadian-born TV host Linkletter
94. Boston Bruins alum Bobby
96. Golf club
99. Sunny courtyards
100. **Ice cream company founded in 1893**
102. Burger topper
103. North Carolina river
104. Some Mexican meals
105. Eight of a kind, say
106. Wood-smoothing tools
107. Eurasian tansy
108. Some fabric workers

DOWN

1. Peak
2. Streetcar
3. Oscar-winning Canadian film: *The _____ Invasions*
4. Rock climber's equipment
5. Like a prickly issue?
6. Proofreader's words
7. Tiny bits
8. Hank Williams hit: "_____ Lonesome I Could Cry"
9. Dawber of *Mork & Mindy*
10. Expensive
11. Print

12. Augment
13. Church area
14. Reindeer's rider?
15. **Calgary-based chocolaterie since 1983: Bernard _____**
16. Queen Street East Toronto neighbourhood
17. Love
29. *Love _____ Many-Splendored Thing*
30. **Confectioner founded in Ontario in 1913**
31. Remits, say
33. Tropical tree type
34. _____ formaldehyde
35. Prepare to shoot
36. Teensy
38. 1966 Catwoman portrayer Meriwether
41. Blue and white pottery
42. Great _____ Lake NWT
44. LBJ or HST
46. "Born as" indicator
48. Universal time abbr.
50. Ignited
53. Dodging
55. Group of concubines
57. Took a chair
58. Métis leader Louis
59. Chicago trains
60. Catch a criminal
61. Shorten by sewing
62. Stamped
63. **Frozen treat retailer since 1986**
66. Obscure
67. Bring home the bacon
68. Opiate or amphetamine
70. Garden of Eden name
72. Middle Eastern garment (var.)
73. Put down in writing?
75. Mercy, in the court
78. Calgary Flames' former home

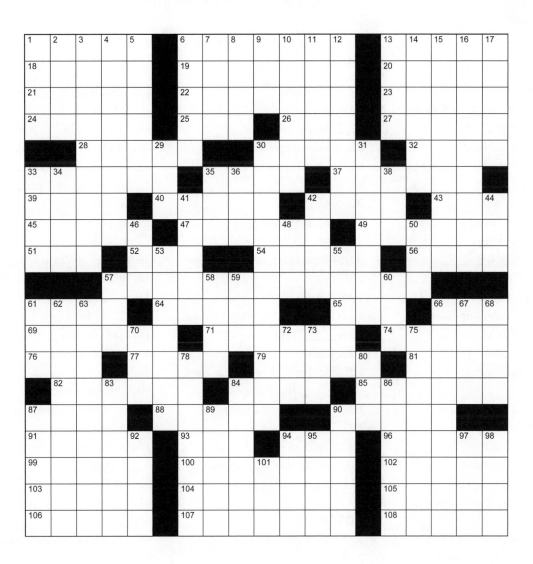

80. Turkish title

83. Popular Banff National Park destination: Lake _____

84. Sooner or later

86. Canadian author Margaret

87. William and Harry's mother

89. Beatles lyric: "He's _____ nowhere man"

90. International accounting firm: _____ & Young

92. Aberdeen refusals

94. Norwegian capital

95. Small deer

97. Active one

98. Tolkien forest creatures

101. _____ La Biche AB

ACROSS

1. 2008 Rush single: "Workin' _____ Angels"
5. Equals in England?
10. Harper and Flaherty, say (abbr.)
13. Kind of meet
17. *State Fair* setting
18. Old-style warship
19. Rainbow shape
20. "The Way We _____"
21. Publicist
23. **Nothing at all?**
25. Impress values upon, say
26. Computer key
28. Some swimsuits
29. Chessman, say
31. Stress
33. South American rodent
37. Requirement
38. "_____ blimey!"
39. '70s music genre
43. Songs of the sea (var.)
45. Like some electrical resistance units
47. Blackball
48. "B-15, G-6 ..." game
49. Famous words to Brutus
51. UAE component
53. Unemotional
55. _____ d'Azur
57. Historic period
58. Mr. King Cole
59. **Pedestrian's light, in Lancashire?**
63. Unreturnable serve, in tennis
65. 2006 *Canadian Idol* winner Avila
66. Smile
67. Celebrity chef Lagasse
70. C&W star Barbara
73. Till bills, in Baltimore
75. Small African antelope
76. Sporting blade
77. Rapscallion
79. Loses mass
81. Belgrade residents
83. California place: Santa _____
84. Seaweed substance
85. Satisfy
86. Juno _____
88. Mr., in Monterrey
90. 51-A, for example
93. '40s presidential monogram
95. Naps
100. **Rainy day footwear?**
102. Like the most sexy voice
104. _____ vera
105. Cashew, e.g.
106. Hepburn/Olivier film: *Love _____ the Ruins*
107. Operate with a beam
108. Repair
109. See 26-A
110. Boy Scout's merit reward
111. Tortoise-like speed

DOWN

1. Native American shelter (var.)
2. Rhino's point
3. Wool sources
4. Spar
5. Pecan confection
6. **Observant person?**
7. Nighttime aid: Sleep-_____
8. Leased
9. _____ precedent
10. Canadian home improvement show host Ruffman
11. Forbids
12. Mouthwash brand
13. Somewhat sugary
14. Gardener's bane
15. Toronto team "Boatman"
16. Clothesline adjuncts
22. Drink
24. Post
27. Canadian heavy metal singer Sebastian
30. "That's right," in Rémigny
32. Medically induced sleep
33. Great Lakes chemical contaminants (abbr.)
34. '45 comedy: _____ *with a Miss*
35. Manual or electric kitchen utensil
36. Corner, in math
40. Blissful place, in *Lost Horizon*
41. Havana's home
42. "Don't bet _____!"
44. Hard worker
45. Visible bedrock
46. Hex
50. Chinese group
52. Supernatural being (var.)
54. Swimmers' hovels?
56. Brockovich portrayed by Julia Roberts
60. Chalky
61. Tense
62. Geeks
63. Canadian PGAer Stephen
64. _____ Breton
68. How a gambler might say, "Sure ..."
69. Québec senator Bacon (1994–2009)
71. Alit
72. Burton Cummings composition: "Share the _____"
74. **Final number?**
78. Alan Alda sitcom
80. Important early epoch
82. Q-tip
84. Breathing malady
87. Make up for one's sins
89. Deteriorate
90. Gouda alternative
91. Stubborn beast?
92. Cultural star

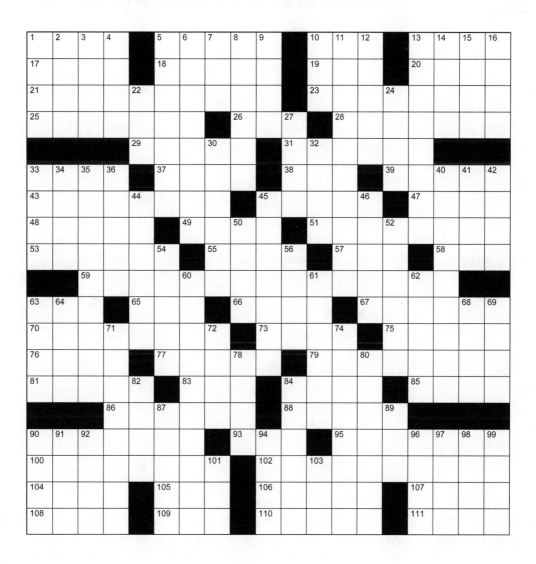

94. Pierce
96. Alternative to acrylics
97. Passion
98. Shell competitor, in Canada

99. Dinner dish
101. Transit-system agency, in Toronto (abbr.)

103. 1982 Hockey Hall of Fame inductee Gilbert

ACROSS

1. Maman's mate
5. Theatrical spat?
10. Chanel or Rocha
14. Homecoming celebration guest, for short
15. Ontario-born *Air Bud* star Zegers
16. Declare
17. Speech impediment
18. Modify
19. Québec motto: _____ *souviens*
20. Helped with a goal?
22. Habituate (var.)
24. At that place
25. Heroic feat
28. Dining
30. Petition for
31. Coastal inlet
32. South American mammals
35. _____ moss
36. Eastern Canada capital city
40. Erse speaker, say
41. Five-cent-coin animal
42. Like some verbs (abbr.)
43. Tokyo tie
45. Alive
49. Get mad, at the ape exhibit?
53. Pointer
54. Cripples
55. Church cemetery
57. Old-style bank transfer
58. Hackneyed, to a baker?
60. Lively
61. Modular furniture piece
62. "The Hunter" constellation
63. Score after deuce, in tennis
64. 1998 Paul Brandt single
65. Bright outside
66. _____ is more

DOWN

1. Good taste?
2. Canadian *24* actress Cuthbert
3. White-fleshed potato
4. Like scientific observations
5. Three-handed card game
6. Transferred control
7. Sidestep
8. FX series: _____/*Tuck*
9. Passes through a gate
10. Spicy cuisine style
11. Spread profusely, like weeds
12. Canadian Norm Macdonald, for example
13. Be indebted
21. Man of La Mancha, say
23. Canadian pollster Nanos
26. Jamaican religion adherent
27. _____ bran
29. Imperial liquid measurement (abbr.)
33. Former Newfoundland premier Brian
34. Suffix with meteor
35. Actor's characterization
36. Kurt Browning's Alberta hometown
37. Botanist's labs, perhaps
38. *The Three Faces of* _____
39. 28th state to join the Union
40. Band's job
43. Single
44. Deep male voices
46. Gamer's paradise in the '80s
47. NHL's best defenceman trophy name
48. Many Justin Bieber fans
50. Like _____ to a flame
51. '93 Rankin Family hit: "Rise _____"
52. He mitigated Draco's laws
56. Naysay
57. Lombardo who led the Royal Canadians
59. Kamloops campus (abbr.)

Canadian Singalong

Cross the country with these tunes

ACROSS

1. Rockies ruminants
6. Heroin street name
10. William Shatner show: *Weird or _____?*
14. Old-style payment to employees
19. Tidal bore
20. Cough medicine resin
21. "Hell _____ no fury …"
22. Famed businessman Donald
23. Third-person pronoun
24. Not for
25. Merged
27. **Stompin' Tom Connors song about an Ontario place**
30. Rod Hull's bird puppet
31. Pakistan neighbour
32. Bit of fabric
33. *Bloodletting and Miraculous Cures* scribe Vincent
36. '72 Neil Diamond hit: "Song _____ Blue"
38. Tombstone acronym
40. Hack at
41. Not light
45. '68 Elvis song: "If _____ Dream"
47. Zest
49. See 12-D
51. Contradict
52. **Tune about a BC city**
55. Big guy's bureau?
57. Grit or grime
58. January to December, inclusive
59. Do math
61. Hardened
62. Margarine container
64. Canadian astronaut Thirsk, for short
66. Data display devices
69. Northwest Québec town
71. "Aloha" accessory
73. Nonetheless

75. Washington neighbour (abbr.)
76. Choreography component
77. RBC ATM insert
80. Heavy weight?
82. Wedding words
84. French menu words
85. Reading room, in Reading PA
87. What the wicked don't get?
89. Cable, old style
91. Brian Mulroney book: _____: *1939–1993*
93. **Song about a prairie city**
97. Hitler's mistress Eva
98. *SCTV* offering
99. Tenderloin meat
100. "Hey!" quietly
101. 2005 Shania song: "I _____ No Quitter"
102. Dashboard gauge indication (abbr.)
104. Bombardier invention: Ski-_____
106. Funereal fire
108. Addis Ababa country (abbr.)
109. Buenos _____
111. About
113. Canadian novelist: _____-Marie MacDonald
115. **Rita MacNeil track from *Flying On Your Own***
123. Found oneself in the woods?
124. Mideast gulf
125. Coral reef isle
126. Caesar's meal?
127. Accra money
128. Cold lake
129. Haggard of C&W fame
130. Dental device
131. Once, at one time
132. To be, to Brutus
133. *Winnipeg Free _____*

DOWN

1. Comprehends
2. Home of Honolulu
3. Matured
4. Cree or Gwich'in
5. Blood products (var.)
6. "Don't go"
7. Delivery recipient
8. Where to say 82-A
9. Liona Boyd instrument
10. Droning noise
11. Full house and flush, say
12. With 49-A, business bag
13. Homophone for 23-A
14. Bacon slice
15. Outcrop
16. Baseballer Babe
17. Sitcom since 2005: *How _____ Your Mother*
18. New mom's blues (abbr.)
26. Chew on
28. Finnish NHL brothers' surname
29. Canadian Mediterranean cuisine company since 1917
33. 54, to Ovid
34. U of T milieu, for example
35. **Prairie song**
37. Sailors' legumes?
39. History Television show: _____ *Stars*
41. Greek fraternity letters
42. **See 35-D**
43. Kia car
44. G sharp or E minor
46. Parliament Hill environs (abbr.)
48. Seize, suddenly
50. Ignore, socially
51. Lacklustre
53. Baseball big name Mel
54. *The Iliad* land
55. Yukon or Nunavut
56. Emitted an electrical charge
60. Former China chairman

61. Sorrowful
63. Stomach woe
65. Wager
67. Bony fish
68. Jacuzzi, say
70. Skip this dance
72. Fury
74. Monkees member Peter
78. Skinny
79. Not quite evening
81. Kind of tide
83. Hold title
86. Hotel room cleaner
88. Flight breaks

90. Little rascal
91. Grad student's degree (abbr.)
92. Verdi aria: "_____ tu"
94. Lasted the test of time
95. Gumbo pods
96. Ultimate degree, in math
98. Mining refinery
102. Meal starch
103. Frolic like a reindeer?
105. Very decorative, in decor
107. Bivouac
109. Half a single
110. Winter coasters
112. Pops

114. Annotator
115. Caulk
116. Hello, in Pamplona
117. *Quod _____ demonstrandtum*
118. Blue-pencil
119. Famous L.M. Montgomery character
120. Split
121. Health troubles?
122. Labatt libations
123. Canadian retirement savings vehicle (abbr.)

56 Double Up

. . . to solve the theme clues

ACROSS

1. Christian feasts
7. Music star Carey
13. Provincial politician (abbr.)
16. Asian dog breed
17. Supreme Court of Canada justice Rosalie (since 2004)
18. Former national flyer: Trans-Canada _____ Lines
19. **Purloined Christmas treat?**
21. Golf ball prop
22. Times on end
23. Chopin's exercise?
24. The Irish _____
26. Dog biscuit, say
28. Math measurement
29. Canonical hour
30. Electromagnetism unit
32. Family member, for short
34. European duck
35. Compensation packages, say
39. "Harper Valley _____"
40. Me, in Montréal
41. Glass units
42. East Indian caste
46. Schleswig–Holstein municipality
48. Bob the bait
50. Town outside of Toronto
51. Removed wool from a ram
53. Protection
55. Direction in Drummondville
56. Medical professionals (abbr.)
57. French secretaries' desks?
60. Scoundrels
62. Wildebeest
63. Québec premier Edmund (1896–97)
64. Fly a Twin Otter
66. Toboggan
68. Wound coverings
72. "Imagine" singer
73. Walked back and forth
75. Brainchild
76. Hostel
77. **Kalahari course?**
80. Stage signal
81. Colour of beavers' teeth
82. '60s CTV series: _____ in Conflict
83. "_____ the fields we go"
84. Prepped for painting
85. Said goodbye

DOWN

1. Portfolio holding
2. Florida reptile, for short
3. '75 Paul Anka song: "I Don't Like to Sleep _____"
4. Throb
5. Use one's resources efficiently
6. Trig ratio
7. Grew up
8. Home sweet home
9. See free
10. Unwell
11. Warnings
12. Second-largest city in Vietnam
13. **Parental concern?**
14. *Remington Steele* star Brosnan
15. Baste, say
20. Former USSR leader
25. Chaste
27. Emotions that flare?
31. Trap
33. Belief system suffix
35. Folklore creatures
36. Biblical ark builder
37. **Truck stop meal?**
38. Canadian history name: _____ Brock
39. Stony Mountain, et al.
43. Friendly relations
44. Nozzle attachment
45. Colony insects
47. Wichita resident
49. Got just right
52. Scouts group
54. 19th-C. US era: The _____ Age
58. Hang around?
59. Tooth type
60. Patchy cat
61. Canadian Monopoly property: Jasper _____
62. Family subdivisions
65. Flaps
67. Supersized
69. Skilled
70. "Mr. Television"
71. Stuffed
74. *Pirates of the Caribbean* franchise star Johnny
78. _____ Francisco
79. Aegean or Adriatic

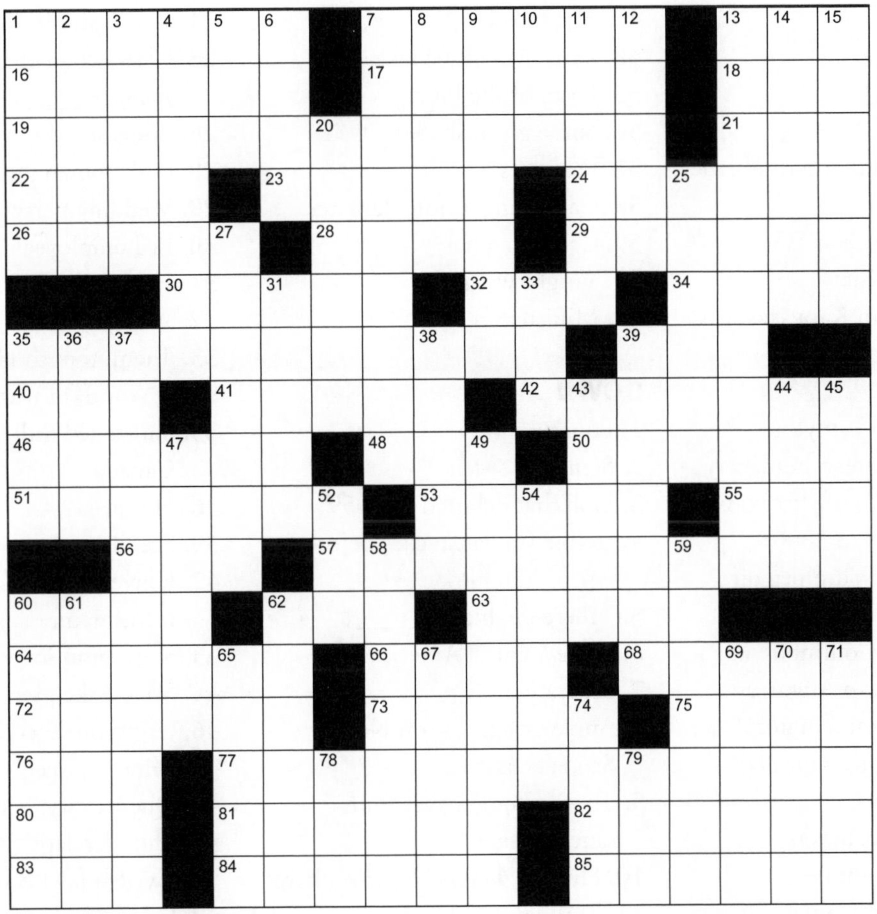

Solution on page 221

ACROSS

1. British bar
4. "How Dry _____"
7. Energetic
13. 19th-C. Canadian poet Valancy Crawford
16. NS-born opera star White
17. Swiss or Spanish
18. 2009 film from Kapuskasing's James Cameron
19. Hares' home
21. History Muse of myth
22. Traditional Korean headgear
23. Canadian Renner who won Olympic silver in 2006
27. Saskatoon-to-Winnipeg dir.
28. Edge on
30. Birthplace of Columbus
31. Buyer beware, to Augustus
34. Sun media commentator Adler
37. Old CBS sitcom: *One Day* _____
38. Some Indian believers
40. It's as good as a mile
41. Toronto Eaton Centre, for example
42. Antwerp country (abbr.)
45. Fishing sticks
46. Wander
47. Not taped
48. Large Manitoba lake
53. Head of the Huns
56. Some green shades
57. Pretenses
58. Canadian author Margaret
59. Catch in a net
60. Wright wing?
61. Minister's msg.

DOWN

1. Puncture
2. Standard orders
3. Doll that debuted in 1959
4. Colbie Caillat track: "Before _____ You Go"
5. "There oughta be _____!"
6. Large Central America city
7. Separate
8. Apple or Cherry, on Nova Scotia's coast
9. They separate naves from sanctuaries
10. Hirsute *Addams Family* relative
11. Through
12. Listen here?
14. Punching doll name
15. Prefix with pen or centre
20. '80s hairstyle
24. Pro's opposite
25. Classic Canadian kids' show: *Romper* _____
26. Longest river in Switzerland
28. Old Roman greetings
29. Wedding party member
30. FBI employee moniker
31. How 9-D are positioned
32. Woeful word
33. Them, too, to Hadrian
34. Ex-royal, in Russia (var.)
35. Shortened milk name, in Canada
36. Not lush
39. Seedling part
42. University of Manitoba sports teams name
43. Show emotion
44. Slave Lake preceder, in AB
46. Grind one's teeth
47. Miners' target
49. Québec city: Sept-_____
50. Thunderclap
51. Twelfth Jewish month
52. Fish with sharp teeth
53. It's just a number ...
54. Wine barrel
55. _____ Hortons

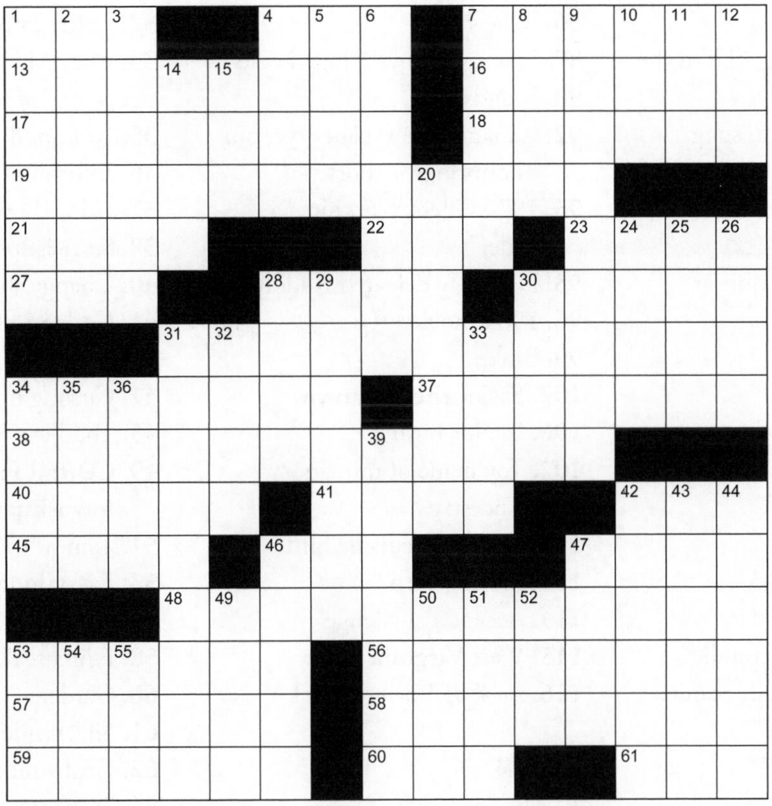

Solution on page 222

58 — Ekal Lake, et al.

North American place name palindromes

ACROSS

1. Signs in pen?
5. Guysborough County NS community
12. 2008 R.E.M. song: "Until the Day _____"
18. 2006 Nelly Furtado song
19. Diamond, for example
20. Former *Hockey Night in Canada* analyst Howie
21. Too much production
23. Dinner dishes
24. Québec city
25. Retain
26. Drug with an opiate
27. Wayne Gretzky scored 894 of these
31. It follows Pi
33. US gov. health org.
34. Least brief
39. South American republic
43. Vancouver Olympics venue: Richmond _____
44. Heart chamber
46. Soak flax
47. Decimal system base
48. Woodlands bird
50. North Dakota place
52. Oozed
54. Northern Canada mammal
55. Espy
57. Violin maker Nicolò
59. Auction goods
60. Brags
63. Dissonant
65. Create
68. Pigs' pens
70. Minister, for short
71. King, in Lisbon
74. In the thick of
76. Cumberland County NS community
79. "Get _____ of yourself!"

81. Sought office
82. 100 yrs.
84. Bucks
86. Relieve
87. Like some mythology beasts
90. Brands, say
92. Canadian newspaper tycoon Thomson, for short
93. 1970 Guess Who hit: "_____ Rider"
95. Narrowly defeated Rudolph?
96. 1984 movie: *This Is _____ Tap*
99. Bloke
102. Saskatchewan town
106. Islands bird?
107. Toy made of mirrors
111. Ancestry
112. European cuisine bird
113. Biblical verb
114. Accept a challenge
115. West Virginia place
116. *Book of Mormon* book

DOWN

1. Fans' favourite
2. Peter MacKay riding: Central _____
3. Ukraine capital
4. Lag behind
5. ABC morning show, for short
6. Rim
7. Bambi's aunt
8. Adam's apple locale
9. Port Colborne ON lake
10. Not immediately
11. Sculptured symbols
12. Little rascals
13. Gypsum, for example
14. _____ the water
15. Historical Florida place name
16. Alternative to Nair
17. Language of old Ireland
22. Coagulate

28. "Gotcha!"
29. Most graceful
30. Blood fluids
32. Lord's Prayer beginning
34. Alice Munro Giller winner: *The _____ of a Good Woman*
35. Not good
36. Informant, in Ipswich
37. Cdn. ID no.
38. StarKist product
40. Change shelf paper
41. Garland film: _____ *Me in St. Louis*
42. Curling match segments
45. Toddler's word
49. Central Frontenac Ontario township town
51. Tam or toque
53. Everything
56. Spring Christian celebration
58. Fujita scale weather event
60. Garden
61. Silvery metal
62. Coal stratum
64. Town near Opuntia Lake SK
65. Golden Québec speed skating Olympian Gagnon
66. Nursemaid in old India
67. Athabasca County AB place
69. See 55-A
71. Gad about
72. Otherwise
73. Caesar's bad day
75. Script's basis
77. Polite Spanish phrase: _____ *favor*
78. First American in space Shepard
80. Reason to take ASA
83. Pen point
85. Who is a jolly good fellow?
88. Three housemates?
89. Clock bird
91. Lisa LaFlamme nightly delivery

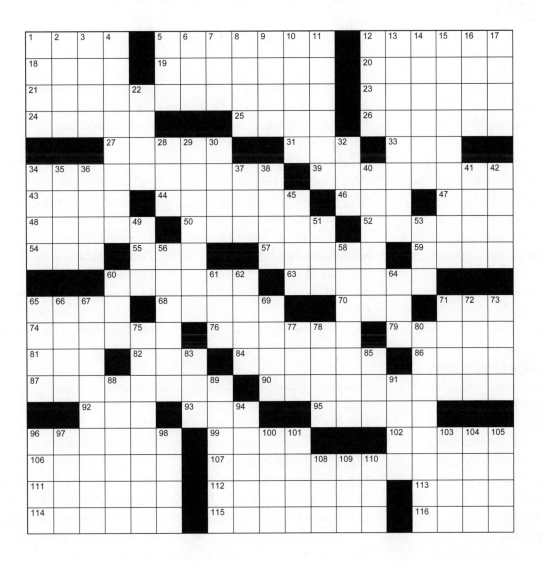

94. Ocean predator

96. Glaswegian, for short

97. Prefix with graph or glide

98. Canadian *For Better or For Worse* cartoonist Johnston

100. Saxophone type

101. Low-level worker

103. Zen Buddhism anecdote

104. Lhasa _____

105. Dampens

108. UN workers' grp.

109. East Indian tree

110. Yoko of note

59 We All Fall Down

Songs you might stumble over

ACROSS

1. Paroxysm
6. *Titanic's* undoing
10. Pierces
15. Jazz singing technique
19. It comes from the heart
20. Winged, in biology
21. Pacific islands nation
22. With the bow, in the string section
23. Bits of dust
24. Old Italian currency
25. 1963 album: *Paul _____ 21 Golden Hits*
26. Praise
27. **1977 Paul Simon single**
30. Magical 1989 Rush album?
32. *Brave New World* drug
33. Finale
34. Restraints for Rottweilers
35. Head shots, in baseball
38. Betty's limb?
39. *Baywatch* star Carmen
41. Mantel vase
42. Conks out
44. City opposite Windsor
46. Millstone, perhaps
49. Passionate about Christ?
52. Schools of thought
53. *The Red Green Show* club: Possum _____
54. Bit in a horse's mouth?
55. Sugary cereal: Froot _____
58. Instrument's sound quality
59. Court order
62. '58 hit: "Purple People _____"
63. Diamonds or clubs, in bridge
66. Feel ill
67. **2006 Dierks Bentley single and album**
70. Cheerleaders' utterance
71. Northern European body of water
73. Covered in frosting?
74. Elizabeth's daughter
75. Popular Nissan
76. Handed out
77. Personals, e.g.
79. Confound a logger?
80. *Moonraker* villain
83. "Bell" vegetable
88. It follows "our" in "O Canada"
89. Auto shelters
92. Look like
93. Sign before Virgo
94. _____ Stone
96. TD green machine (abbr.)
98. How oil-field workers might act?
100. Islamic fundamentalist group
102. Trimmed with ermine, say
105. Nursery furniture piece
106. Online news group
107. **1991 Crowded House hit**
111. Love you forever, in texting
112. '70s tennis star Chris
114. Christopher Columbus ship name
115. Blazing
116. Meadows (var.)
117. Early _____
118. Gravitational forces, for short
119. They get shifted in a standard
120. Anticipated arrival times (abbr.)
121. *Kama* _____
122. While lead-in
123. Surrealist painter Max

DOWN

1. Edmonton Oiler Gagner, et al.
2. Swimming spot
3. Craftsmen
4. Put one's foot down?
5. Fourth Estate
6. *South Pacific* show tune: "_____ H'ai"
7. Omit an o, say
8. _____ to go
9. Tommy Douglas, to Kiefer Sutherland (var.)
10. Cartoon created by Calgary's Todd McFarlane
11. Bright birds
12. Drunkard
13. Sheep bleat
14. Person of interest, say
15. Auction environs
16. **2000 Savage Garden #1**
17. Critical
18. Fusses
28. Lasso
29. Like, in Laval
31. Stoolie
34. Floral "jewellery"
35. Hobo
36. Earlier, to an Edwardian
37. Red Chamber politician (abbr.)
40. Peter Sellers co-star Herbert
43. Ruminants' grub
45. Scale notes
47. Hungarian, for example
48. Get boiling mad
50. See 12-D
51. Italian dessert: Panna _____
53. To read, in Terrebonne
56. Poetic contraction
57. Cost
58. 2,000 pounds, in the US
59. Canadian truck-trailer manufacturer
60. Theatre district
61. **1983 Culture Club smash**
62. Sailor (abbr.)
63. Coffee _____
64. Community south of Winnipeg: _____ Chênes
65. Doze off

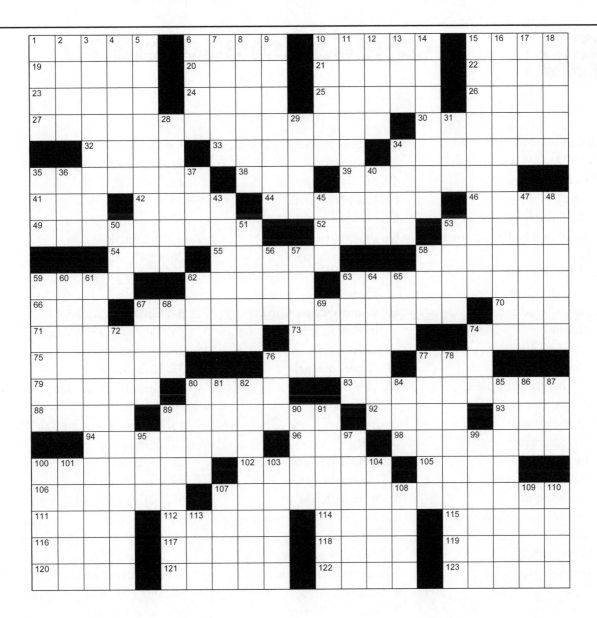

67. Lame

68. Ontario Curling Association (abbr.)

69. Mulroney cabinet minister Carney

72. Right place, right moment

74. Cleopatra biter

76. Chinese food additive (abbr.)

77. Quick glance

78. Shipping delay fee

80. Canadian singer Arden

81. It often appears to the right of you

82. Hiker

84. Xmas mo.

85. Ancient Rome commoner

86. Sushi source

87. Toronto venue: _____ Thomson Hall

89. Cheese shredders

90. *SCTV* character Camembert

91. Odd

95. Honest _____

97. Forte

99. Disagree

100. Tutu material

101. To date

103. Extreme

104. Physics units

107. Regina winter celebration: Kona-_____

108. Brewer's kiln

109. Bungles

110. Exam

113. Vancouver Island University (abbr.)

60 Canada Cornucopia 20

ACROSS

1. NAFTA word
6. River in Germany
10. Sieve
14. Muslim women's group
15. Emperor who fiddled around?
16. Just
17. They cover seeds
18. Concrete piece
19. Halt who goes there?
20. Blue hue
21. Yukon capital
23. Month of Purim
25. The Beaver State (abbr.)
26. Biblical carrier
27. Spring bloomer
31. Large marbles
33. Turkey of old
35. Quit pouring, say
38. Fertilizing soil
39. *Our Miss Brooks* star Arden
40. Rice wine
41. Wheat variety
43. Groups of seven (var.)
46. "Sure . . ."
48. Most sudsy
49. Every bit
51. Not post
53. Glance at
54. Jacques Plante's hockey safety invention
57. *SCTV* star Thomas
61. Intangible quality
62. Clearasil target
63. BC explorer Fraser
64. Two words that follow woe
65. '70s NHL stars Dryden and Hodge
66. Country where Canada provided earthquake relief in 2010
67. Capone nemesis
68. Votes in favour
69. Terminated

DOWN

1. Demonstrative pronoun
2. Uncommon
3. Opera highlight
4. Canada's highest cascade
5. North Sea feeder
6. Reverently preserves
7. Supermarket section
8. Sister of Clio
9. WWI PM Borden
10. Just okay
11. Within Wyoming, say
12. Dentist's instruction
13. Ilks
21. Dry riverbed, in Africa
22. Cure
24. Portuguese title
27. Crooks' Hollow and Fanshawe, in Ontario
28. PDQ
29. Building safety warnings
30. Adores
32. Caribbean resident
34. Take back a truck, say
36. HI instruments
37. Nuisance
42. Great Plains dwelling (var.)
44. Pushpin
45. Environment Canada's US counterpart
47. Unsettling
49. Once more
50. Nasty person who bugs you?
52. Howie Mandel or Alex Trebek
55. Liberal Arts and Engineering Studies (abbr.)
56. Empress of Russia (1730–40)
58. Surrounded by
59. Go to the polls
60. Noddy series author Blyton
63. Ship pronoun

61

CanadianZ

Last but not least

ACROSS

1. Farmer's land measure
5. Make modifications
10. Fleas, for example
16. Snare or bass
17. Spaghetti or vermicelli
18. Stage platforms
19. **Acclaimed children's book illustrator Werner**
21. Confederates
22. Put in place
23. Outrigger canoes (var.)
25. Soup scoop
26. Areal
28. Small stature
30. WWII bombing campaign, for short
33. Synonym for 17-A
34. Yokel Simon, perhaps?
38. _____ & Bradstreet Canada
39. Loves
40. Hymn of praise
42. Dressed in
46. Sings alone
47. River in France
48. Sheer fabric
49. Large number of murderers?
50. Parliamentary periods
51. Sagan's universe?
52. Period
53. Koalas' shrubs (var.)
55. Man raised from the dead by Jesus
59. Rent again
60. Flossflower plant
62. By Mae, maybe?
67. Early Hudson's Bay Company employee's coat

68. Major city on 47-A
71. Foolish
72. Picks up the tab, say
74. **1984 Juno-winning singer Alfie**
76. Prince William title: _____ Strathearn
77. Leamington Ontario county
78. 2000 DeNiro movie: _____ *the Parents*
79. Coniferous trees' secretions
80. Bone china pioneer Josiah
81. Colloquial name of Calgary's second-oldest building: King _____

DOWN

1. Woodworking tools
2. Curl one's hair
3. Sensuous Latin dance
4. Old-style ant
5. Car loan interest rate (abbr.)
6. Like a tent at dusk, perhaps
7. Old Russian royal title
8. Sicilian rumbler
9. "The mouse _____ the clock"
10. Horse-and-buggy _____
11. Extra seat on a motorcycle
12. Vancouver _____
13. **Detroit '52 Stanley Cup winner Larry**
14. Threatening words of a thug
15. Appraise
20. Foodstuffs
24. Weekend confection?
27. Molson offerings
29. Sentence subject, often
31. Sot

32. **Canadian media entrepreneur Moses**
34. Jordan of 35-D
35. Reality show: *Canadian* _____
36. Mammal with six species in Canada
37. Where Jack and Rose "flew" in *Titanic*
41. Come after
42. Snug (var.)
43. Not taut
44. "Thanks _____"
45. He loved Lucy
47. Arranges
48. Like an electrochemical reaction
50. _____ *de suite*
51. Normandy city
52. Alberta oil and gas town: _____ Valley
54. Held onto
55. Former's opposite
56. Old Greek gathering places (var.)
57. *Air Bud* **movies star Kevin**
58. Sheep in central Asia
61. Labyrinths
63. Garden goblin?
64. Tore down, in Tottenham
65. Chipped in chips
66. Like non-vegetarian lasagna
69. Grate
70. _____ facto
73. The City by the Bay's orchestra (abbr.)
75. Paul Bunyan's tool

62

Repetitious

Is there an echo in here?

ACROSS

1. *Lion King* character's mark?
5. McCain _____ (Canada)
10. Clock changing time (abbr.)
13. Dump dwellers
17. **Couturier Chanel**
18. Caper
19. Warm season in Sorel-Tracy
20. State where Canadian Beckie Scott won Olympic gold
21. Maori chant
22. Rwandan Civil War side
23. **Society Islands island**
25. Precise
27. Witnessed
28. Downpours
29. Virile (Sp. pl.)
31. Pro _____
33. Emblazoned
34. Household pet
35. _____ Valley AB
36. Canadian analgesic product: _____ A535
38. Nasal passages
40. Laundry detergent brand
41. Alter land use
43. Mat for Mats?
45. Ti-Cat rival
48. Royal flush card
49. Has trouble pronouncing
51. Valley in California
55. Like accountants' tables
57. Penny _____
58. Weighty books
59. Act on feelings?
60. Tony winner Hagen
62. It paves the way?
63. Arabic chieftains
64. Anti-authority type
65. Part of the Hindu trinity
67. Providing of provisions
69. 1899 war name
70. American cowboy Bill

71. Mr. Van Winkle
72. Actress Myrna, et al.
73. Equity market instrument (abbr.)
75. Outfit add-on
78. It monitors Delta (abbr.)
81. Armoury ransackers?
83. Skating jump type
84. Popular sushi fish
87. Comics' Olive
88. Canadian grocery store acronym
89. Quirks
91. Canadian cinema chain: _____ Players
93. Moves a mum, say
96. Cannabis pipe
98. Caribbean "pole" dance
99. **Hawaiian fish**
100. Book that features 74-D (with "*The*")
102. Male deer
103. Hawk in the nest
104. _____ *de guerre*
105. '76 Olympics icon Comaneci
106. **Extinct bird**
107. Musician's break?
108. Information overload, in texting
109. _____ Slave Lake
110. Portent

DOWN

1. Conspire about a plan?
2. Like circles sharing a radical line
3. **Anti-aircraft fire**
4. Cocky insect?
5. Portly
6. Duty
7. Aquatic animal
8. Illness
9. Tiny bit
10. Red ink item

11. Ottomans
12. Scotties and Yorkies
13. Hick
14. Post-haste
15. **Fish sauce**
16. National forest in California
24. Like a pretentious sculptor?
26. Skedaddled
30. Khartoum country
32. Perform unction
37. '96 Celine Dion hit: "_____ You Loved Me"
39. Not in the basement
41. Carpenters' groovy tools?
42. Upstanding?
44. Deviation
45. Biting
46. Canada's 25th Governor General LeBlanc
47. *The* _____ *and Mail*
50. Persevere
52. _____ acid
53. Canadian '88 Olympics skiing medallist Karen
54. Nincompoops
56. Actor Gibson
58. Letter after sigma
61. Long-legged bird
66. Attributing writing?
68. Satire
70. Touching
74. Trojan War king
76. Mackerel-like fish
77. _____ Canadian Superstore
78. Previous
79. **Sailor's affirmative**
80. Top dogs, say
82. Understand the deep sea?
84. **Aboriginal drum**
85. Song about the dawn
86. Weather map line
90. Contemptuous in tone
92. Perform incorrectly

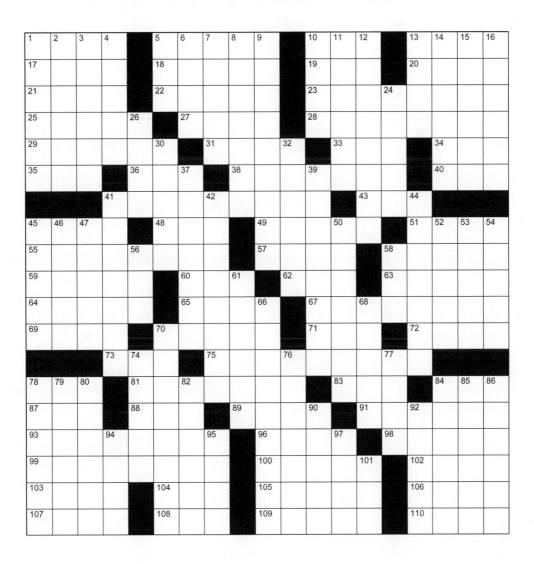

94. Santa checks it twice

95. See 51-A

97. Terra's Greek equivalent

101. "Can't Help Lovin' _____ Man"

ACROSS

1. Canadian polling firm: _____ Reid
6. Appear to be
10. Canadian hockey great Bobby
14. Welsh dog breed
15. Not busy
16. Asian buffalo
17. Ontario nuclear research facility: _____ River
18. Brief
20. Slice of cake, say
22. Domestic pigeon
23. Sickly looking
25. Roots Canada's initial merchandise
28. BCE, for example
29. Toward shelter, nautically
31. Belly button type
33. Alberta-born NHLer McAmmond
34. Come in waves
36. Montréal-born folksinger McGarrigle
38. PC or Mac, say
44. Nike slogan: Just _____
45. High seas fleet
46. East Indian religion adherent
50. Tress tangles
52. Responded to a charge
53. Canaanite city
55. _____ for the mill
57. Those with clout
58. Indulge in misery
60. Advantages of brewing coffee?
62. Medical patient's history
65. Like expectations not fulfilled
68. PEI's MacLellan who wrote "Snowbird"
69. Mischievous character in Scandinavian myth
70. MS Society of Canada fundraiser: _____-Thon
71. Units of work
72. At that time
73. Title holder

DOWN

1. Anglican Church of Canada (abbr.)
2. Japanese drama form
3. Anchors
4. Juicy fruit
5. *Oliver Twist* character Bill
6. Son of Jacob
7. Western Canada restaurant name: _____ Japan
8. Big tree
9. Old CBC show: *Making Ends* _____
10. Strong dislike
11. No can do
12. Latin "body armour"
13. Long-time NDP leader Jack
19. Filbert, for example
21. Rockies weather phenomenon
23. Canadian airline founder Max
24. Plant emollient
26. Thespian who's a lawmaker?
27. Prefix meaning "Chinese"
30. National park east of Edmonton: _____ Island
32. All together
35. Trace Adkins tune: "Better Than I Thought _____ Be"
37. Month that follows Mar.
39. _____-Pong
40. MLB official, for short
41. Calgary-based oil and gas company
42. Canadian *Blood Sports* author Robinson
43. Room warmers, for short
46. Drain detritus
47. More silly
48. Albertan who sang "Hallelujah" at 2010 Olympics
49. HGTV network star Mike
51. Scores off the rim
54. *Hockey Night in Canada* host MacLean
56. Central Nova Scotia town
59. Hive
61. Had info
63. Scale note (var.)
64. Tina Turner's ex
66. Central Netherlands municipality
67. La Brea black stuff

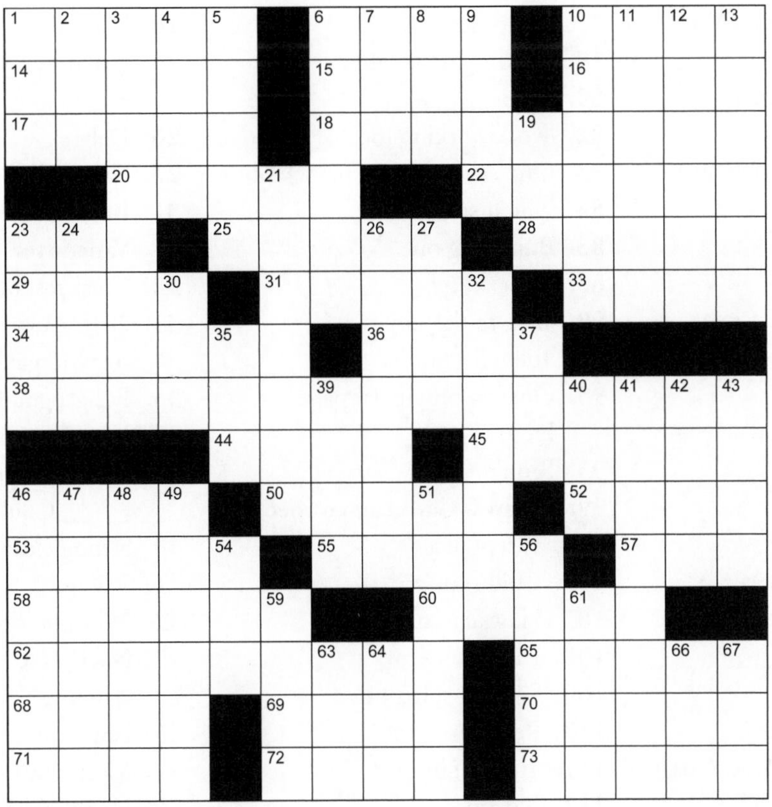

Solution on page 223

Bridging the Gaps

... with a Canadian attention span

ACROSS

1. Tip one's hat, say
5. Florida city
10. Military manoeuvres (abbr.)
13. Wading bird
17. UN civil aviation agency (abbr.)
18. Former Pennsylvania senator Specter
19. Charolais sound
20. Greek curd cheese
21. Equestrian's grip
22. NHLers' objectives
23. Boxing bout, say
25. **QEW crossing at St. Catharines**
28. Make certain
29. _____-cone
30. Cribbage player's piece
31. Québec city name until 2010: Notre-Dame-du-_____
34. Dine at home
37. Coral reef component
39. BC First Nations name: Coast _____
41. Emeril Lagasse word!
44. Submarine equipment
46. Canadian golfing great Sandra
48. BC national park
49. Like DNA in court, say
52. Not on the level?
54. Hoity-toity tunes?
55. Belgrade country
57. Mount Hood state (abbr.)
58. Cape Verde island
61. Canada/US boundary lake: St. _____
63. **Famed Niagara Falls span**
65. Calgary Olympics ski jumping underdog: Eddie the _____
67. Sandwich meat
68. Samuel's biblical teacher
70. Tuberous garden plant

72. Not tanned
73. Like some swimming pools
76. "I Get a Kick Out of You" composer
78. Wedding dress fabric
80. Saran _____
82. Woodworking tools
83. One-striper in the navy (abbr.)
84. Not at sea
86. Bumbling one
88. Riser
90. Take to the slopes
91. Tolkien cannibal
93. Ontario provincial park: Presque'_____
95. Brought in the harvest
99. **Ottawa–Gatineau connector**
103. Pasta sauce
106. Cold shower?
107. Hawaiian tuber
108. Landed
109. Sinking ship's call
110. Religion in India
111. Tropical birds
112. Bluenose coin
113. 911 responder (abbr.)
114. Affirmatives
115. Opposite of 114-A

DOWN

1. Funereal music
2. Atlantic _____
3. PNE and CNE, say
4. Swiss dish
5. Forces in physics
6. '85 Camaro model: _____-Z
7. Jai _____
8. Thaws
9. Harmonious
10. City in Siberia
11. Singer's vocal chord malady
12. Rainy day headgear
13. Wishy-washy

14. Quilting party
15. Bryan Adams hit: "_____ Only Love"
16. Warmed the bench, say
24. Grammy Award winner: Lady _____
26. Delete
27. Shower bar?
31. **Burrard Inlet bridge in Vancouver**
32. Cigar residue
33. 2010 *Dancing with the Stars* star Margaret
35. BC geographic region
36. Nigerian currency
38. Gordon Lightfoot #1: "If _____ Could Read My Mind"
40. Strong cleaning solution
41. Wasaga _____ ON
42. '06 *Canadian Idol* winner Eva
43. **Northeast New Brunswick crossing**
45. Fanatical
47. Most wintry
50. Handheld Nintendo game system
51. Linear particle accelerator, for short
53. 22nd letter
56. Detest
59. US sitcom star Tim
60. Lascivious looks
62. Flushed, facially
64. Stews made in pots?
66. Fourth mo.
69. Not upper, in type
71. Gymnast's equipment, say
74. Key role in *The Matrix*
75. CTV news reporter: John Vennavally-_____
77. Willow twig
78. _____ Cruces NM
79. Query

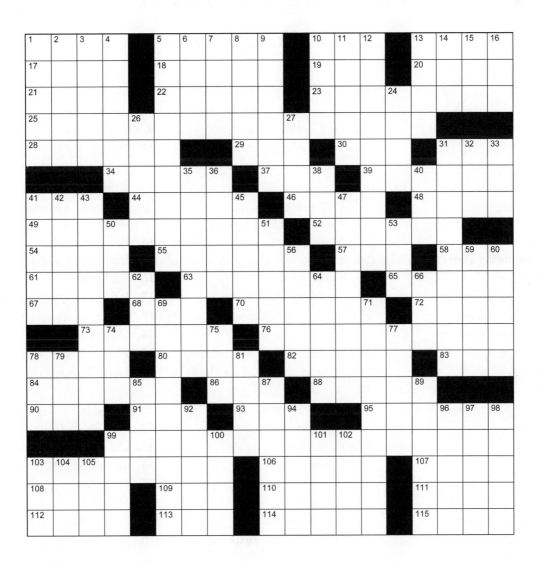

81. Analgesic's target
85. Reddish-brown horse shade
87. Gaudy
89. Wicker furniture a.k.a.
92. Data storage unit

94. Canadian newspaper advice columnist Tesher
96. Oscar Peterson instrument
97. Supernatural
98. Smelting waste
99. House dust bug

100. Malt kiln
101. Comfy rooms
102. Surrender
103. US TV drama: _____ Men
104. Boxing's Muhammad
105. Cup part

65 Book of the Month Club

Read up on this

ACROSS

1. Stomach, say
6. Quickly, quickly
10. Toddler's owie
16. _____ and running
19. Positive integer
20. Sumptuous
21. Where Christian soldiers go?
22. Old Swedish currency
23. **Ray Bradbury short story collection**
26. Last of 26, in the States
27. Mynas that mimic
28. Bewildered, on a boat?
29. Saccharine
31. Exhort
32. Mary Chapin Carpenter track: "I Have _____ For Solitude"
33. Homeland Security operative (abbr.)
34. Erode
38. Desert travellers
40. '79 Bette Midler film
44. _____ It to Beaver
45. Skin lubricant
46. Call to a captain
47. Health services overseer in some provinces (abbr.)
48. House of Commons staff
49. **V.C. Andrews offering**
52. Clever comment
53. Anne Laurel Carter book: *Under a Prairie _____*
54. Fly
55. Knowledgeable about, say
56. Tossed
57. On an even _____
58. Big first for baby
59. Howie Mandel or Monty Hall, say
61. **Kovic autobiography/Cruise movie**
68. Ancient Greek theatres
69. Town on the Thames
70. _____-Defamation League
71. One way to drink scotch
72. *Doctor Zhivago* star Sharif
73. Flowers that are toxic to cats
76. "_____ sell his own mother!"
79. Psychic power
80. **36th James Bond novel**
83. Strike out instruction, for short
84. Employ
85. Gershwin and Levin
86. Castle trenches
87. Acclaimed children's author Eric
88. Shade provider
90. Spirit in the Koran (var.)
92. Wood for building
93. Approves, for short
94. Fava and lima
95. Duct drop
97. Climb ev'ry octave?
100. Russian martial arts type
101. Mortify
106. *Royal Canadian _____ Farce*
107. **Dean Koontz suspense novel**
110. On the _____
111. US chain that bought many Zellers in 2011
112. Observer
113. Partitions
114. Delivery from Santa
115. Tucks in securely?
116. Simple
117. Trout relative

DOWN

1. _____ and crafts
2. Thai money
3. Notion
4. Fashion designer Christian
5. Omit
6. The Association hit: "_____ Comes Mary"
7. Biological groups
8. Chopping tools
9. According to
10. Punted, say
11. Burdens
12. Possessed
13. Long-time Canadian shoe company
14. Famed Canadian pilot Marion
15. Homeric journeys
16. Trickle out
17. It follows "and" in "O Canada"
18. Imperial measurement
24. Canadian _____
25. 1977 Pontiac muscle cars
30. Pierre Berton book: *Marching as to _____*
32. As stubborn as _____
33. *The Tommy Hunter _____*
34. Old-style handouts
35. Turtle's protuberance
36. Off-colour
37. Map abbr.
39. Funeral home write-up
40. Dance-a-_____
41. Brass that looks golden
42. What Canadians do frequently in winter
43. Joey's Only, say
45. Slopped
46. Take in a stray
49. Perennial plant
50. Rwanda native
51. Jungle mimic?
54. Many millennia (var.)
56. Title for a Mecca pilgrim (var.)
57. Bow
58. Wayne Gretzky, to Walter
59. Gift recipient
60. Small newts
61. Cram for an osteology exam?
62. "Ukrainian" town name in ON and SK

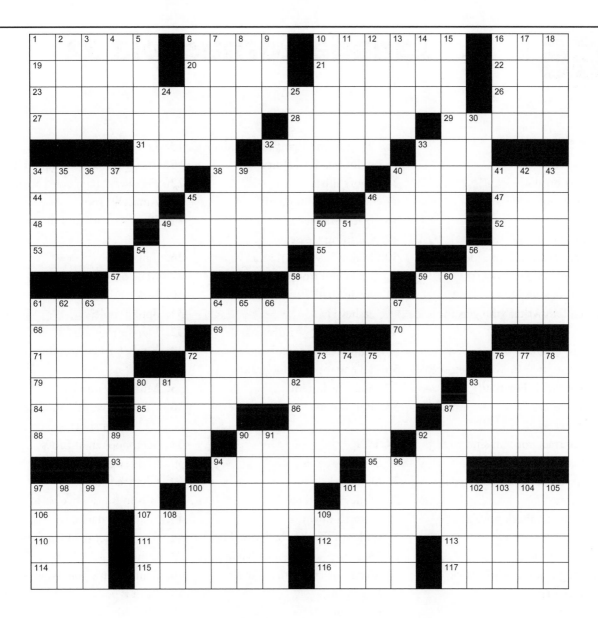

63. Grim gatherer?
64. Some engines
65. And others (Lat.)
66. Shape
67. Chinny chin chin wisps
72. Speed skaters' track shape
73. City in France
74. Old W Network DIY show: *Anything _____ Do*
75. Some atlas lines
76. Former BC MP Dhaliwal
77. Her magazine?
78. Red _____ AB

80. Computer insertion
81. Cupid's counterpart
82. "Für Elise" key
83. Castors' creation
87. Long-billed birds
89. Yahoo! rival
90. Showed how a product works
91. Baroque-style collars
92. Not clerical
94. Police officer's shield
96. Manicurist's board
97. Antigonish NS community: _____ Springs

98. "Later" to a Latino
99. Major employer?
100. Balkan native
101. US boxer Oscar De La _____
102. Muslim religious leader
103. Canadian navy rank: _____ Seaman
104. Share a secret
105. Formerly, formerly
108. Life of the carnivores' convention?
109. Par 4 start, say

ACROSS

1. Residence
6. Short breaks
14. Show up
16. Not guilty
17. Rooms in *une maison*
18. SK-born NHL president Campbell (1946–77)
19. Safekeeping spot
20. Tabloid writer who gets the axe?
21. Last (abbr.)
22. "Fantastic," in Winnipeg-speak
23. Michael J. Fox film: _____ *to the Future*
24. Jacket
25. Contract you can sink your teeth into?
27. Former Governor General Jeanne
28. John Steinbeck novel: *To _____ Unknown*
29. Prehistoric
30. Sought water with a stick
31. Tack on
33. Tolerate
37. Gist
38. Old-style shoe cover
42. Crummy
43. Multi-tasking
45. '92 golden Olympic Canadian swimmer Tewksbury
46. Short shirts
47. "Mmm mmm good!"
48. British range
49. Clothing crease
50. Major WWI battle for Canadian troops
51. Avian that's crazy about cashews?
53. United _____ Loyalists
55. Skin cream ingredient
56. Like many wedding cakes
57. Spice rack item
58. Philosophy

DOWN

1. Small batteries
2. Daring
3. Disney World city
4. Watered down
5. Order of Canada ballerina Hart
6. 1967 Stephen Leacock Memorial Medal for Humour winner
7. Intertwine
8. Quick bite
9. Tourtière ingredient
10. Diamonds, in slang
11. Iffy at best
12. Gated community, say
13. Left as is, by the editor
15. Toronto clock setting (abbr.)
22. *Rosemary's Baby* star Farrow
23. Amaryllis root
24. Large Canadian union, for short
26. Talk up
27. Male of a family
30. Reservations?
31. Spot a mole?
32. Duo's pronoun
33. Yearly farmers' reading?
34. Clots
35. Museum employee
36. Commonwealth Stadium CFLer, for short
38. Scrapbooker, at times
39. Old-style ant
40. Changed states?
41. '40s mystery novelist Josephine
43. Snap alternative
44. _____ Energy of Canada Limited
46. Stanley Park pole type
49. Bean type
50. All ready
52. Common contraction for a guy?
54. Nigerian language

67

Hill Billies

Parliamentary personages

ACROSS

1. Puts on a happy face
7. Prune a photo
11. Yolk holder
14. Take more than your share of ham?
17. Newfoundland, for example
18. New Wave singer Lovich
19. Poor press?
21. Odours
22. Smooth
23. **29-year NDP MP from Winnipeg**
24. **Canadian Wheat Board chief-turned-senator**
26. Integrated Digital Environment (abbr.)
28. Phony
29. '76 horror film (with "*The*")
30. Disproves false claims
32. Lost lover?
36. Soon, to a bard
37. Notable Swiss mathematician
41. Eyebrow element, for some
42. Window ledge
44. Spinning toys
46. Went by horseback
47. Ontario _____ of Appeal
49. Unworldly one
51. How the Siamese birthed her babies?
53. Bestows a quality
55. Wood type
57. _____-Magnon
58. Graham Greene novel: *The _____ of the Affair*
59. **Longest-serving PM**
63. "Pipe down!"
66. Freelancer's enc. to a publisher
67. Made with a Singer
68. Farley Mowat's first book: *_____ of the Deer*
72. Built a barrel

75. Morse code signals
77. Not liquid
78. Roman god of love
79. Ice mass
81. Sold-out shows (abbr.)
83. Warbled like a wren?
84. Dashboard switch
86. Sun News Network commentator Levant
88. Licorice liqueur
90. Bay Street-set TV drama (1996–2000)
92. Robert's stack?
93. "Goodness gracious!"
96. Toddler's snooze
97. **Minister of national defence during the Gulf War**
102. **'50s Métis MP from Saskatchewan**
104. Sunlight rival
106. More cozy
107. Blink of an eye
108. Canadian Ken Taylor's '79 diplomatic posting
109. Saudi _____
110. Salon job
111. Brandon-born singer Moore
112. Small price to pay?
113. Docilely

DOWN

1. Shell game, say
2. Canadian "Marina del Rey" singer Jordan
3. Privy to
4. Peru city
5. Charm, in Chattanooga
6. Some seeds
7. Tabula rasa
8. Press the accelerator
9. Ontario Natives
10. Just hanging around?
11. Bro or sis

12. Hollywood actor/director Woody
13. **PC MP defeated by John Turner in Quadra**
14. Traditional Maori dance
15. Exclude
16. Expression of frustration
20. Rock cleft
25. Coniferous tree secretion
27. Purchase for a Kindle
31. Frog one's knitting
32. Riot spray
33. Press on?
34. Gulf War missile
35. Droning sound
38. Single
39. He succeeded Churchill
40. Funny Foxx
43. Property encumbrances
45. Comic _____
48. Taunt
50. Disconcerted
52. Shades
54. Winter wrapper
56. Fuzzy fruits
60. _____ over (fell)
61. Sting operation
62. Happy Valley–_____ Bay NL
63. Jack family fish
64. '90 Dryden/MacGregor book: *_____ Game: Hockey and Life in Canada*
65. Ungulate's foot
69. _____ du jour
70. Bits of fuzz
71. Rim
73. Canadian TV reality show: *To Serve and _____*
74. Twelve drummers drumming, for example
76. _____ boom
80. Inconsistent
82. Old-style topper

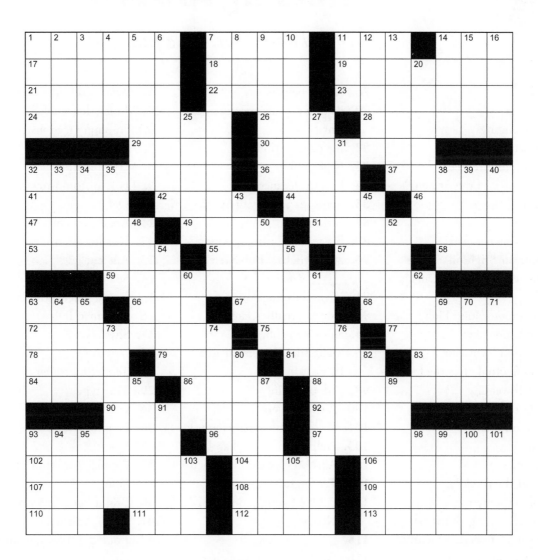

85. **Chrétien government minister of foreign affairs**

87. Have a goal

89. Lady of Spain

91. Kanata's Scotiabank Place, for example

93. Tokyo ties?

94. Sharpen skills, say

95. It can precede bowl or bunny

98. Muslim holy man

99. Mock (var.)

100. 2006 Olympics golden Canadian Jennifer

101. Airline passenger's seat adjunct

103. Highway 66 abbr.

105. Winnipeg-born former PGA pro Halldorson

68

Horsing Around

Fodder for some fun

ACROSS

1. Campus grp.
5. Musical endings
10. Pork serving
14. Sticky campfire snack
19. "The _____ of the Ancient Mariner"
20. Demean
21. Batten down a mast
22. Babble, in Brighton
23. Conference Board of Canada subj.
24. US composer John Philip
25. Earthen pot stew
26. Glaciation formation
27. **Be ineffectual after the fact?**
30. Eiffel Tower city
31. About this
32. Finish off a cake?
33. Syrup of _____
35. Dummies
38. **Win at the track?**
43. Cooking spray name
46. Revolutionary geometry shape?
48. Margaret Atwood, sometimes
49. Demolition explosive
50. Yellowfin tuna
51. Worked with a wrought iron worker's tool
53. Choral composition
54. Art _____
55. Ontario-born *SCTV* actor John
57. Nose holes
59. Some Greek consonants
60. Jason's wife, in mythology
61. Skier's lift
62. Movie set documents
64. Sigh of relief
65. **Climb the corporate ladder?**
71. Red Chamber vote
72. Rotary engine
73. Vancouver Island historic site: Fort _____ Hill

76. Santa's helpers
79. Baking powder measurement amt.
82. Big cake sections
83. Night noise
84. But, in Bécancour
85. Actresses Sevigny or Webb
87. African fly
89. Big name in campgrounds
90. 2005 Michael Bublé release: _____ *Time*
91. Nightclub singalong
93. Not paternally related
94. Sunscreen abbr.
95. **Make like Queen Elizabeth II?**
98. Park plaything
100. Aussie hollers
101. St. John's university (abbr.)
103. Helps out: _____ hand
107. Alliston ON car manufacturer
108. **Try again?**
114. '72 Neil Young song: "A Man Needs _____"
115. _____ *Brockovich*
116. WWII torpedo launcher
117. Surface species in *The Time Machine*
118. Guts
119. Zest source
120. Political power
121. "Round and Round" '80s band
122. Greek mythology nymph
123. Gives way to gravity
124. Weekly gossip magazine: _____ *Canada*
125. _____ spell

DOWN

1. Just picked, say
2. Nouveau _____
3. Love, in Longueuil

4. Encamped in the Outback?
5. Money that moves?
6. Symphony reed instrument
7. Apply stucco
8. Very, to Verdi
9. Look for tomorrow?
10. Oaf
11. Angel's aureole
12. Northern European capital
13. Ancient Jews
14. Spanx garments, say
15. Half a percussion set
16. Hammed it up
17. Shyness
18. '70s hit: "_____ Tu"
28. Tender foot? (var.)
29. Tide type
34. Furtive summons
36. Hypnotic state
37. Sweet
39. Popular Toronto museum (abbr.)
40. Bright lights description
41. "_____, Brute?"
42. Roofed walkway, in ancient Greece
43. Warsaw _____
44. *Moby-Dick* captain
45. US hip hop star Nicki
47. Letter's flourish
52. US chain in Canada since '94: Home _____
54. Remove antlers
56. Hive he-men?
58. Pompous promenade
60. Mother's Day month, in Sherbrooke
62. Montréal duo that hit with "Love Song"
63. Nautical pole
64. Consumed
66. Accounting experts (abbr.)
67. More than plump

68. Ambulance alarms
69. Put in place (var.)
70. Cozy corners
74. Bit of rain?
75. Tone-_____
76. Kuwait leader
77. Older newbie
78. Seer
79. Spacecraft engines
80. _____-happy
81. Not wealthy

83. Sowing machine
85. Two-four, for example
86. _____ out a living
88. Killer heel?
91. Pummelled the dough
92. 1815 Jane Austen novel
96. English lady of legend
97. Ottoman Empire administrator
99. Goes in
102. Lofty lord?
104. _____ Lama

105. Tessa's golden ice dance partner
106. Japanese dog
107. '70 Guess Who hit: "_____ Me Down World"
109. Diva's solo
110. William Lyon Mackenzie _____
111. Finishes up
112. Canadian Tire buy
113. Tow

ACROSS

1. Canadian "Oh, What a Feeling" band
8. Where optic nerves cross
15. Mexican or French follower
16. More severe
17. Cast out
18. Occurrence
19. A parent, in Papineauville
20. To deny, in Dorval
22. Small songbird
23. Country bordering the Adriatic (abbr.)
24. Ear canal, for example
26. Place in Parliament
27. Interest Rate Option (abbr.)
29. Canadian folksinger Ken
31. Canadian jazz great Oscar
34. Restricted, at the movies
38. Voter
39. Popular bouquet flower
40. Pretend to be an artist?
41. Canadian commercial property giant: _____ Fairview
42. Artificial intelligence computing language
44. Ali's simile insect
45. Sudden bump
48. Women's tennis star Williams
50. Fathers, for short
53. Measha Brueggergosman musical moments
55. The "A" of ABM
56. Bit of chocolate
57. Errors
59. Balsa tree: _____ *pyramidale*
61. Slithery sea creature description
62. Terrier type
63. Rained and snowed simultaneously
64. CBC or Global

DOWN

1. Espresso foam
2. Star in Orion
3. What orthodontists can fix
4. Sage
5. *You _____ Your Life*
6. Hockey rink, in Roberval
7. Home heating device
8. Angel baby?
9. Fortune
10. Official Québec flower: Blue flag _____
11. Of interest to the municipal tax department?
12. Ocean's edge
13. Journalists and reporters
14. Bing Crosby tune: "_____ You Glad You're You"
21. British boys' school
24. _____ and pestle
25. Fathered
28. Garbage bin
30. Speedy Gonzales catchphrase word
31. Canadian Neilson chocolate patty
32. "Evil Woman" grp.
33. Average answers?
35. Shutterbug's lens option
36. Pitcher's stat
37. Digital-to-Analog Converter (abbr.)
39. New Brunswick CFB
41. Ontario grows the most of this crop
43. Rented
45. Bay at the southern end of Hudson
46. Architectural window projection
47. Hosiery material
49. Wall recess
51. To like, in Lachine
52. Hit bottom?
54. Spades or hearts
56. Bird's pouch
58. Get the most out of
60. Worked (up)

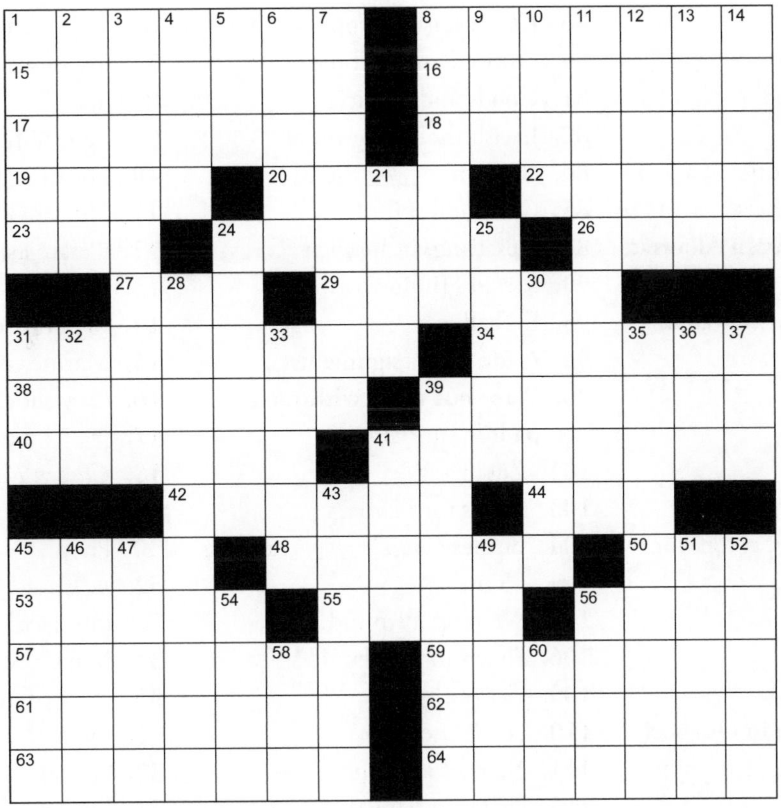

Solution on page 225

70

Pick a Number

Map out these place names

ACROSS

1. Scold
7. Permit
12. Baja money
16. '56 CBC series: *It's the* _____
19. Good-looking god?
20. SW US tribe
21. International oil org.
22. Soccer stadium cheer
23. **Small community in Alberta?**
25. Milk source for a calf
26. Language for the deaf (abbr.)
27. Asian duck
28. Mob melees
29. Entr'_____
31. Garbage
33. Boating blade
34. Calgary Flame Kiprusoff, for example
35. Reed instrument
36. For each
37. Adorable
38. **Place to meet up in Québec?**
41. Musicians' moments to shine (var.)
44. Architect Christopher
45. Newbie, in Nottingham
46. Like some mystical religious beliefs
50. Collective farm, in Israel
56. "_____ That a Shame"
57. Ballerina's jetés
58. Simile's centre
61. Sweetheart
62. '66 Governor General's Award winner: *A Jest of* _____
63. Left
64. Castaway's isle
66. Crop up
67. **Ontario archipelago for a good dressing?**
71. Slacken a shoestring

74. Juno-nominated band: The Northern _____
75. Very, in Verdun
76. *Cheers* star Danson
79. Toy or standard breed
81. Goods and Services _____
82. Jewish mourning ritual
84. "Comin' _____ the Rye"
85. Cathedral spire
87. Upsetting, in Ipswich
90. Sacred Hindu writings
93. Eyeball
94. Attorneys' assignments
95. **Place not to be without a paddle in PEI?**
101. Zig or zag
103. Plazas for Plato
104. Beatles song: "_____ Leaving Home"
105. Wrap up a wound
106. Poke fun at Adam?
109. Get pushy?
110. Feudal fields
111. Nape of a sheep
113. Unaccompanied
114. Wee bit
115. Famed guitarist Lofgren
117. **BC place for one less Dalmatian?**
120. Single thing
121. Passage to a mine
122. Ornamental shrub
123. Forestry industry worker
124. Pickering-based electronics company
125. Parliament Hill journalists Martin and McGillivray
126. Lower leg, to the butcher
127. Nanaimo bars, say

DOWN

1. Male opera voice
2. Swelling

3. Irish Canadian?
4. Over again
5. Can's cousin
6. _____ de corps
7. City in 42-D
8. Cite
9. The facilities, in Swansea
10. Possess
11. Horseradish, in Honshu
12. Ceramics, say
13. Fencing weapon
14. Big body of water
15. Marine creatures (var.)
16. Lazy shoe factory employee?
17. _____-Lorraine
18. *Citizen Kane* star Orson
24. _____ *kleine Nachtmusik*
30. Price
32. *Jack and the Beanstalk* interjection
34. Make a scene
35. _____ Chaplin, née O'Neill
36. Bypass
37. Geezer
38. Ego's excursion?
39. Some PVR buttons
40. Grate on
41. Bachelor's blowout
42. Seventh-most populous US state
43. Extend credit
44. "_____ to ya?"
47. Margarine, by another name
48. Put the sows in the sty
49. Musical syllables that precede do
51. Necklace components
52. Pubs
53. Mentalist Geller
54. "_____ the season …"
55. Alphabet letter, in Louisiana
59. Ship's distress call

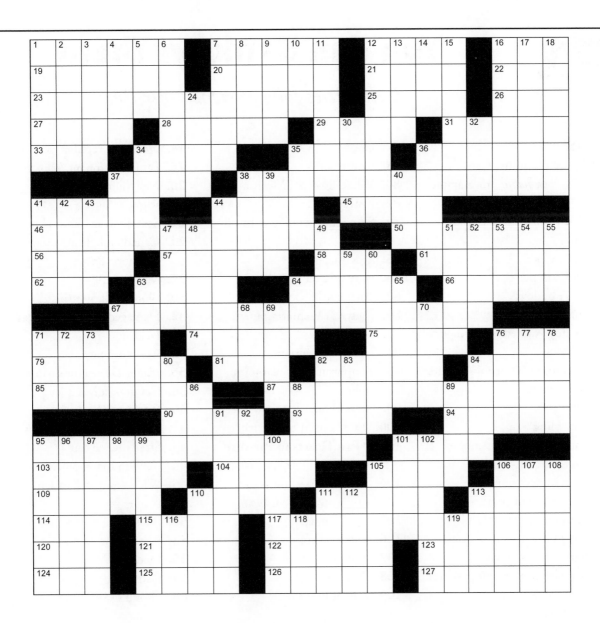

60. Wayne Gretzky: NHL's _____ leading scorer

63. Young seal

64. Plugs, say

65. Immature amphibian

67. It ebbs and flows

68. Wanted poster letters

69. *Canada's _____ Top Model*

70. Orderly

71. Canada Post competitor

72. Anti adverb

73. Foot digit

76. '50s public affairs show on CBC: _____ *Week*

77. Enniskillen river

78. Canadian Pointer, et al.

80. Two-time Canadian Olympic silver medallist Stojko

82. Philosopher's spice?

83. Big wrestler?

84. Autocrat until 1917

86. Jellied or smoked delicacy

88. Some deer

89. Frosted

91. Ceases

92. Pang

95. Town south of Calgary

96. *The Night of the _____*

97. Dozed (with "off")

98. Part of a joule

99. Mythological creature

100. Rigs a ship again

101. Medicine bottle

102. Canadian fiction writers Marian and Howard

105. Edge

106. Red, in Repentigny

107. Miniature map

108. Molson Canadians

110. _____ Flon MB

111. Vegetarian burger type

112. "Let's get goin'"

113. Theatre seating area

116. Wedding vow

118. "_____ la la!"

119. Discovery Channel show: _____ *It's Made*

Solution on page 225

71

You Can Bank on Them

Celebrities who enriched our lives

ACROSS

1. Children's aprons
5. CTV's *Flashpoint*, for example
10. _____-centre
13. Open Broadcast Network (abbr.)
16. Berry type
17. Museum piece
18. Joey's buddy?
19. Some Saturns
21. **"A Boy Named Sue" singer**
23. Baldness
25. Long-time Montréal Alouettes QB Calvillo
26. Meadow
28. Like bling
29. Short scouting mission?
31. Conductor
33. Proofreader's notation
37. Runners' transport?
38. Ideal following?
39. 2009 Canadian/American horror series movie
42. Circular amusement park ride
44. Sobbed
46. Adolescent
47. Adjust tires, say
48. TV actress Ward
50. Slithering reptiles
52. Strauss waltz river
54. "_____-dub-dub"
56. Wonderland beverage
57. *Barney Miller* actor Jack
58. **Laverne & Shirley star**
62. Rage
65. Scot's refusal
66. _____-dieu
67. Long-time rock group: Iron _____
71. Newspaper names in Montréal and Picton
74. "If all _____ fails …"
76. "You're So Vain" singer Simon

77. Goofs
78. Construct
80. White-flowered Mexican plant
82. Instruct
84. SK statutory holiday: Family _____
85. Ares' mater
86. Petty quarrel
87. Toxic substances
89. Daily CTV entertainment news show
91. Tudor-era legislation
93. Temporomandibular joint (abbr.)
95. Greased one's hair
100. Took a short transit trip
102. **"Two Tickets to Paradise" singer**
104. W Network show: *Come _____ With Me Canada*
105. _____-pitch
106. Old gold coin
107. Toil
108. Peculiar
109. Pale or bitter brew
110. Pelts
111. Canthus infection

DOWN

1. Gulf of California peninsula
2. Graphic representation
3. Bangkok currency
4. Math abbr.
5. Skin trouble, in winter
6. Uses a blue box
7. Chicken _____ king
8. Purposely deceived
9. Sore spot
10. Word heard when Greece scores?
11. Dentures
12. Broadway bombs
13. Give an inflated review

14. *Hee Haw* regular
15. Famed astronaut Armstrong
20. Nelly Furtado hit: "_____ It Right"
22. Scandinavian land (abbr.)
24. Canadian light infantry unit, for short: Princess _____
27. Muslim title
30. Bloody Mary garnish
32. Damaged merchandise tag
33. Jackfish
34. Apia currency
35. *Happy Days* actress Moran
36. Get gussied?
40. Presidential rejection
41. "Not _____ many words"
43. Straightened out
44. '72 film that won eight Oscars
45. What you perchance to do?
49. Node
51. Buckingham or Kensington
53. Related through mom
55. Seed coat
59. Cad
60. Group of six
61. Prevaricators
62. Michael Bublé cover: "_____ a Kick out of You"
63. Steak order
64. **20th-C. US poet**
68. Lozenge
69. Lanchester of film
70. "No," in Novosibirsk
72. Ushered
73. Canadian NHL "bad boy" Avery
75. East–West ancestry
79. See 49-D
81. *Swan Lake*, et al.
83. Sword end
85. Colorado Avalanche captain Milan
88. Tortilla topping

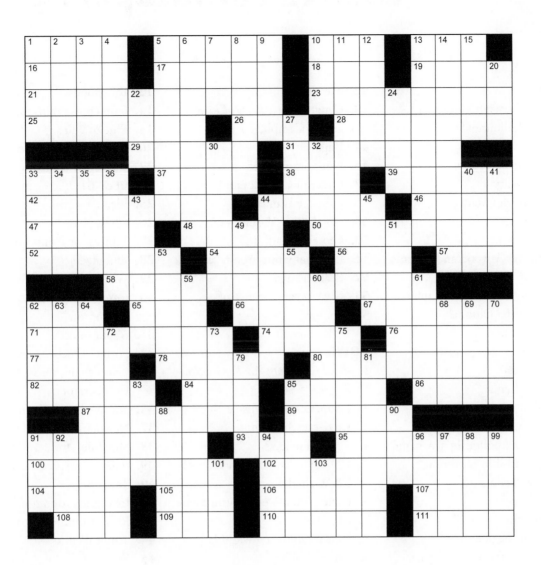

90. Max Webster front man Mitchell

91. Photoshop document (abbr.)

92. Cincinnati state

94. Prescription drugs, for short

96. Bullies bovines?

97. Briny navigation unit

98. Mysterious (var.)

99. '60s TV star Dick Van _____

101. Female deer

103. 601, to Justinian

ACROSS

1. Tennessee neighbour (abbr.)
4. Actress Lollobrigida
8. Twist
13. What cashiers scan
15. Taiwan city
16. Purcell Mountains range
17. Quiet time
18. Smells (var.)
19. Margaret Atwood and Graeme Gibson
21. Driving exam, for example
22. One of the Dionnes
23. Pig's home
24. Tackle
25. Passerine
26. Sacred hymn
28. Biblical apostle
29. Old-style ankle covering
30. Canadian political party name
33. Chapped skin condition
34. Shows feelings
35. Existence
36. Entertain
37. Puts in the pen
38. BC-born former Bruins star Neely
41. A Deadly Sin a.k.a.
42. Metallic sounding
43. Ontario-born *Party of Five* actress Campbell
44. Bugbears
46. Not domesticated
47. Order of Canada tennis inductee Daniel
48. Good thing about food?
50. Crotch-to-cuff line
51. Like many mushroom caps
52. Beatle Ringo
53. Give the appearance of
54. Pot top

DOWN

1. *Royal Canadian Air Farce* actor Roger
2. Cosmetics queen Estée
3. Large merchant ship
4. A lot, to sailors?
5. 1997 Paul Brandt Canadian #1 C&W single
6. Babies' intensive-care unit name
7. Classifies
8. French tennis star Monfils
9. North Bay lake
10. Forsaker of a faith
11. Makes over
12. Falsehoods
14. Golf course transport
15. Pine or palm
20. Rail-service crown corporation
22. Car repair company in Canada since '61
25. Blender setting
26. Chess pieces
27. Miniver or Doubtfire
28. Elite flyer?
29. With glee
30. *Caroline in the City* actress Thompson
31. About to occur
32. Former Québec premier Robert
33. Cover again, through The Co-operators?
35. Yes! We have none of these?
37. Newmarket-born actor Carrey
38. Shreddies, for example
39. Italian newspaper since 1896
40. Thawed
42. Investment duration
43. Rush drummer Peart
44. Tropical cuckoos
45. Frost
46. To's opposite
49. Golf ball peg

And the Territory Is . . .

Exploring the North

ACROSS

1. Converse online?
5. *Pequod* captain
9. Contemptuous expressions
13. 2000 Giller Prize winner: _____ *Ghost*
18. Van Halen member David Lee
19. Weaken in intensity
20. Oil of _____
21. Classic Canadian headgear
22. **Third-largest land mass**
25. Farmer's treatise?
26. Where a confession might be made
27. On one's way
28. Shakespeare's village?
29. Tel Aviv country
30. "_____ My Heart in San Francisco"
32. "Swedish" chocolate bar
34. Common Internet acronym
35. Harbour boat
36. Angler's catcher
38. More organized
40. Ore area
41. Tore
43. Nancy Drew's beau Nickerson
44. Singapore and Monaco, for example
46. Ukrainian port
49. Break in the day?
50. Close up a gap
51. Warps
54. Separates the herd
56. Ottoman Empire bigwig
60. Energetic
61. 2011 Canadian TV launch: _____ News Network
62. Have a tab
64. Ex-Vancouver Canuck Sami
65. Pool tool
66. **Official bird**
71. Charlottetown prov.

72. Bagpiper's skirt
74. White wine beverage
75. _____ *dolorosa*
76. Meadow munchers
78. Ogled
81. Raise old gardening issues?
83. HGTV series: _____ *Virgins*
84. Taking a cruise, say
86. Use a shuttle
87. Hags
88. Exhibit's main attractions
92. Acronym for some early Canadians
93. Domesticated
97. Amniotic sac
98. Hilltops
100. NWT licence-plate bear type
103. BMO no., say
104. Canadian hockey legend Bobby
105. Former Governor General Michaëlle
106. More mature
108. Open the wine
110. Transfer to the Internet, say
112. Ex-Edmonton Oiler Jarret
114. Behaviour (var.)
116. Laughs like a lion?
117. **Official flower**
119. Crazy Muppet?
120. Dairy Queen Blizzard type
121. Extraterrestrial
122. Old-style flu
123. _____ a high note
124. Broadleaf, for example
125. Old Justin Timberlake band: *N _____
126. Golfer's props

DOWN

1. Gives attribution to
2. Secludes oneself
3. On the lam

4. Greek consonant
5. As busy as _____
6. Robust constitution
7. Lunched
8. Light brown
9. Canadian university degree: _____ Science
10. Order of Canada folksinger Mills
11. Quits: _____ up
12. *Danny and the Dinosaur* author Hoff
13. Rose oil
14. *Cheers* barfly
15. **Capital city**
16. Central Switzerland tourist destination
17. Establishes oneself
19. Stroll
23. Paul Anka composition: "_____ A Lady"
24. Downy
28. Arabians and Clydesdales
31. Yeats sonnet: "_____ and the Swan"
33. Florida _____
37. On shelf, in retail-speak
39. A grad gets one of these
40. West Edmonton and Square One
42. Old-style second-person verb
45. St. Anthony's cross shape
47. Former prairie province premier Gary
48. Therefore
49. **And the territory is . . .**
51. Pulls into the pier
52. **Majority population group**
53. Cemetery pillar
54. Lop off
55. European country (abbr.)
57. Become narrower
58. **Northernmost community**

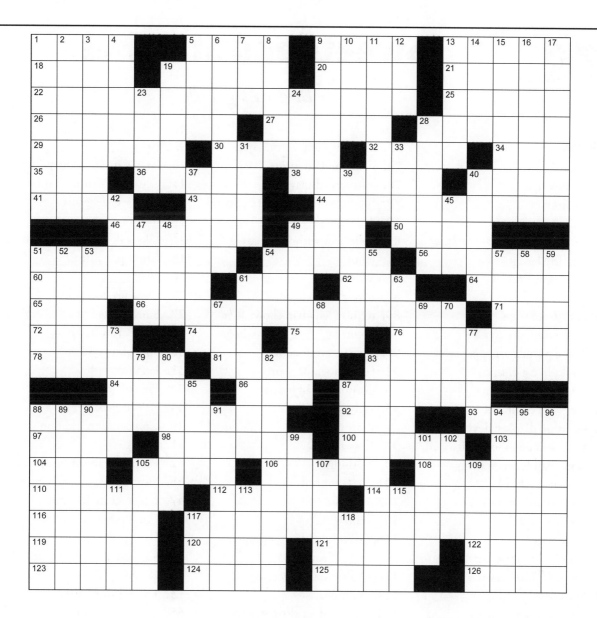

59. Loud

61. Elves' soft drinks?

63. Chinese food wrap

67. Baby goat

68. Clothing damage

69. Elvis's middle name

70. Scruff of the neck

73. Fish on open waters

77. Gusto

79. Kreskin's extra sense

80. Cleaned airplane wings in winter

82. Mollusk

83. Foreshadow

85. American Educational Research Association (abbr.)

87. Canadian public sector union (abbr.)

88. Famine, for example

89. Whaler's weapon

90. Two of four words in the territorial motto

91. Severe scolding

94. Provisions for royal children (var.)

95. Australian pop singer Kylie

96. Restaurant's main meals

99. Window's bottom edge

101. Record keeping, for short

102. Great Barrier _____

105. Harper immigration minister Kenney

107. Defendants' supplications

109. Diamond weight

111. Lamb side dish

113. Cherry or apple

115. Chairman or vice-president, in brief

117. Internment camp prisoner, for short

118. Underhanded

Solution on page 226

74

Sweets and Starches

Bad but good!

ACROSS

1. Visage
5. Meadow male
8. French roast
12. Carman's contentment?
17. Kirkland Lake *Growing Pains* star Thicke
18. Rap sheet ltrs.
19. Née
20. Like dryer traps
21. Irish political party
23. Apple portable media player
24. Looks like a creep?
25. Requiring payment
26. Neither's companion
28. **Graphic display device?**
30. Like women's short hairstyles?
33. Canadian federal energy regulator (abbr.)
35. 1947 prairie novel: *Who _____ Seen the Wind?*
36. Rake part
37. Exerciser's target, for short
38. *The Old Man and the _____*
40. Scrivener
43. Hydroelectric project
44. Hollywood star Brad
46. Paraffin a.k.a.
48. Half-moon tide
50. **Office furniture?**
53. '70s Canadian NHL star Clarke
57. Curved sabre
59. Patty Hearst's kidnappers (abbr.)
60. Attractive quality?
61. Indy 500 unit
62. Banjo sound
64. Rude look
66. River in Thailand
67. Canada Revenue _____
69. French pronoun
71. Enlivens
73. Sleeping spot on the train
74. **Fish condiment?**
76. '60s record player
78. Island group north of Scotland
79. A deadly sin
82. Politician without a party (abbr.)
85. Workshop
87. *Poivre*'s mate
89. 09/00 Canadian show: *Who Wants to _____ Millionaire?*
90. Business transaction
92. Gumshoe, for short
93. Torquay troublemaker
95. Famed Canadian thoroughbred: _____ Minister
97. **Easy task?**
99. Nothing
101. In favour of
102. Repent
103. Hibernia
106. Meech Lake catchphrase: _____ society
110. Adjust a shoelace, say
111. Visionary
112. 2011 Giller Prize winner Edugyan
113. Like Broadway signs
114. Took a shot?
115. Hindu titles
116. Short snooze
117. 1982 Disney film

DOWN

1. Scale notes
2. Former women's boxer Laila
3. **Volunteer job?**
4. World-weariness
5. Canadian politician Bob
6. Related by blood
7. Sole female NHL goalie Rhéaume
8. Slugger's stat.
9. *Alley _____*
10. Grey Cup or Stanley Cup
11. Old-style writing fluid
12. _____ Québécois
13. Illumination
14. Like a decorative table surface
15. Chest parts (var.)
16. Solar _____
22. Own up, for short
27. Summarize
29. To be, to Caesar
30. Soft bun type
31. Japanese sash
32. Fit and well
34. Bails out Barry?
39. Communion location
41. Rinds
42. People arranged in a painting
45. Stompin' _____ Connors
47. Czech currency unit
49. Cambodian dictator: _____ Pot
51. Chinese fruit trees (var.)
52. Ringed planet
54. **Lab equipment?**
55. Scottish hillside
56. Cravings for sushi?
57. Chunk
58. Animal enclosure
60. In formation
63. Idiot
65. Sanctuary sections
68. Math degree?
70. Leave the straight and narrow
72. Postpone: Put on _____
74. Like classic movies?
75. Ohio Goodyear headquarters city
77. Preferred cheese in Athens?
80. Lab Dr.?
81. "Whoopee!"
82. Driver's licence, say
83. Less of a mess

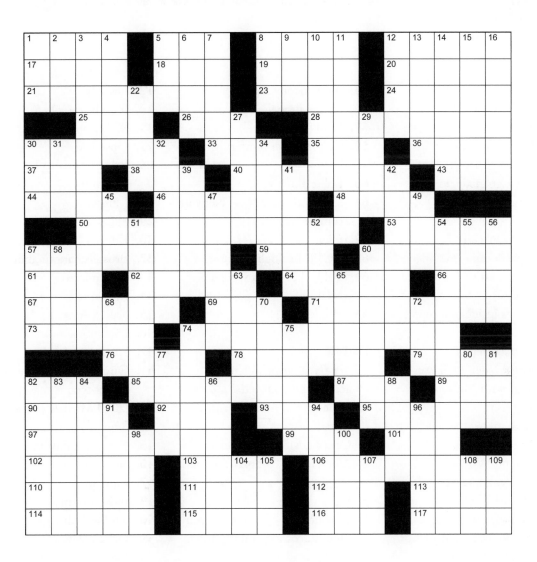

84. Early MB tribe that went south
86. Grosser
88. NDP, say
91. Stalin's predecessor
94. Obama's VP

96. _____ Pelee National Park
98. Old CBC show: *This _____ in Parliament*
100. Giller-nominated author Moore

104. Portuguese king
105. Trauma centres (abbr.)
107. Small drink
108. Dove's cry
109. Former US C&W network

75

Canada Cornucopia 25

ACROSS

1. Defeat The Donald?
6. Offspring of Eve
10. Wedding band colour
14. Wife of a rajah
15. 30-year Canadian ladies clothing chain
16. *Rara* _____
17. Like the Quechua
18. Secret wedding
20. Emulates Patrick Chan
22. Responses
23. Gambler's inside info source
25. Affirmatives (var.)
27. Years, to Yvon
28. He sang "When Irish Eyes are Smiling" with Mulroney
31. Wriggly fish
32. National monetary policy setter
35. Traumatize
38. Physics unit
39. Montrealer Mike who led the '80s NY Islanders
40. Stocking again
43. Irish Republican Army (abbr.)
44. Sense of foreboding
45. Astern
48. Acid type
51. Food Network Canada host Lawson
53. Big Vancouver park
56. Not as short
57. Plaid
59. Country that borders Mount Everest
60. Roll call reply
61. Sometime Sun News Network commentator Jerry
62. Elicit
63. CCCP, in English
64. 2011 U.S. Open winner McIlroy
65. Hinder

DOWN

1. *The Bachelorette*'s Rehn who actually got married
2. Cape Breton musical family name
3. Opens a Molson Canadian
4. Alberta food company: Sunterra _____
5. Pierce
6. "The dog _____ my homework"
7. Ontario cottage country town
8. Black, to a bard
9. What some concert performers do (var.)
10. Canada Winter _____
11. Across the ocean, say
12. Flax pips
13. It ends in Oct.
19. Wool source
21. Observed
24. Bring home big bucks in autumn?
26. Murder
29. Spiny shrub
30. Knitted blanket
32. Brussels nation (abbr.)
33. Surrendered
34. Eggy quaff
35. See 48-A
36. Dies
37. Splashes
41. Ontario Power Generation power type
42. '2009 Michael Jackson movie: *This* _____
45. _____ impossible
46. See 19-D
47. More pungent
49. Indy entrant
50. Squid's squirt
52. Omit a vowel
54. *Cogito,* _____ *sum*
55. Four quarters, combined
57. Canadian piano prodigy Wesley
58. Arid

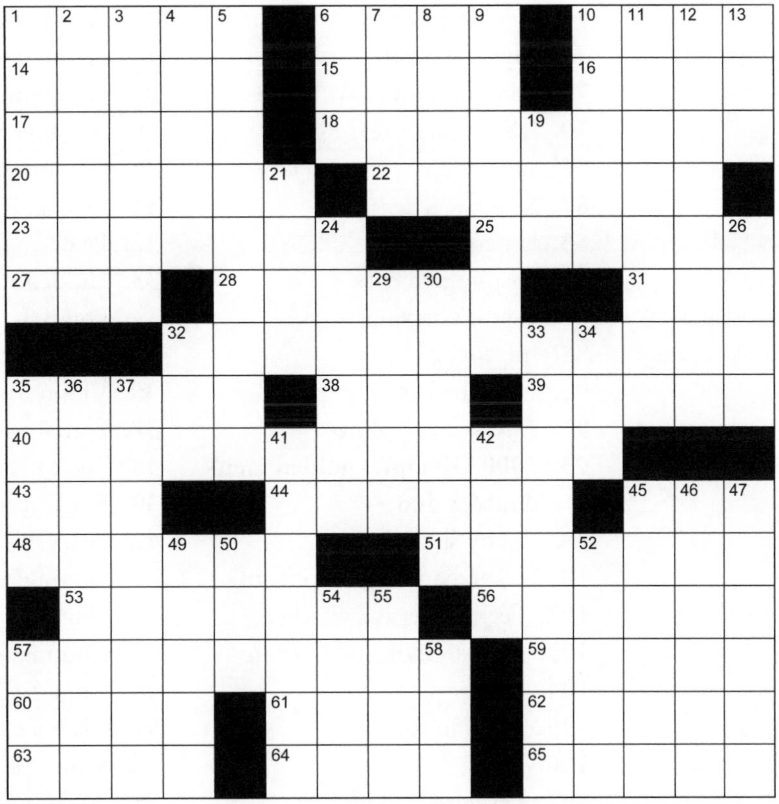

Solution on page 226

76

Canadian Combos

Groups that met with success

ACROSS

1. Arrogant person
5. Jet's collision avoidance system (abbr.)
9. National "out of this world" agency (abbr.)
12. Air pollution
16. Volcanic eruption flow
17. St. John's _____
18. Billiards kin
19. Mr., in Mannheim
20. Road to Rome, in olden days
21. Proctor & Gamble skin care line
22. Sway
24. **MLB Canadian nonet**
27. Viewed
28. Pasture calls
29. Come about
30. Tiny Tim's instrument, for short
32. Bad timing?
36. KFC limb
37. Disappear
40. "I'm working _____!"
41. 2000 Miss Universe Lara
43. Old-style clock description (var.)
45. Jim Morrison's entryways?
47. Sold-out sign at the theatre
48. '90s BC premier Clark
49. Once
50. Undisturbed, in archaeology
52. Québec ski resort: Mont-Sainte-_____
54. Flap
56. Successful CFL receptions (abbr.)
57. **Musical quintet since 1970**
61. Well put
64. Couture house since '62, for short
65. Ex-Calgary Flame Fleury

66. South American pack animals
70. German industrial area
72. Ceramic unit
74. Solemn promise
76. Mystical board
77. Flue substance
79. US baseball great Roger
81. Alt.
82. Spoof
83. Expert
85. Soap ingredient
87. Geisha's craving?
88. Improvise
90. Hear the herald angels sing?
91. *Exodus* actor Mineo
93. **2000 Olympics golden men's doubles duo**
99. Patchy skin disease
101. Canadian actress Botsford
102. Feels under the weather
103. Russian indigenous group
104. Identical
105. John, in Russia
106. Prod
107. Level, in London
108. Business attire component
109. US politician Gingrich
110. Lapsang souchong, et al.

DOWN

1. Skirt feature
2. International military alliance (abbr.)
3. 2006 CBC music documentary: *Shakin' All _____*
4. Atmosphere pressure description
5. Like some sloths
6. Behemoth
7. Kaffiyeh wearer
8. Fountain pen, in Fontainebleau
9. Marriage related
10. Up till now
11. Comrade in arms

12. "Thar _____ blows!"
13. **2008 Olympics golden octet**
14. Pacific pod member
15. Developed
18. Fragment
23. Common
25. Negative vote in Neuville
26. California university acronym
31. Be cognizant of
32. Place CCR was stuck in
33. Unidentified quotation notation
34. Uncles, in Seville
35. Violin name, for short
37. Barbarian
38. Took to civil court
39. Egg layers
42. '80s CBC Friday evening offering: *Good Rockin' _____*
44. Handy
46. Command to Rover
48. Large Swiss city
51. Clear a clog
53. Slangy negative
55. '52 Winter Olympics city
58. Got off a horse
59. Uncouth ones
60. Reuben sandwich filling
61. Rainbow shapes
62. Unprocessed
63. **Long-time a capella quartet**
67. Brian's wife/Ben's mom
68. '69 smash: "Leaving on _____ Plane"
69. Michael Bublé cover: "_____ the Last Dance for Me"
71. Took the train
73. Production interval
75. Pull back
78. Islam sect
79. '70s Israeli prime minister
80. Varnish
84. Shut

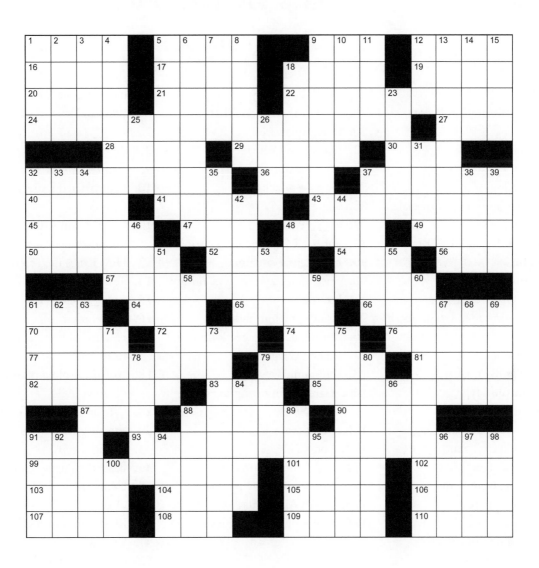

86. Southern constellation
88. Musical instruction: Allegro _____
89. Jasper National Park ski resort: Marmot _____

91. Joust, verbally
92. China's continent
94. Toronto area: _____ York
95. Pews' place
96. Emerald Isle a.k.a.

97. Aquatic organism
98. Employs
100. Street, in Saint-Raymond

77

Up in the Air

Songs that soared

ACROSS

1. Canadian created apple, for short
4. Venomous snake
9. TSO or CPO, for short
13. Untamed
19. Suffix with sermon or special
20. Internet bucks
21. This and that, in Trois-Rivières
22. Big birds
23. Old Ford letters
24. _____ Gritty Dirt Band
25. Honours awarded by Elizabeth (abbr.)
26. Old-style sofas
27. Canadian Football _____
29. Transmission type
31. Run out of time?
32. **Beatles song for Carl Sagan?**
36. California city: San _____
37. Part of an actor?
38. "Gallows" word game
43. Skiers' US mecca
46. Homemade racer
48. In the centre, politically
49. Pointed weapons
51. + (abbr.)
52. Ward off
53. '70s CTV talk-show host Hamel
54. Jack Kerouac character Paradise
55. Prevalent Canadian mammal
57. Glassy mineral
59. Manufactured
60. Starch converting enzyme
62. Spur wheels
64. See James Bond?
66. Bevel edges (var.)
67. **Elton John song for Wernher von Braun?**
70. Evicts
73. Padlock hinge
75. 1979 Nobel Prize-winning nun

76. Tax dodging, say
78. "_____ there, done that"
80. Catch unawares
82. Dreary, to Dickens?
84. _____ standstill
85. Surprise attack
86. Some bucks
87. _____ mode
88. Former 24 Sussex resident John
90. House tax evaluator
92. Nasty comment posters, on the Internet
95. Group of felon finders
96. Get off at Union Station?
97. Is just the right size
98. Panoramic view
100. **Carole King song for the USGS?**
106. Summon back
110. Loonie
111. _____ one's laurels
112. Weakness-inducing disease
113. North American Native group
114. Liberty Island neighbour, in NYC
117. Go quickly
118. Propelling a gondola
119. Spray
120. South American river rat
121. Freddy Krueger's street
122. Contend
123. Not in favour of poker?
124. 10-year-old, say
125. TV chef Rachael

DOWN

1. *Resident Evil* films star Jovovich
2. Montezuma, for one
3. BC tree: Western red _____
4. **Wings song for a Williams sister?**
5. Most chilly?

6. Yukon premier Duncan (2000–02)
7. *Id* _____
8. The rain in Spain?
9. *All in the Family* star Carroll
10. Constructed again
11. Chop
12. Swiss region where you hope nobody bugs you?
13. How ladies used to ride
14. Texas town
15. _____ voce
16. Rush order?
17. Patriarchal lineage, in old Rome
18. North Carolina motto: "_____ quam videri"
28. Pyle on *The Andy Griffith Show*
30. Saintly glows
33. Young sheep
34. Basketball nets
35. Geneva's river
39. Orca
40. Kuala Lumpur residents
41. Somewhat
42. Hawaii state bird
43. NE India state
44. Hindu mystic
45. Believer in many gods
47. Arm-twisters, say
48. High-IQ org. since 1946
50. '75 ABBA hit
52. Appropriate for cinematic treatment
56. Not 'neath
57. Clean with a broom
58. Dogs and cats
61. Hero's beloved, in myth
63. Gumbo mallow
65. **Sheryl Crow song for Apollo?**
68. Riverbank critter
69. Maiden name preceder
71. Big bags

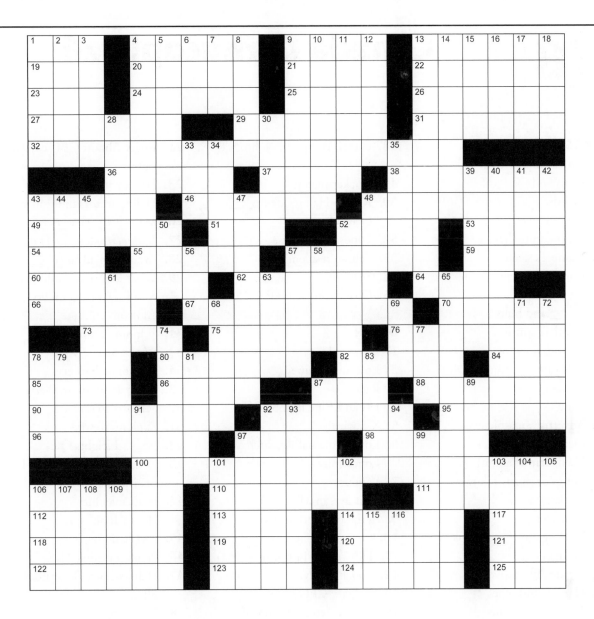

72. Drum type
74. Gentle teasing
77. UK consumption tax
78. First Newfoundlander (Gushue) to win Olympic gold
79. Naturalness
81. Shania Twain hit: "_____ Needs to Know"
83. Cocoon contents
87. Out on the ocean
89. Gads

91. Yachting
92. '90s YTV music show
93. Argo or Maple Leaf, say
94. Formal title
97. Old Netherlands currency
99. Military rank indicator
101. Puffiness cause
102. Vertical
103. 2006 Christina Aguilera song: "Ain't No _____ Man"

104. "There you have it," in Terrebonne
105. Arch foe
106. _____ Nui
107. Ether form
108. Prisoner's accommodation
109. Female friend, in Québec
115. Bliss Carman poem: "_____ Tide on Grand Pré"
116. Caustic substance

78

Canada Cornucopia 26

ACROSS

1. Against the current
9. Loamy soil
14. Practise
15. Beginnings
17. Most comprehensive
18. Siamese's sleep?
19. Canadian singer Bryan
20. Living things
22. _____ and bolts
23. Spaniel's spittle
24. Bigwig, for short
25. '70s Juno-winning vocalist Gallant
26. Spud
28. Advertise an athlete?
32. Occur, old style
33. Used a crowbar, say
34. Long- or short- follower
35. Advisories
36. Considers
37. DEA agents, for example
38. Trudges
40. Senate affirmative
41. Harvest and blue
42. 1,504, to Tiberius
46. Hunters' signs of success?

48. Chuck Berry hit: "Johnny B. _____"
49. Wicker material
50. Rideau Hall resident: _____ General
52. Dinosaurs' demise
53. Tehran residents
54. Seabirds
55. Give the royal nod?

DOWN

1. Not rural
2. Lost, in Lachine
3. Piglet
4. Jets and Blue Bombers
5. X-ray units
6. Environmental Research and Education (abbr.)
7. Various
8. Subways, in Montréal
9. In the neighbourhood
10. _____ even keel
11. Hibernated in summer (var.)
12. Touchy-feely?
13. Calgary CFLer
16. Sony video game console (abbr.)

21. Roger Abbott CBC co-star Luba
23. Fruits with pits
25. Halifax and Hamilton, say
26. Many YTV viewers
27. *Beaujolais nouveau*, et al.
28. Arrange in advance
29. What Donovan Bailey, et al., won for Canada in '96
30. Glutton
31. Sulphur compound
32. Writes on the Web
34. Corporate backers
38. Justin Trudeau, to Pierre
39. Minoan colonnade
41. Explores for ore
42. _____-Heights QC
43. Canadian actor Peter or his British uncle Robert
44. Paul Anka hit: "_____ Like to Sleep Alone"
45. Left-hand page
46. Prefix meaning "three"
47. Halifax-born Oscar nominee Ellen
48. DNA bit
51. Anatomical duct

79

Who Am I? 2

An iconic Canadian

ACROSS

1. Frosts
5. Bucket
9. Has to
13. Tousle
17. Hue
18. Arm bone
19. Tolstoy's Karenina
20. Go _____ length
21. Precipice
22. Felix Unger's opposite
23. Thailand, old style
24. Like a *Cinderella* stepsister
25. **His 1980 fundraiser**
28. Zap in a microwave
29. Take as one's own
30. Teems
31. '80s sitcom: *One Day _____ Time*
32. '90s Dubya job
34. Cherry stones
36. Hilo garland
37. Light Brigade's Balaclava attack
40. WWII military alliance
42. Sherpa's homeland
44. Less emotional
46. **Best picture award for his biopic**
48. Lions' home
49. Mix-up?
50. Literary captain
51. Suffolk and Norfolk environs: East _____
53. Malarial fever
55. "Are you a man _____ mouse?"
57. Where sociologists might work (abbr.)
58. **National honour he was accorded**
62. Military activity (abbr.)
65. Lobe locale
66. Vietnam's northwest neighbour
67. *The Far Side* cartoonist Gary

71. Tuber
73. US "monster" lizard
75. Razz
77. **His flag-bearing mom at the 2010 Olympics**
78. Air, like the CBC
80. Tabulated
82. Solidifies
83. Not mono
84. Petawawa or Trenton (abbr.)
86. *I Dream of Jeannie* star Barbara
88. Opposite of WNW
89. Grand _____ National Historic Park (NS)
90. Milieu of Canadian retailer Marks
92. Shoulder wrap
94. Calista Flockhart show: _____ McBeal
96. **Thunder Bay Trans-Canada section honouring him**
100. Unit at the bakery
101. Tortoise competitor
102. Old married couple?
103. First caucus state in presidential campaigns
104. Fictional '30s Japanese spy
105. Nights before some holidays
106. Project detail
107. Screwdriver, for example
108. Highest point
109. Spiciness
110. Reusable shopping bag
111. She, in Sept-Îles

DOWN

1. Dating couple, say
2. Canadian foreign aid program administrator (abbr.)
3. Carving a cameo, for example
4. Place
5. Thumbtack
6. Doled out

7. Get _____ the ground floor
8. Toil, in Tallahassee
9. Old-style five iron
10. 93-D, for example
11. Ginger cookies
12. Subdued
13. **One of these was named for him in BC's Selwyn Range**
14. Open
15. Polio vaccine developer
16. Red eye cause
26. Old CBC quiz show: *Reach for the _____*
27. Thanksgiving season
31. NHL feeder league
32. Nuts about Stefani Germanotta?
33. Pair that can take a yoke?
35. Canada's easternmost point: Cape _____
37. Okay place for horses?
38. *Hazel* producer: Screen _____
39. Love god
41. Grain storage structure
43. Namibia neighbour
45. Common noun suffix
47. The Old Sod
49. Confectionery: Laura _____
52. Slow movement, in music
54. Western Canada agricultural cooperative (abbr.)
56. Muslim greeting gesture
59. Sister of 61-D
60. Actor's audience statement
61. War god
62. Table scraps
63. Leonard Cohen, sometimes
64. Hot part of an iron
68. Abrasive cleaning pad
69. Sports names Mel and Steve
70. It's at 11 Wall St.
72. **He is ...**
74. Teaches at university

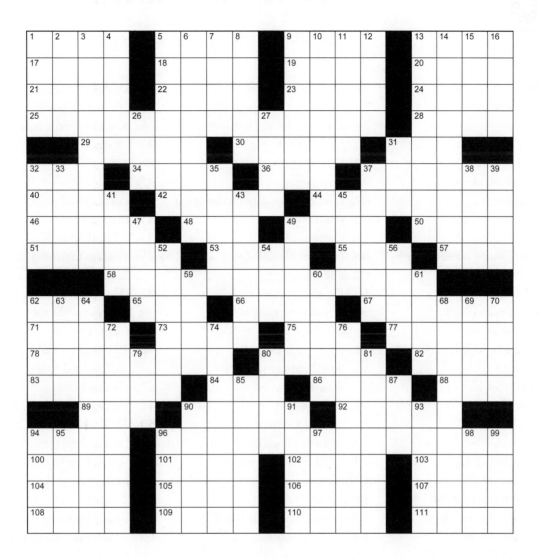

76. Mattress topper
79. Ganders' flying formation
80. Start of a magician's catchphrase
81. Bust open, like flowers
85. Treed expanse

87. Shrew
90. Italian wine
91. Discharge
93. Canadian labour leader Bob
94. Small place name in five provinces

95. Roller coaster component
96. Old CBC kids' show: _____ *Hélène*
97. 1986 Vancouver event
98. Military desertion acronym
99. Connecticut university

ACROSS

1. Mexican meal shell
5. Spew
9. Canadian Environmental Law Association (abbr.)
13. Help control the pet population
17. Neighbour of Saudi Arabia
18. Years ago
19. Telesat Canada satellite name
20. Estimator's phrase
21. Netherlands city
23. Seaweed/sushi dish
24. Fondest desire
25. **Completely inferior cellar reno?**
28. Trudeau met him in China
29. Salé and Pelletier, for example
30. Sibling on *Frasier*
31. Paddles
33. BMO banking machine (abbr.)
36. California wine county
38. **Something to take for 59-A?**
41. Political party "enforcer"
43. Goose egg, in soccer
44. Mork and Alf, for short
45. Saint Petersburg country
46. Taboo things
48. _____'easter
50. Upper limit
51. Esquimalt and Nanaimo Railway (abbr.)
52. Crossword alternative
54. Will beneficiary
58. Letter add-on (abbr.)
59. **Builder's level of angst?**
62. Takes too many drugs, for short
64. Old lace mate, at the movies
65. Hot dog condiment
69. '87 Canadian film: _____ *Heard the Mermaids Singing*
70. Those elected

71. Tennis court mesh
73. '56 shipwreck: *Andrea* _____
74. Group of four
76. US attorneys' grp.
79. Pollen sheath
81. Insect eggs
82. **Like emotionally challenging renovations?**
84. Canned herring
86. Harden, like Jell-O
87. Life and _____
88. Big hurry
90. Ericsson who explored Newfoundland
92. Sports enthusiast
93. **Small reno inspired by *Hawaii Five-0*?**
99. Provo neighbour
101. Singer Clapton
102. Céline Dion, for example
103. Architectural moulding style
104. Take a break
105. Sups
106. Historians study these
107. _____-majesté
108. Doctrines
109. Blunt blade
110. '50s British bombshell Diana

DOWN

1. Suit _____
2. Armoury supplies
3. Broken arm covering
4. Coming up next, at the pub?
5. _____ knot
6. Support from below
7. Sign of healing
8. Macho fellow
9. King Arthur's castle
10. Tooth coverings
11. This way
12. Similar to
13. Piglets' parent

14. Uptight flowers?
15. Hired guns, say
16. Takakkaw Falls park, in BC
22. Oomph
26. X or XXL
27. Add
32. Promotional pitches
33. Bract bristles
34. Biblical pronoun
35. Gordon Lightfoot classic: "If You Could Read My _____"
37. Warm welcomes, in Waikiki
39. BC river and valley name
40. Corn cob
42. 2005 Disney film: _____ *Heffalump Movie*
47. Go downhill?
49. Québec singing star Simard
50. TV drama: _____:*NY*
53. Lake Victoria land
55. Roadhouse
56. Jockey's strap
57. Too too much
58. Road safety cone
60. 1982 Eddie Murphy movie: *48* _____
61. Media mogul Turner
62. Way too big
63. Those in custody
66. Eye part
67. Location
68. Verb that might follow 34-D
69. *Addams Family* character
70. Metrical feet
72. Follow too closely
75. Pirate's quaff
76. Ancestral reversion, in biology
77. Cuts in two
78. Makes a scene?
80. Wash
83. "_____ No Business Like Show Business"
85. Grime

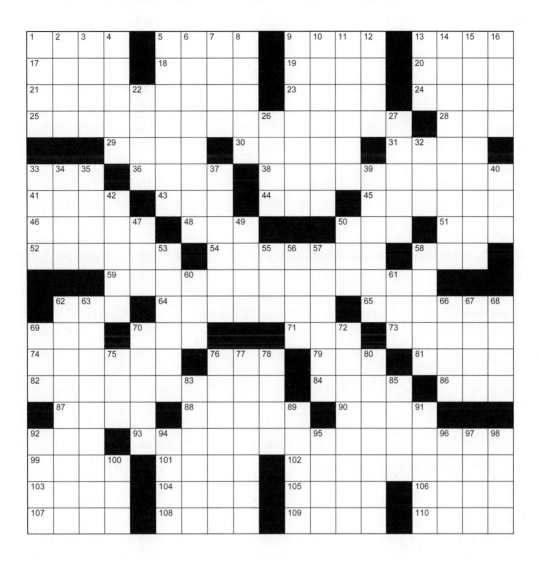

89. Fred Davis, for one
91. Released from incarceration
92. Guess Who hit: "Dancin'
_____"

94. Garr who had a *Tootsie* role
95. Crack, in the winter
96. French bread?
97. Winter Palace ruler

98. Thomas Hardy heroine
100. Canadian hip hop singer
Michie

ACROSS

1. *Edmund Fitzgerald*, for example
5. Water-to-wine miracle site
9. '80s CBC drama: *Street* _____
14. Fill the hold
15. Cy Young Award winner Hershiser
16. Nitrogen compound
17. Cause ochlophobia?
19. Devilfish
20. Most annoying
21. More bland
22. Give a duke his due?
23. Crumpled up, like paper
24. US insurance co. since 1845
25. TD Square, in Calgary
26. Operated
28. Montréal landmark: Notre-_____ Basilica
31. Roman, say
34. Form of discrimination (var.)
36. Harvest goddess
37. Parts
38. Not alike
41. MLB Cincinnati team
42. Peterborough's prov.
43. Install a shower stall
44. Make a choice
46. Sounds made by a banned '70s toy
48. Hunter-gatherers, in 53-A
52. *Faust* playwright
53. Southern Africa country
54. Not conventional
55. Mercy seekers
56. Swelter
57. Harbinger
58. Kind
59. Blue Jay's bargain?
60. Redden who logged 11 years with the Ottawa Senators
61. Three on a die

DOWN

1. Incline
2. Shelter from a storm
3. That is, in old Rome
4. Excessive cheer
5. Former Global network newsman Rae
6. Sprang up
7. Salamander
8. Municipal councillor (abbr.)
9. Thin, like a membrane
10. Electronic message
11. Canada Dry _____
12. Created a chronology
13. Cordelia's father
18. King _____ ON
21. Neighbour of Java
23. Model wood
25. Canadian arboreal emblem
27. Scottish loch name
28. Pedestal part
29. 1415 battle
30. Plant to peck under
32. Works hard
33. _____ Territories
35. AB-born Grammy winner Joni
39. '90s BC premier Harcourt
40. Regular dance performance?
45. Silent letters?
47. Sunny lobbies
48. Like old-style corsets
49. Lord's lodgings
50. Among (Fr.)
51. Truly cruel
52. Oodles
53. Church platform
55. Imprisoned soldier in wartime (abbr.)

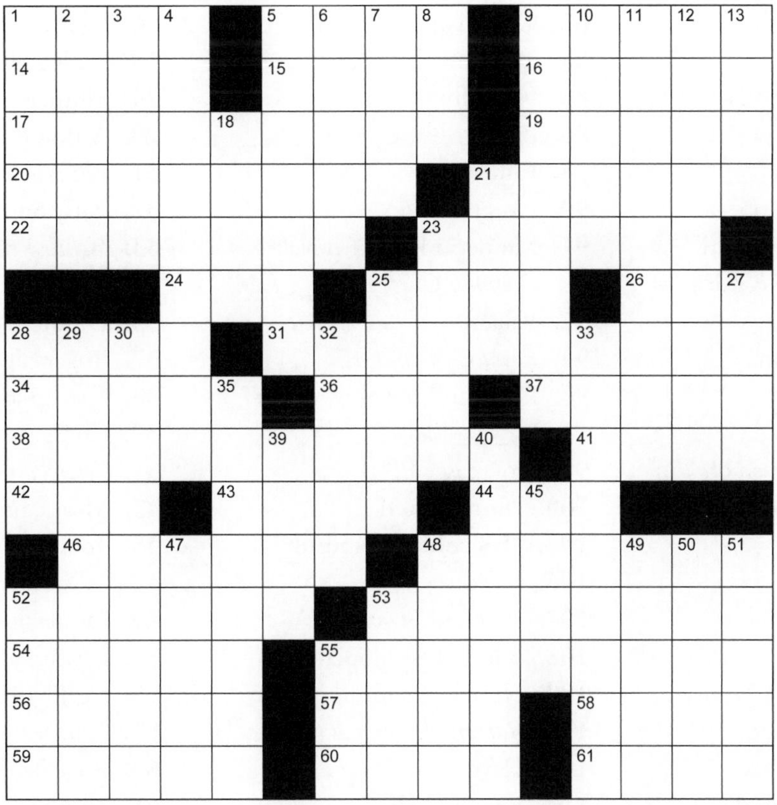

Solution on page 228

Talking to Thespians

Words to Canadian actors

ACROSS

1. Alka-Seltzer jingle word
5. 1987 thriller: _____ *Attraction*
10. Inuit-invented jackets
17. Amble
18. Stratospheric fireball
19. Blood poisoning
20. State categorically
21. Muse holding a globe
22. **"Wait a minute, Brent!"**
23. **"For heaven's sake, Rick!"**
25. Hard _____ rock
26. Feminine pronoun
27. Four-sided shape
28. Sandwich fish a.k.a.
30. "_____ Got a Crush on You"
32. _____-aux-Chats QC
34. Poverty
36. Beaufort _____
37. Bananas Foster cooking technique
40. Beery family actor
42. Willy Wonka creator
44. Catastrophes
46. Beverage topped with marshmallows
48. Crucifixion artwork
50. Asian bug?
51. Hissy fit
52. "Michael, Row the Boat _____"
54. Michael J. Fox sitcom: *Family _____*
56. Class
58. Finger opposite
59. **"Just joking, Margot!"**
63. Speedometer letters
66. Art lover's destination, in Toronto (abbr.)
67. Remarked
68. Vacillate, near the swing set?
72. Not in the wind, at sea
74. Paramedic (abbr.)

76. Made tracks
78. a.k.a. mother-of-pearl
79. Visit an issue again
82. Carnelian
84. '90s Canadian skier Kate
85. Hairy fly
86. Barbary beast
88. Father
90. Postgrad deg.
91. Mordecai Richler novel: *Solomon Gursky _____ Here*
92. Valiant
94. *Royal Canadian Air _____*
96. Doug and the Slugs ditty: "_____ Bad"
98. Prov. east of NB
100. **"Sure, Janet!"**
104. **"It's cold, Raymond!"**
106. Motor
107. Womanizer, say
108. Injected with opiates
109. NHL forward, hopefully
110. *Raising Arizona* actor Nicolas
111. Have
112. Renters' belief?
113. _____ bomb

DOWN

1. Baby buggy
2. Alice Munro book: *No _____ Lost*
3. Stretch too far
4. Fisherman's spot?
5. Grizzly's ancestor?
6. Winged
7. Bit of colour
8. Farewells, in Frontenac
9. Acquired knowledge
10. Cornered
11. We, in Winslow-Sud
12. Beefy soup ingredients?
13. Yankee's enemy, in the South

14. What Canada's Wonderland provides?
15. _____ and kin
16. Gratify a hunger
18. Cadged from a hobo?
24. Thither
29. Artless one
31. Big tanks
32. Early South American empire
33. *Gentlemen Prefer Blondes* author Anita
35. Hindu loincloth
37. Rogers Sportsnet analyst Rob
38. Get-up-and-go, Italian style
39. Compass point in Spain
41. *Peter Pan* captain
43. Meat cuts
45. Tobogganed
47. "Vissi d'arte," for example
49. Impressionist Edgar
53. Lawn manicuring devices
55. Curling rink captains
57. Avid
60. Rogers Centre roof style
61. Think tank nuggets
62. Get what you sow?
63. Canadian pianist _____-Andre Hamelin
64. "Not guilty," e.g.
65. Dictionary entry lead-ins
69. Maligned mammal?
70. London landmark: Marble _____
71. Dandelion, for example
73. Early Icelandic literary collection
75. Nicholas II, for one
77. Trawler's hauler
80. Labour unrest, say
81. Most meagre
83. Dresser component
87. Convey emotion
89. Bobble

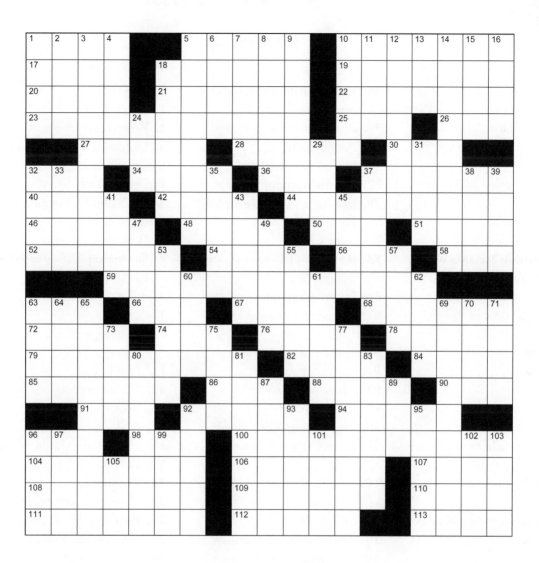

92. Canada geese

93. Encourage a hen?

95. Approximate age, when appraising antiques

96. Recipe amount (abbr.)

97. Sandwich cookie

99. '74 Top Ten hit: "_____ Tu"

101. Offer employment

102. '89 hurricane that hit Eastern Canada

103. Flow copiously

105. _____-relief

83 Terrorisms

Little shots of horrors

ACROSS

1. Monastery head
6. Guitarists' solos
11. River that splits Calgary
14. Flair for fashion
19. Canadian singer McLachlan
20. Totally
21. Tropical cuckoo
22. Secure the sloop
23. **Frightening Mélanie Watt children's book?**
26. '50s decor, today
27. Prolonged time period
28. Toggy or anorak
29. Urge on a cowgirl?
30. Milk plants
32. It's a blast?
33. Baby barn bird
35. Recurring payment
37. Montréal stadium moniker: The Big _____
38. Manitoba community: The _____
40. **Brat you want to stay away from?**
45. Calyx parts
48. Ex-NHLers Duguay and Hextall
50. Reform Party's Red Chamber concept (abbr.)
51. Nimble
52. Solitary person
53. E'en if
55. _____ Vegas
56. Old-style colony type
57. Overwhelms
59. Northern Alberta Institute of Technology (abbr.)
61. Without any difficulty
62. Clay/lime soil
63. Half a bikini
64. Not portly
65. Yonge, in TO
66. **Sidney Sheldon daytime reading?**
74. Pharaoh's symbolic snake
75. Pimple problem
76. Indochinese language
77. Canadian author Christie
78. MB-born '70s Philadelphia Flyer Bobby
82. Dam kin
83. Radium in BC, for example
85. Nigeria city
86. Hibernation home
87. Primitive "calculators" (var.)
89. Collect a lot?
90. Poet Pound
91. Cartoon collectible
92. Charges of 1-A
93. Tooth type
95. **Frightening NBC show?**
98. Large Canadian metropolis (abbr.)
100. Sue Grafton book: _____ for Lawless
101. All decked out
103. Like Caesar's committee?
105. Precious stone
108. Drag one's feet
112. Doris Day song word
114. Christian _____
115. Canada neighbour (abbr.)
116. Hearing related
117. **Arizona park you don't want to visit?**
121. Low-life
122. "_____ had it!"
123. Enthusiastic wave?
124. Commencement
125. Greens meal
126. Salt
127. Waste product
128. Windsor MP Brian

DOWN

1. Holding, say
2. Eggs' accompaniment
3. Mohawk for whom an Ontario city is named
4. Dinghy stick
5. **1915 film for wusses?**
6. Qatar currency
7. Foot part
8. Something that's asked often? (abbr.)
9. Agues
10. Ladies' falls?
11. Spanish-speaking US community
12. Half of two
13. '72 Stampeders single
14. Big step
15. Stadium seating level
16. Himalayan creature of legend
17. Entice
18. Traditional poem
24. Carpenter's connector
25. Buzzi and Westheimer
31. Pot builder, in poker
34. Filled pastries
36. Kilt crease
37. Without secrecy
39. It follows fah
41. Some grains
42. Raja's mate
43. Kind of history
44. Count on
45. Sub system?
46. Accustom to (var.)
47. Ancient Persia dignitary
49. Zigzagging, say
52. Bean type
54. "The Maple _____ Forever"
55. Car with a bar
56. Whittle down
58. Verbal invective
60. _____-mémoire

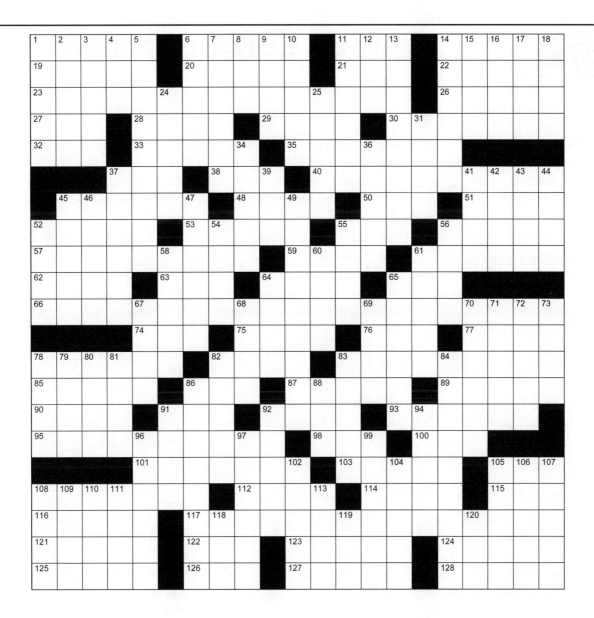

61. Group values
64. Quarterback takedown
65. Electrical interference
67. Trees bearing acorns
68. Come on down?
69. Group of particles
70. Skin layer
71. Of birds
72. Laundry cycle
73. Beer barrels
78. Treble or bass
79. Take it easy
80. Taj Mahal site
81. "I am woman, hear me _____"

82. BC community on the Fraser River
83. *The Terminator* catchphrase: "_____ la vista, baby!"
84. **Place to go when you're scared?**
86. Worn out
88. Get groceries?
91. Astronomer Sagan
92. Less restricted
94. Standoffish
96. Like writer Aesop?
97. Rockefeller's preferred mollusk?
99. Vipers
102. Towelled off

104. Pelts
105. Canadian band: The _____ Who
106. Pluralizing letters
107. Photo finish?
108. Backtalk
109. Hawaiian Islands dance
110. Seed cover
111. Parental name
113. Way off yonder
118. "Little" '60s singer
119. Whitesnake hit: "Here _____ Again"
120. Genetic material (abbr.)

ACROSS

1. Mistry Giller-Prize winner: *A _____ Balance*
5. Welland Canal feature
10. Grey or Stanley
13. Had an easy time on an exam
14. Nonsensical
15. Bangladesh cash
16. _____ Nurses' Association of Ontario
18. Algerian port city
19. Stomach soreness
20. Habeas corpus, for example
22. Chats
25. Removed a computer file
26. *Heroes* star Larter
27. Ontario township abutting Lake Superior
29. Round Table title
30. Spellbound
32. Strapping tape brand
34. Iraq city
38. Gun dog developed in the US
41. Savoury sauce
42. Canadian education plan savings vehicle (abbr.)
43. Canadian Brass instrument
44. Emergency Lighting Equipment (abbr.)
46. Seized vehicle, say
48. Crawl space?
49. Okanagan Lake "monster"
53. Frozen desserts
55. Ship's ordinance experts (var.)
57. Old-style servant
58. Beaufort and Bering
59. Skylab attire
63. Circus act venue
64. Italy's third-longest river
65. Singer/songwriter Sedaka
66. Canadian _____ Patrol
67. Clicks one's fingers
68. Capital on a fjord

DOWN

1. 2006 Nickelback hit: "_____ Away"
2. On thin _____
3. Refusals
4. Court pronouncement
5. Well-read ones?
6. Bryan Adams single: "_____ Night Love Affair"
7. '60s Maple Leafs star Brewer
8. Knock-_____
9. Marsh plants
10. Insertion mark
11. Tsar's ruling
12. Like a leaded glass window, say
15. Broad-minded
17. Sullivan had a really big one
21. Excuse
22. Civil rights org. in the US
23. Pool problem
24. Curse
28. *The Mary Tyler Moore Show* star Ed
31. Fence part
33. Church recesses
35. Stuns
36. Confute
37. Residents of 34-A
39. Sorrow (var.)
40. Those not for
45. Gets rid of
47. They lack refinement?
49. Hops kilns
50. Movie from Winnipeg's Vardalos: *My Big Fat _____ Wedding*
51. Neighbour of a Saudi
52. Purple plant (var.)
54. *The Beachcombers* star Gerussi
56. Netherlands Caribbean island
60. Porcini
61. Blue Rodeo single: "_____ I Am Myself Again"
62. _____-mo

85

Destination: Ottawa

Take a tour of the National Capital Region

ACROSS

1. Santa _____
4. Give temporarily
8. Violinist Stern
13. '71 Guess Who single: "_____ Flasher"
19. Handel or Haydn
21. It's got the beat
22. More sour
23. Bleach
24. **Ex-prime minister's museum home**
26. **1 Sussex Drive**
28. Red Sea peninsula
29. Middle of the month, to Tiberius
30. Shinto shrine plaques
31. Hair goop
32. Pills
34. '80s US tennis star Andrea
39. Foul substance
41. Properly
42. Brunei bigwig
43. Milk type
44. Law enforcer, for short
45. Relinquish a right
50. Octets
52. Be slow
53. Newfoundland town
54. Blackberry drupes
55. Alps vocalist (var.)
57. Rushes forward
58. Marxist's mate?
60. Lennon's missus
61. Antiquity, once
62. Ontario time zone (abbr.)
63. **Parliament Hill attraction**
68. Not forward
71. Brewery product
72. Paddling stick
73. Adulthood, say
77. Minor-_____
79. Crime against the state

82. Talk at length
83. Sudden
84. "Yo!"
85. Wrapped up again
87. Busybody
88. Something to chew on
89. MDs
90. Mansbridge and C. Newman
91. Vancouver-born *The Proposal* star Reynolds
93. Fair fun
94. Potatoes, colloquially
95. Scolder
99. Juno Award category
100. Hair colouring
102. Church exclamation
103. Month following Adar
105. **Memorial Chamber locale**
112. **Cold War museum in Carp**
115. Pool purifying agent
116. National skiing body: _____ Canada
117. String section instrument
118. Oil field on the Grand Banks
119. Took it easy
120. Shoe parts
121. Got ready to drive
122. Not even

DOWN

1. Serving whiz, on the courts
2. *The Little Red Hen* denial phrase
3. In the centre of
4. Singer Falana
5. Son in Genesis
6. Lower regions description
7. Berton book: *The National _____*
8. "_____ never work!"
9. BC coastal waters appellation: Salish _____
10. Provided entertainment
11. Easter month, often

12. Toonie, say
13. _____ fibrillation
14. Scale note (var.)
15. Roast in the sun
16. Chopin piece, for example
17. Change the clock
18. Long lock
20. *The Black Cat* scribe
25. Devour
27. Was without
31. Wrigley product
33. **Shopping enclave**
34. Apple or orange drink
35. Seaweed-based thickener
36. Cultural
37. **Home of the Mackenzie King estate**
38. Navy rank (abbr.)
40. Upslope
41. Three _____ Night
42. Navy commando
43. Struck down, old style
44. Canadian wrestler Huynh who won 2008 Olympic gold
46. Tiny insect
47. *Monty Python* star Eric
48. Some neckline shapes
49. Once, once
51. Canadian C&W band: Prairie _____
52. Horne of jazz
53. Soviet prison camp
56. French wine valley
57. Actress Bonham Carter
59. Bathurst _____ NU
64. Eminent
65. Not a one
66. Total failures
67. Solvent solution
68. Kill with comedy?
69. Zeus daughter
70. Story about knitting?
74. Rage

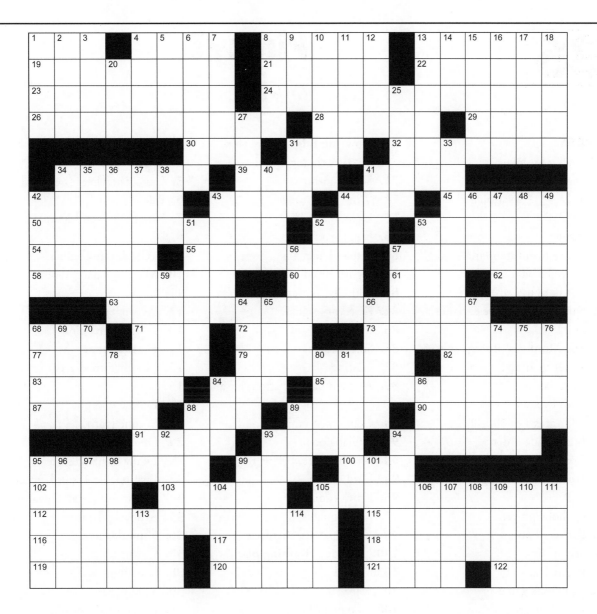

75. Busy bodies?
76. Finales
78. Kind of feeling
80. Nickname of NY Yankees star Alex
81. Withdraw
84. Attila, for one
86. Tax return maven (abbr.)
88. Lesser Antilles Amerindian
89. It accompanies chips
92. Pined for, old style

93. Cause annoyance
94. Electronics expert
95. *M*A*S*H* role
96. 2005 Genie-nominated movie
97. Honks
98. _____ for human consumption
99. Royal title in Indian (var.)
101. Pleasure boat
104. 1934 Morley Callaghan novel: _____ *Is My Beloved*
105. Flames and Oilers

106. North Sea feeder
107. Pigeon-_____
108. Iconic hockey surname
109. Lush
110. Writers Bagnold or Blyton
111. Peruse
113. Letters on a compass
114. Building addition

Solution on page 229

86

Piracy?

Talk like a tar

ACROSS

1. Makes a mistake
5. Big gulp
9. Bar U _____ National Historic Site (AB)
14. "Quiet!"
19. Office furniture item
20. Chip for salsa
21. Get used to (var.)
22. Former Portuguese currency unit
23. **The Monkees' storage space?**
26. Water mammal
27. Materialize
28. Send by sea?
29. Old capital of 100-D
30. Burger side order
31. Coalesce
33. **Horatio's undoing?**
36. VIP
40. Catholic prayer
42. Backyard hut
43. See 36-A
44. Planted
45. Children's game
48. Poisonous gas
52. US territory in the Pacific
53. Lion's share
54. They often hang near the fireplace
56. Toronto cultural attraction, for short
57. Play part
58. 1961 W.O. Mitchell short story collection: *Jake and the _____*
59. Exploits an advantage
60. Gloom's mate
61. Warm up leftovers
63. Pressure measurement in a vacuum
65. Not WSW
66. '80s Calgary Flame McDonald

67. **How you might solve this puzzle's theme clues?**
71. Social no-no
74. Win _____ mile
75. Lighten a load
76. Feudal servant
80. Stable shade
81. Lighthearted on a liner?
83. Old CBC series: _____ *Alive*
84. Director's signal
85. Electees
86. Soft colours
87. Nesting place
89. Anthem line: "... from far and _____"
90. Gentlemen (abbr.)
92. Hullabaloo
93. Weather Network word
94. Field worker
95. Chick's sound
97. Functional
99. Attractive, in Aberdeen
100. **Marley's climbing plant?**
105. Postal _____
107. Similar
108. Jungle primate
109. Parmigiana preceder
111. Florida fruit
116. Old-style courtly dance (var.)
117. **Bunyan's comment about the cold?**
120. Revise
121. Cheapskate
122. Attack
123. Baby hawk
124. Clef contents
125. Some jingle composers
126. Binge
127. Flap

DOWN

1. Old Icelandic literary work
2. Bring in the crops

3. Answer an invitation (abbr.)
4. Terrier type
5. Canadian Tire, for example
6. Pale
7. Where Elvis and Kurt star
8. "Gee!"
9. Go back into business
10. Mandela's party (abbr.)
11. Zaps
12. Personal motto
13. Long-legged birds
14. Derisive ones
15. Modified roadsters
16. Up to
17. Dofasco output
18. Equine (var.)
24. Door part
25. Like weathered skin
32. Fashionable 1860s hairnet
34. When you see an alligator?
35. Artie and Tommy
36. Humidor item
37. Construe
38. Unwilling
39. Stately tree
41. Doc for a dachshund
44. '90s Canadian decathlete Mike
46. Back lanes
47. Peek or boo?
49. Wrinkle remover
50. Sinclair Ross short story: "The Lamp at _____"
51. Gemini's US counterpart
54. '56 Farley Mowat book: *Lost in the _____*
55. _____ and terminer
58. Knock out, colloquially
59. Paid athlete, for short
60. East Indian trees
62. Like night, old style
63. Car manufacturer in Woodstock and Cambridge
64. Authorized

66. Scotiabank transaction, say
68. Wellness product manufacturer: _____Forme
69. Cricket club
70. Egg producer
71. Cut down to size
72. Top-of-the-line
73. Choir member
77. Heir
78. 1948 Pulitzer poet W.H.
79. Suspicious
81. Foundations of MLB?
82. Viva voce

83. Old-style copy
86. Canons' payments in bygone days
87. Science class, sometimes
88. Signal that the danger's done
89. *W5* question
91. Eastern Washington city
93. Less fancy
96. TV type
98. Ontario waterway: Trent–_____
99. Riverbank
100. Kyoto country

101. 1836 battle site in Texas
102. Musky mammal
103. Garden pest
104. Rational religion
106. Tatted cloth
110. Bullets, et al.
112. Help out
113. Grammy-winning R&B singer
114. Diploma recipient, for short
115. Imperial Oil station name
118. Alphabet letter
119. Jerk

ACROSS

1. Kind of point
6. Cookbook abbr.
10. Town northwest of Edmonton: _____ Hills
14. Insect stage
15. Open to new ideas
17. Everglades reptile, for short
18. Put under anaesthetic, old style
19. Capture
20. Israel currency unit
21. Inner spaces?
23. Small amphibians
27. Evaluate
29. Bone in the arm
30. Play a Les Paul
31. Burlington-to-Pickering highway: 407 _____
32. *London* _____ *Press*
33. Prince Edward Island _____ Museum
34. 10^{100}s
36. Queen's Park city
37. Like a ball on the field
38. 1993 single by 51-A: "Already _____"
39. Slice
40. It precedes *obstat*
41. Invalid
42. Roman Empire invader
43. Some cards
44. Lined paper
46. Pulsates
48. Process featured on *Intervention Canada*
51. 2012 Canadian Music Hall of Fame band inductee
54. Michael Moore film: *Capitalism: _____ Story*
55. Visit many rural ridings in a day
56. Of lesser importance
57. Embargoes
58. Watering tube
59. Perfume

DOWN

1. Mediterranean edibles
2. Arabian Peninsula land
3. Disaster
4. Gathering places, in ancient Athens (var.)
5. Screen siren Sophia
6. Railway bridge supports
7. Famed Canadian doctor Norman
8. Outline
9. Look-sees
10. Sharp heel
11. '78 Jackson/Ross film: *The _____*
12. Short street?
13. Vaughan's Hanlan Road is named after him
16. Word root meaning "before"
22. Like an afro
24. Quebecer, for example
25. Egyptian king's scolding?
26. Not crunchy
27. Prairie capital
28. Lacking muscle strength
30. Ticked off
32. Ranch newborn
33. Small lakes
35. Shines
36. Arduous
38. Peanuts
41. Black magic
42. Sometime Rankin Family song language
44. Foam
45. Studies late into the night
47. Store sign info (abbr.)
49. Cosmetics company in Canada since 1914
50. *Sesame Street* puppet
51. Canadian consumer protection org.
52. Half a Teletubby
53. Coffee server

88 Hometown Glory

Cities celebrate their Canadian bands

ACROSS

1. Nat King Cole's salad?
5. Wing it
10. Faux pas
15. Butts into a ewe?
19. '76 Elton John duet partner Dee
20. _____ River AB
21. Girder
22. Asian animal
23. Glass Tiger front man Frew
24. German industrial area
25. **Finger 11 ON environment**
27. Titles
29. Net
31. Lading
32. **April Wine NS base**
35. California peninsula
36. Basil sauce
37. '03 event where Mike Weir tied for third
38. Siamese's plant?
40. 20th-C. German artist Max
44. Scatter
45. Ness, in Scotland
46. Consisting of three
49. Math subj.
50. 11th US president
51. Wilhelm's rolls?
52. '40s movie and music star Ritter
53. Superior, to a Shawinigan resident?
54. School dance
55. Maid or butler
56. Recalcitrant child
57. Joy
59. Up to then, for short
60. Reception areas
62. UN monetary organization (abbr.)
63. **Rush ON place**
65. Jogged

66. Teetotalled
70. Mr. Willie Winkie
71. Sculpture, say
75. Italy city: San _____
76. See 31-A
78. _____ the Impaler
79. _____-di-dah
80. Treat poorly
81. Italian verse style
82. Canadian *Top Chef* judge Simmons
83. 19th-C. Irish–Canadian painter Paul
84. Turrets
86. '99 Bryan Adams album: *The _____ of Me*
87. Archie's political appellation for Meathead
88. Room at the top?
89. Ridiculous
91. Golden '84 Olympics US gymnast Bart
92. Did nothing
95. Skin opening
96. **The Stampeders AB stomping ground**
97. 2 p.m. performance
100. Duke, say
101. Loudness units
102. **Hedley BC hometown**
104. '80s Canadian tennis star Kelesi
106. Canadian actors Jackson and Green
110. Extended family
111. Diatonic
112. Sap a shoreline
113. Black and white cookie
114. Not his
115. Severe pain
116. Slip cover?
117. CTV _____ Channel

DOWN

1. Cousin of reggae
2. *Diamond* _____
3. Alias abbr.
4. **Crash Test Dummies MB domain**
5. Yeti, say
6. Neuter
7. Aberdeen gal
8. Skating surface
9. Under
10. Big Mediterranean rock
11. _____ in the oven
12. Iron, in Île-Dupas
13. Vancouver inlet: _____ Creek
14. Gives off
15. *Senecio* flower
16. Not pro
17. 1992 Neil Young song: "Harvest _____"
18. Carolled
26. Secretaries, say
28. Some
30. 1977 Steely Dan album
32. Con man's '70s dance?
33. Stellar?
34. Cuirass, old style
35. Endorse
36. Buddy, in Barcelona
38. *Bon Cop, Bad Cop* Canadian actor Feore
39. _____ Member's Bill
41. TNT component
42. Sauna mist
43. Some BlackBerry messages
45. Canadian coinage bird
47. Confined
48. Like main roads
50. Highlighted
51. **The Grapes of Wrath BC city**
54. Arizona Native group
55. Gentleman's title
56. Ulna or radius

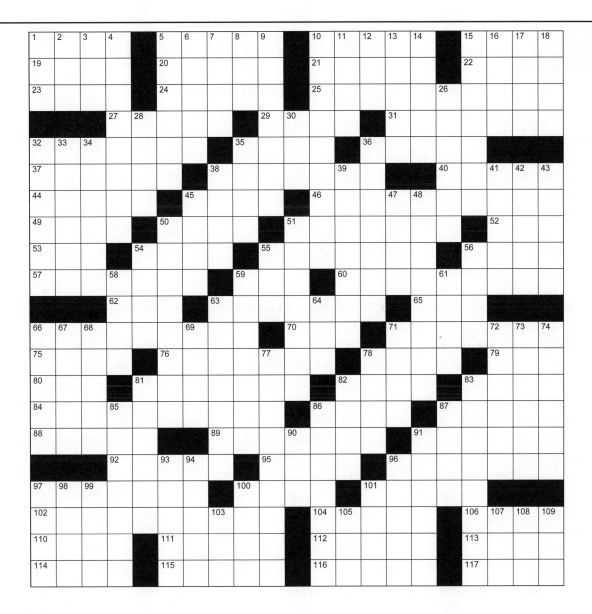

58. Josip Broz a.k.a.
59. Hot drinks
61. South African currency
63. Afternoon serving piece
64. Not pos.
66. Oranjestad country
67. Attack
68. Refine metal
69. Snub or Roman
71. Dart
72. Canadian two-time Olympic speed skating medallist Kraus
73. More fetid

74. Hypothesis
77. With vapidness
78. Urn
81. Triangle ratio
82. Simmons' DNA unit?
83. **The Tragically Hip ON home ground**
85. What seers see
86. Delivered, in the delivery room
87. Totem _____
90. Our, in Val d'Or
91. *Jesus of Montreal* won the *Prix du Jury* here

93. Seed coat, in science
94. Confuse, old style
96. Some students
97. Sound barrier word
98. Accomplished
99. Chairlift alternative
100. Kukla, _____ and Ollie
101. Wild plum
103. Mrs. Lennon
105. Miscue
107. Bauxite, for example
108. Kitten's sound
109. Brillo rival

Skipping a Long

Just as it sounds

ACROSS

1. NHL award: Art _____ Trophy
5. Western Canada grocery store name
9. Poetry, in Beijing
12. Couch
16. Glass tube
17. Kerr role in *The King and I*
18. Got taut
20. Domestic pests?
22. *Hamlet* castle
23. **Slightly misdirected WWI song?**
25. Coquette who owns fur coats?
26. Some soccer scores
27. Cathode Ray Tube (abbr.)
28. Repulse
31. Policy nerd
32. Cornering a bear, say
36. _____ Baba
37. Agog
39. Manitoba Native group
40. Likewise
41. Vocalized
43. Christie classic: *Death on the _____*
44. Legal document
45. '80s Blue Rodeo hit: "Diamond _____"
46. Like high-schoolers
48. Abound with
49. Railcar restaurant
50. **Sooner-than-expected date with Bob Dylan?**
53. Bubbling
55. Parting word, in Palermo
56. Like the moon's surface
59. Sharpen
60. Something to swab
61. Furniture wood
62. Ex-Winnipeg Jet Hawerchuk
63. See 48-D

64. '42 film noir: *This Gun for _____*
65. Caged the cows
67. Winnipeg's Vardalos of *My Big Fat Greek Wedding*
68. Female deity
70. Song for a pair
71. Weight watcher
73. Take the cake?
74. Town NNW of Lesser Slave Lake: _____ Prairie
75. Chilly
76. **Emphatic Simon and Garfunkel statement about an architect's style?**
83. Dead discussion point
84. Times without end
85. Folded egg serving
86. Old Keebler snack: _____ Skins
87. Land, in Lévis
88. Hourly pay
89. Approx.
90. *Dr. Strangelove* star Pickens
91. Are, in Argentina

DOWN

1. Melee
2. Major compositional work
3. Old CBC kids' show: _____ *Park*
4. Cooking slowly
5. What sepals form
6. "You can bank _____"
7. Person-to-person
8. Gluing
9. Strides
10. Lend a hand
11. Clandestinely
12. Parliament Hill chamber
13. Aroma (var.)
14. Rage
15. King Kong, for example

16. _____ Beta Kappa Society
19. "Yes _____!" (var.)
21. Castanets dance
24. Variety
28. Hops drying oven
29. Chimney component
30. Got the bugs out
31. Untamed grain?
32. Boat with three hulls
33. Nomadic labourer
34. Zilch
35. Attendee, briefly
38. Awls, say
39. New moon shape
42. Travelocity's "roaming" ad mascot
44. CBC Radio One *Ontario Morning* host Chen
45. Copied Marcel Marceau?
47. Canadian 2006 Olympic bronze curler Nixon
48. One of 52
49. Morse code tap
51. Deciduous tree
52. Raze
53. Nova Scotia UFO site: _____ Harbour
54. Somewhat, in music
57. 1986 Nobel Peace Prize winner Wiesel
58. Beloved
60. Antipathy
61. Abstain from alcohol
64. Funeral procession vehicle
65. Young hens
66. Igneous rock type
69. Desecrate
70. East Indian entree
72. A-lists
74. Clay pigeon sport
75. HMV purchase
76. Math cube mind-bender
77. Blood type, for short

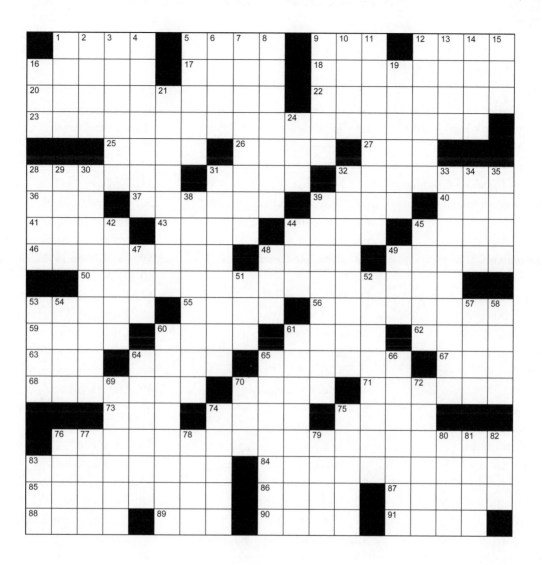

78. Crazy, colloquially

79. Himalayan hominid

80. Encircle

81. '34 British film: *Give* _____ *Ring*

82. Former Canadian trading floor (abbr.)

83. Joni Mitchell composition: "Both Sides _____"

ACROSS

1. Soprano's neighbour
5. She sang "Thank You" in 2000
9. Said, old style
14. Curb, with "in"
15. Adam and Eve's environment
16. '70s Governor General Jules
17. Horse hair
18. Bean curd food
19. Make amends
20. More pale
22. Target of a 5/2/11 raid
24. Doppelgänger
26. Moor expanse
30. Ancient fertility goddess
31. Sheep disease
33. Ambience
35. In the know
36. 1759 battle site in Québec
42. Afghan or basset
43. Drain of energy
44. Less insightful
47. Small lumps
52. Cozy corner
53. Schizophrenic
55. Walloped, old style
57. There's one of these of Queen Victoria on Parliament Hill
58. Secret stash
61. Ivy League university
63. Trick
64. Poppy-based narcotic
65. Canadian hockey great Esposito
66. Weight watcher's regimen
67. Juno-winning rapper
68. Vision organs
69. Old-style corset

DOWN

1. Naval force
2. Rental documents
3. Canadian soldiers' headgear in WWI
4. Iroquoian language
5. Debris
6. Marriage vow
7. Clear the car windows
8. Unwelcome obligations
9. Close a door with force
10. CFB in Ontario
11. In olden days
12. Canadian folksinger Tobias
13. Prior to, poetically
21. Shopping and banking, say
23. Rainbow curve
25. Agrippina the Younger's son
27. Brilliantly coloured fish
28. Former currency in Venice
29. Judge
32. Unusual repast in Wales?
34. Not fore
36. Unit of loudness
37. Canadian apple type
38. Shortened word in CAA
39. Symbol on Nunavut's flag
40. Hokkaido Native
41. Capital of Belgium
45. Economic Development Officer (abbr.)
46. Put in data again
48. Not-for-profit group overseers
49. Get a sense of?
50. Upset stomach symptom
51. Like messy weather
54. Family folk–country group from Lakefield
56. The same, in Sept-Îles
58. Liver oil fish
59. Mo. when the Easter Bunny comes
60. US counterpart of CSIS
62. Fib

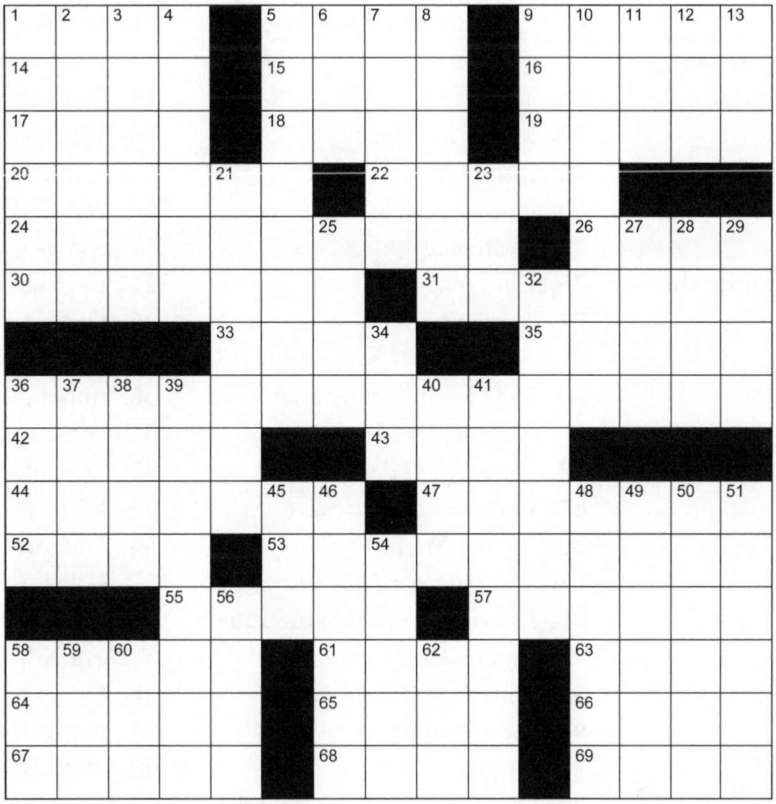

Solution on page 230

91 Canadian Boys of Summer

Diamonds of MLB

ACROSS

1. Yukon neighbour
7. Not as loose
13. Marijuana
18. **2006 AL MVP Morneau**
19. York Region ON town
20. Cineplex _____
21. Southern manner of speaking, say
22. Easter event: Good _____
23. **'90s third baseman for the Twins Koskie**
24. Equestrians' grips
25. Positions
26. Fatty
27. Lamb or pork serving
29. American Hockey League (abbr.)
30. In pain
31. Historical record keeper
35. Key of *Eroica*
37. Lived
40. Early car name
41. Smaller
43. Not have enough for all
45. Andy's radio partner in the '30s
47. Law, to Lucius
48. Rehab candidates
50. Solo for Maureen Forrester
51. Prepare for printing, old style
53. Prevent, through the courts
54. Canadian fiddling icon MacMaster
55. Big birds
56. **2004 NL Rookie of the Year Bay**
57. Cronies
58. _____ *diem*
60. Where Canadians served in the '50s
61. Boxer George who's in charge?
64. Shakespearean play royal
65. Canadian high jump record holder Debbie
66. Scale notes
67. Cape Breton singing star MacNeil
68. Type of well
70. More raw-boned
73. Irish myth otherworld: _____-nan-Og
74. Heartache
75. Land maps
77. Tormented
79. Highway 407 fee, in Ontario
80. 1982 NFB documentary from Gwynne Dyer
82. Formerly, once
83. Improves an essay, say
85. Milano Mr.
87. *The Metamorphosis* scribe Franz
91. **Lawrie who joined the Blue Jays in 2011**
92. John Turner's middle name
93. Broadcasting
94. Hunter's gun
95. "Footloose" lyric: "I'll hit the ceiling _____"
96. **1991 Baseball Hall of Fame inductee Jenkins**
97. Pretended
98. Aware of shenanigans
99. Assignations

DOWN

1. Not completely closed
2. US playwright: Clare Boothe _____
3. Botany sac
4. Unpleasant odour
5. Theory of relativity?
6. Termite
7. Laurier's US counterpart
8. Gold-coloured
9. *David Copperfield* antagonist: _____ Heep
10. Walk like a one-year-old?
11. Stats for 96-A or 42-D
12. Beam from the sun
13. Fun park four-wheelers
14. Venerate
15. Computer geek
16. **2010 NL MVP Votto**
17. Some
25. Keyboard instrument
26. Gives, temporarily
28. Unfertilized plant seeds
30. Impolite drinking sound
31. What I smell?
32. French cognac: _____ Martin
33. Work well together
34. Number of NHL teams (1942–67)
36. Old refrigerant
37. One who does 83-A
38. Dry
39. Remain
42. **2007 NL Golden Glove winner Martin**
44. Ice road trucker, say
46. Always, in music
49. Ancient colonnade
52. Petition for damages
53. *The National* anchor Cameron (1959–66)
54. Pub
56. Knee or elbow
57. Artistic charlatan?
58. Talon
59. Nestlé confection
60. Native African village
61. ID a manicurist?
62. End in _____
63. Old-style ointment
65. Former premiers Vander Zalm and Davis

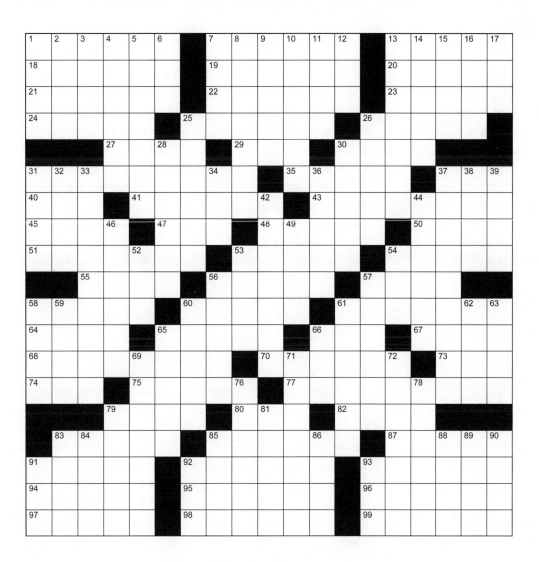

66. '72 Neil Young hit: "Old
_____"
69. Saw a Dalmatian?
71. Sincere
72. Like bolder investments
76. Steals a debit card?
78. Like a clear night sky

79. Lord or lady
81. Nimble
**83. 2003 NL Cy Young Award
winner Gagné**
84. Skilled
85. Rani's dress
86. Store-bought cookie type

88. Newtons' fruits?
89. Purl, etc.
90. Ripens
91. Lingerie department purchase
92. Right this instant
93. Rearward, on ship

Solution on page 230

ACROSS

1. Town, American style
5. Chin indentation
10. '60s sitcom: *Mayberry* _____
13. _____ state of affairs
17. Composer Stravinsky
18. Phone greeting
19. That woman, in Lisbon
20. Noon, in Neuville
21. **Kona cocktail**
23. Osgoode Hall _____ School
24. Ferrari founder
25. Some Fiats
26. TD Canada Trust employee
28. 19th-C. boys' fiction author Horatio
29. Caribou horn
31. Lack of activity
33. Toque, for example
36. Barracks bed
37. Pass by
40. St. Lawrence River site: Île d'_____
41. Lots of amusement
42. Canada's former name, for short
43. Vancouver Island municipality: _____ Bay
44. Sultan's stove?
45. Swallow again
47. Ancient Scandinavian language
49. Ontario-born ex-NHLers Ramage and Blake
51. _____ inept
53. Hemlock and spruce
54. Cries of triumph
56. Acceptable for Islamic diets
57. Fox hunt disruptors, in England
58. Type of office asst.
60. Plant part
62. Untidy one
65. Circle width
67. Comport with, old style
69. 6/12/17 Halifax explosion ship
70. Dash lengths
71. Ski resort trail
72. MDs
73. Deride: Pour _____
75. Northeast BC town: Fort _____
77. Hurricane centre
78. Four-sided shape
79. Friendly
81. Explosive device
82. Packing heat
84. Darrin's *Bewitched* mother-in-law
86. 1980 Doug and the Slugs hit
90. Early baby talk word
91. Tudor Henry's Roman numeral
92. **Russian libation**
94. Allege
95. Holiday lodgings
96. Disdainful look
97. 2003 comedy: *Anything* _____
98. Half a couple's set
99. _____ trip
100. Seaweeds
101. Pig's food mixture

DOWN

1. Dining apparel for infants
2. Tangerine/grapefruit hybrid
3. Profligate
4. See 81-A
5. Purity
6. *All Quiet on the Western Front* star Ayres
7. Joy giver
8. Air ace (var.)
9. Slave away at
10. Cede
11. Canadian fashion magazine
12. Bird that burgles
13. Earhart who disappeared in 1937
14. **Asian drink**
15. Wood-shaping tool
16. Last name in fashion
22. Airport building
27. 2011 Grey Cup ring receiver
28. Georgia city
30. Rodeo rope
32. Tear up
33. Rime
34. Therefore, to Octavia
35. **Birmingham beverage**
36. **Caribbean quaff**
38. Prepaid postal enclosure (abbr.)
39. Scrapes by
41. _____ Tuck
42. US journalism pioneer Nellie
46. Reddish yellow, in Yellowstone
47. Paella pots
48. Spheres
50. Wooden levelling wedge
52. Strings for shoes
55. Barometer without liquid
57. Hamilton audiences?
58. Protectorate the British left in 1967
59. 10-cent piece
60. Kingston _____
61. Microwave button
63. 1847 Melville novel
64. Beethoven's birthplace
66. Canned fish
68. The following day, to a bard
72. Changed one's hair colour

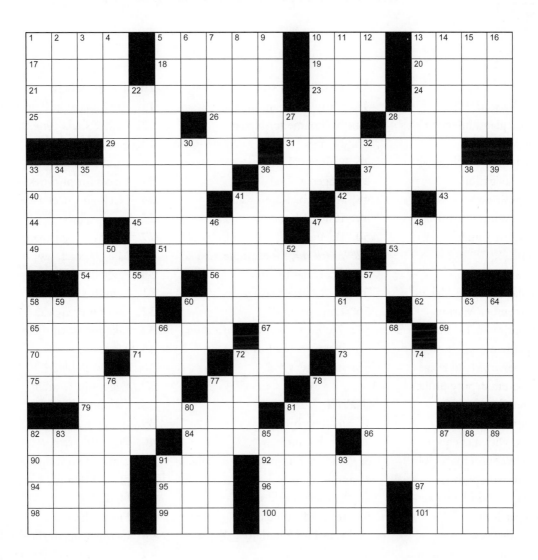

74. Antennae enclosures
76. Sullies a reputation
77. Pacific weather phenomenon
78. Prickly plant
80. Human, say

81. Apt to lie down?
82. Eastern nursemaid
83. Give five stars
85. Russia's seventh-largest city
87. Cattle male

88. As well
89. Insightful
91. Try to win
93. Mushroom with a big top

93 Canada Cornucopia 31

ACROSS

1. Noah's silly son?
4. Sebaceous gland infection
8. Most reticent
14. Guided missile technology: _____ navigation
16. Ballet position
17. Québec Winter Carnival figure
18. Vivacity, in Vanier
19. Not out
20. _____ best friend
22. Canadian Aviation Hall of Fame member Marion
23. Jungle primate, for short
24. Bumper bang
25. France–Switzerland range
26. Trudeau-era deputy prime minister Gray
27. Shut up
28. Cheated with a cheque
29. CRA US counterpart (abbr.)
30. Places to park parkas
32. Ontario's 23rd Lieutenant-Governor John
33. Part of the eye
34. Restaurant with the slogan, "Always so good for so little"
38. The Way, in Asia
41. Doctrine

42. First lady of scat
43. Dirty old man, for short
44. Nickname for Nadal
45. Natters
46. Calgary NHLer
47. Anger
48. Attire for Karen Kain
49. Pencil adjunct
50. Boeing rival
52. *Maclean's*, for example
54. Apartment renter
55. Narcissist's malady
56. Loses ground?
57. *The Real Housewives of Atlanta* cast member Leakes
58. Gangster's rod

DOWN

1. Small barbecue
2. Not that one
3. Western Europe ancient stone monuments
4. Put one's foot down?
5. Sir Sandford Fleming's invention: Standard _____
6. Edible tuber
7. Earth or air, in olden days
8. Exhausted by shopping?
9. *Bonanza* brother

10. Toy dog's bark
11. Air Canada inflight reading
12. Coffee stick, for example
13. Foursomes
15. Parallelogram
21. Places for pismires
24. Neck-and-neck race
25. Lively dances
27. *Tourtière ingrédient*
28. Make a scarf, say
30. Ancient coffin
31. Length x width
32. Out on the ocean
34. Like furrowed rocks
35. More tired
36. Towering blaze?
37. Egg-white protein
38. Cajoling
39. Its capital is Yerevan
40. Pig out
43. Downtown Calgary gathering place: Olympic _____
45. Updrafts
46. Picture holder
48. Get in sync, in the orchestra pit
49. *Ghostbusters* character Spengler
51. One-hit wonder from Canada's Daniel Powter: "_____ Day"
53. Grow older

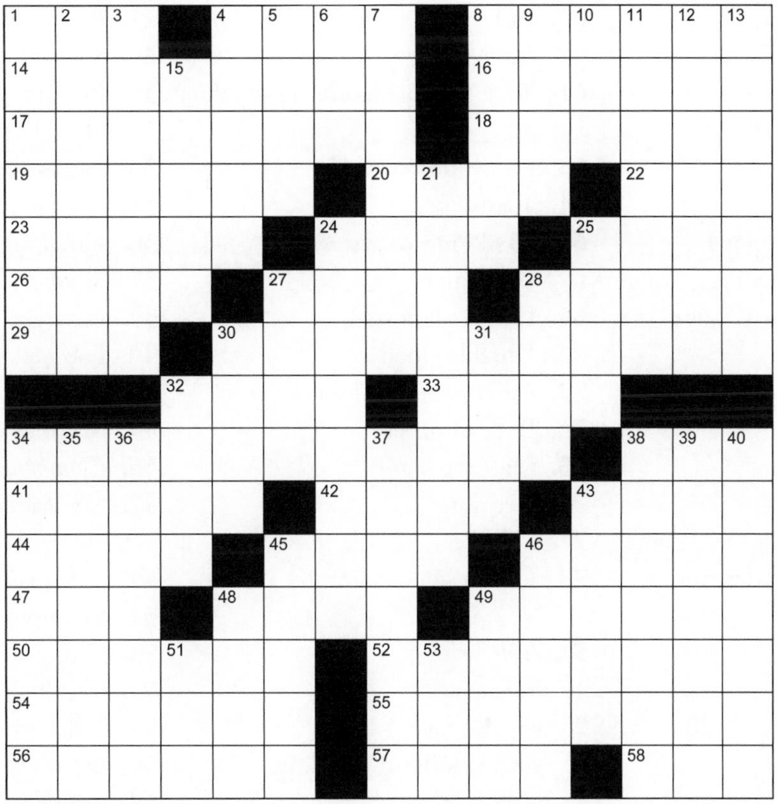

Solution on page 231

94 For the Foodies

Good old Canadian eats

ACROSS

1. '70s Swedish pop group
5. Brawls
10. Put on a housecoat?
16. Sweetheart
17. Go on a tear?
18. Helsinki hot spots?
19. Touch down
20. Stubborn
22. "Gentlemen, start your _____"
24. Courtroom proceeding
25. Part of a cell nucleus (abbr.)
26. Topes
28. *Tarzan* star Ron
29. Skate part
30. Coins
32. Abbey expanse
34. Niagara Escarpment trail name
35. Northern Canada description
36. Tons
37. Sales booth
38. Misfortunes
39. US rights grp. since 1920
40. Sty sound
41. Plays with?
42. **Québec pork spread**
44. Greek vowels
48. Singers Brickell or Adams
50. States of rage
51. Writer Ephron
52. Like posh communities
54. South American cuckoos
55. '70s Montréal Canadiens star Steve
56. Spiteful
57. Unencumbered
58. "Where _____ a will …"
59. Ultimatum ender
60. Farley Mowat book: _____ *of Slaughter*
61. '87 k.d. lang record: *Angel with a* _____
63. MGM lion name
64. Toast type
66. 1998 Prairie Oyster hit: "Canadian _____"
69. Lamps on posts
72. Durable wood
73. Parliament Hill home
74. Piece of paper
75. Marine avian
76. Get snug
77. Dawdle
78. Owner's document

DOWN

1. Proficient
2. Noggin, say
3. **Newfoundland pudding**
4. Book on tape, say
5. Sculptured wall item
6. Hair tint
7. Suitable
8. Central Asian hut
9. Scantiest
10. Writer's opinion piece
11. Catch a carpenter?
12. Hairpiece, colloquially
13. Taxing
14. **Trail biscuit**
15. Sprawling property
21. Cairo's waterway
23. Black, in Bécancour
27. Room, in Repentigny
29. Sorrowful
30. Roasting rod
31. Horseback sport
33. **Cheese curds dish**
34. Storage vessel
36. Ranch unit
37. Smooch
39. Etcher's liquid
40. Loonies, perhaps?
43. Projecting window
45. **Acadian meat pie**
46. *Commedia dell'*_____
47. US academic admission exams (abbr.)
49. *L.A. Law* actress Susan
52. **Synonym for 14-D**
53. Groups together
54. Middle East scholar
55. Tibia
56. BC town
57. Tripped
58. Reliable
60. Bristles
62. John Jacob's flower?
64. Whimper
65. Old-style Turkish honorific (var.)
67. Compos mentis
68. Scraped by on limited resources
70. Dine
71. That girl

Sayonara to Cinema

At the movies

ACROSS

1. "Darn!"
5. Ripped
9. Shiny motorcycle finish
15. Out of harm's reach
19. Individually
20. Christie classic: _____ *Under the Sun*
21. Looked at lecherously
22. Bothers
23. Give as an example
24. Glacial snow ridge
25. 1904 Sara Jeannette Duncan novel: *The _____*
27. Place for a proton
28. Apothecary's measurement
30. Go wild
31. **1957 Rock Hudson movie (with "A")**
35. TV's *The Biggest _____*
36. One hundred of these equal one dinar
37. Montana or Maine
38. 30-year CBC series: *Hymn _____*
39. In a perfect world . . .
42. Appearances
43. Common Canadian interjections
44. Hamilton-born NHL goalie Emery
47. BC city
48. Fish stabilizers
49. Once known as
50. Wait, old style
51. Go on the hunt
52. _____ shui
53. Caribbean entertainers
56. Deli meat
59. Masticate
60. National Hockey _____
61. US Civil War soldier moniker
64. **1972 avant-garde offering**

67. Saturn's spouse
68. Air element
70. Yokel
71. Works together, old style
73. *One Thousand and One Nights* catchphrase
75. Hewed
76. '72 Edward Bear hit: "_____ Song"
80. Perfume since 1932
81. Singer Tormé
82. Lake in the Rockies
83. Chinese dinner dish: _____ Chicken
85. Pigpen
86. Ontario-born *SNL* star Aykroyd
87. Mill's output
89. Biblical reptile
90. British school town
92. Oscar winner Vivien
93. Booby _____
94. Light-to-dark shading
96. **2005 cartoon movie featuring Shaggy, et al.**
102. 2010 Olympics venue: Pacific _____
105. Illness with a rash of symptoms?
106. Swiss psychologist Carl
107. Retaliatory punch
110. _____ of passage
111. Toothbrush brand: _____-B
112. Away from the wind
113. High and mighty
114. Black cat, perhaps
115. Port Stanley ON lake
116. Large group at church?
117. Toiled like a helot?
118. *Runaway Bride* star Richard
119. Reddish-brown stone

DOWN

1. Some Tim Hortons coffee
2. Indian dish with yogurt
3. Donald Sutherland, for example
4. Canada's Wonderland, et al.
5. With loving care
6. Superimpose
7. Ti-cat to an Argo, say
8. Vote in
9. Prevailing moods at the Weather Network?
10. Skirt's edge
11. Gym iteration
12. End of a threat
13. Mother, in Magog
14. Make the final cut?
15. Old West bar
16. **1965 spaghetti western**
17. *All That Jazz* director Bob
18. Glyceride, e.g.
26. *Cheers* contemporary: _____ *Forgiven*
29. Watering the garden, say
32. Ridge on fabric
33. Operated
34. Yukon's Logan, et al.
38. Thin varnish
39. Magazine no.
40. '90s CTV series: _____ *South*
41. Before, to bards
42. _____ wage
43. Reform Party goal (abbr.)
45. Do math
46. Affirmatives
48. Leg arteries adjective
49. Place name in NB, NS and NL
50. Ovine utterance
52. US DoT org.
53. "Quiet, please!"
54. Parlour furniture piece
55. Crooked
57. Top-notch pilots

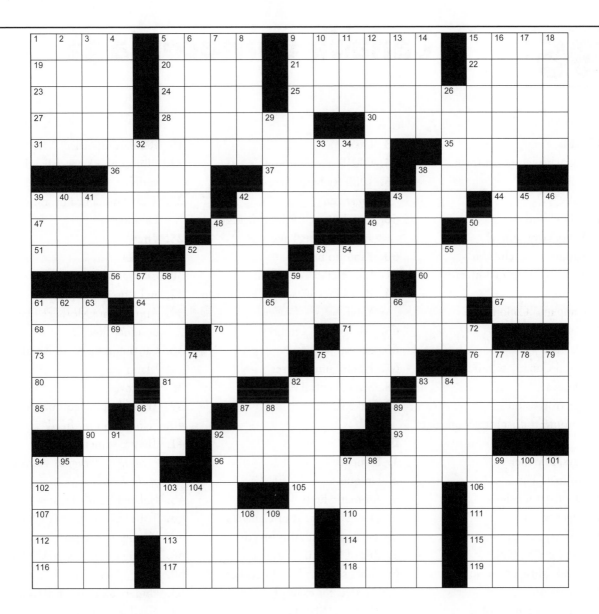

58. Annual CFL award: Most Outstanding Offensive _____

59. Annual August event in Toronto (abbr.)

61. National retailer since 1973

62. Canadian living abroad, say

63. **Genie-nominated film from 1989**

65. Canada's first chess grandmaster Yanofsky

66. Bronzed in the summer

69. Bearded antelope

72. Messy meals?

74. Ottawa NHLer, for short

75. Square dance step

77. Jungle swinger

78. 1789–95 Nootka Sound landmark: Fort _____ Miguel

79. Bit of potato?

82. Scrooge, say

83. Canadian Gesner invented this hydrocarbon liquid

84. Riyadh resident

86. Old-style second-person verb

87. Set

88. City in Brazil, for short

89. More portly

91. Aspects, in astrology

92. 11th Greek letter

94. Philosopher William of _____

95. Cash, colloquially (var.)

97. Young'un, in Yorkshire

98. Doorbell sound

99. North African grain

100. Walking _____

101. See 21-A

103. Sushi fish

104. Caspian Sea feeder

108. 54, to Tiberius

109. Shelley work, e.g.

ACROSS

1. Saskatchewan resort town
7. Heels
11. Tally
14. Yellow bird
15. Vera's salve source?
16. Kung _____ chicken
17. Scotiabank annual literary award
19. Capp and Capone
20. More bloated
21. Decrees
23. Royal Canadian building, in Ottawa
24. Electrolysis bit
26. Toronto tourist attraction: Bata _____ Museum
27. Pays, in poker
29. Animals' lair
30. Doomsayer's signs
31. Eager to go
33. Red Serge org.
35. Duplicating DNA
37. Greek Muse of music
42. Excursion
44. Crete resident of old
45. Places in Portugal?
49. Pal, on the streets
51. Three notes, in music
52. Pickering neighbour, in Ontario
53. Oozes
55. Old Testament book
56. 1980 Richard Gere film: *American _____*
58. City between Prince George and Williams Lake
60. Kimono belt
61. Like a crafty criminal?
64. Rita MacNeil song: "Flying On Your _____"
65. Nipigon, in Ontario
66. See-saw
67. Haranguing horse?
68. Sea in central Asia
69. Take stock

DOWN

1. Sprocket
2. Unique
3. Aromatic herb
4. Over 90 percent of Canada's dairy cattle are this breed
5. Bits of land, in Mistassini
6. Crocs style with a closed heel
7. WestJet, for example
8. Thrilla in Manila victor
9. Tim Hortons order, say
10. Plant starter
11. Geronimo, e.g.
12. Ontario premier McGuinty
13. Crashes anywhere
18. Remain unsettled
22. Philosopher's specialization suffix
23. Trudeau-era health minister Lalonde
25. Then
28. Tizzies
30. Of the eye
32. Axl Rose band (abbr.)
34. Appropriate Mother's Day bouquet flower?
36. Cutting remark, in Rhode Island
38. Improves
39. Train sleeping compartment
40. Felons who are freed
41. They're sometimes split
43. *Hannibal Rising*, to *The Silence of the Lambs*
45. Isolated body of water
46. Tribe that surrounded Superior
47. Putting in the pen
48. Losing tic-tac-toe row
50. _____ Dei
53. Underwater object detector
54. Nasal partitions
57. Stephanie Plum partner, in Evanovich books
59. Witnesses
62. Reggae relative
63. Surgeons, et al.

Stephen Leacock Memorial Medal for Humour winners

ACROSS

1. Extravagance, perhaps
8. Stuffs
13. Block, biologically
20. Bait
21. Netherlands city: The _____
22. Where the Winnipeg Jets flew in 1996
23. Anther locales, in flowers
24. Oxlike antelope
25. Most rosy
26. Separated
27. **2004 winner for *Village of the Small Houses***
30. Wise guy?
31. Denouement
32. _____ record
33. Surgery tool
35. Large container for 36-A
36. Spanish table wine
38. Rigatoni relative
41. Not a bit
42. Expel
44. Alice Cooper hit: "_____ Mr. Nice Guy"
46. Asinine
48. Biases
49. Merit
51. Smooths wood
52. PNE or CNE
53. Early developmental stage
57. Golfer's fabrication?
58. Squash type
62. See 45-D
63. Legendary nightclub: _____ 54
65. Place to find a pupil
66. Prospector's find
67. "Little" Dickens girl
68. **1958 winner for *Girdle Me a Globe***
70. Politician's helper
71. Surrealist Salvador
72. Swiss artist Paul
73. Merry at Noel?
75. Not in mint condition
76. More colloquial
78. Soupçon
79. Doughnut kin
81. Clams or bread?
82. Unspoken
84. Famed US general Robert
85. Mountain climber's journey
88. Best kind of bun?
90. Holy places (var.)
94. *Canada's Got Talent* judge Martin
95. _____ *Like It Hot*
96. *The Time Machine* group
98. Old Russian rulers
99. Rum cocktail: Mai _____
100. Hightail it
102. Ward workers (abbr.)
104. Soft food, say
105. Has
107. **2000 winner for *Black Tie and Tales***
112. Score before 15, in tennis
113. Not in the loop
115. Soft palate adjunct
116. Satellite, say
118. Disproves
119. Bills of fare
120. Vermin-catching cats
121. '73 Keith Hampshire hit: "The First Cut Is the _____"
122. Oscar winner Kathy
123. As one

DOWN

1. London ON university
2. *Shrek* sequels star Banderas
3. Success in Hollywood, say
4. US news magazine since 1923
5. Early Toronto Maple Leafs star Bailey
6. Winning Canadian filmmaker's award
7. Artificial
8. Canadian cooking show: _____ *at Home*
9. Unhealthy breathing noise
10. Thickening agent, in food
11. _____ bean
12. Diligent
13. What one side of parliament officially does
14. Crepe de _____
15. Bamboozle
16. Albanian currency units
17. Left on the table?
18. Gross out
19. Degrees
28. Newbie, say
29. Without, in Montréal
32. Canadian *Away from Her* director Polley
34. Fired up again
37. **1986 winner for *No Axe Too Small to Grind***
39. Brits' thank-yous
40. Right-leaning type style
41. Lymphatic protuberance
43. **1981 winner for *Take My Family ... Please!***
45. Greek god
47. Dominion of Canada's official flag
48. Some days of the week (abbr.)
50. Memo
52. Business collapse, say
53. Nickelback and Hedley
54. *Carousel* song: "_____ Nice Clambake"
55. BC place: _____ Coola
56. Early German painter
58. Evidence of guilt
59. Aplomb
60. Viper

61. Must-haves
64. Quit, colloquially
65. Slick, in winter
69. Antiseptic liquid
72. Highlands garb
74. If they, in Île-Goyer
77. Ladies' mates
78. Scotch _____
80. Udder adjuncts
82. Folklore little person
83. 1921 silent film: ____'able
David

85. Stun
86. US Natives
87. Loonies and toonies
88. Choo-choo's sound
89. When repeated thrice, a '70
movie
91. Truman's old-style coats?
92. Peter, Paul and Mary surname
93. Badmouth
95. Most mad about losing?
97. Kind of tax
101. Is concerned

103. Fifth-largest Ohio city
106. Trade
108. 65-A container
109. Small litter member
110. Labatt _____
111. Burns' babe?
112. CTV anchor LaFlamme
114. Had breakfast
117. Behind

98 — Dinner in Blackpool

What's on the menu?

ACROSS

1. Not fem.
5. Sales associates, for short
9. USSR successor
12. '85 Bryan Adams hit: "One Night _____ Affair"
16. Norse myth mom
17. Modern pentathlon tool
18. Bonding substances
21. *Dreamgirls* star Sharon
22. **Beginning of the meal?**
24. Preferred house style in Massachusetts?
26. Not together
27. Birds of peace
29. Skin, anatomically
30. One who lacks knowledge
34. Mermaid's milieu
35. Hewed
40. Student's aid
41. Like some editions
43. Shoe brand: _____ Blahnik
44. 93-A, for example
46. Limpers' aids
47. South American marmoset
48. Sunbeams
50. Toyota product
51. Dress in Madras
52. Kingston Online Services (abbr.)
53. **Trendy place to eat it?**
57. Make a note
58. Hot *M*A*S*H* character?
59. Chemical suffix
60. Kind of portrait
61. Cause of stomach woes
63. A deadly sin
65. Approaches
68. Romance novel verb
69. Committed a hockey infraction
71. *Desperate Housewives* role for Marcia
72. Got some rest
73. Cut off
74. Eye inflammation
76. Parent, in Port-Cartier
78. Destroys, in Dulwich
79. Satirical Canadian political party
84. Arctic headgear?
88. **Entire entree?**
90. Archipelago segment
91. Focus
92. Shania Twain hit: "Come On _____"
93. "We stand on guard for _____"
94. Sci. subj.
95. 100 lbs., in America
96. Caution
97. Still-nesting hawk

DOWN

1. A Spice Girl
2. Square footage
3. Rice Krispies ad character
4. Scottish, to Seneca
5. Garbage pickup, say
6. Widespread outbreak
7. Ballpoint
8. Bits of time
9. U of A and UBC
10. Thought up
11. Islam moral code
12. Labatt _____
13. 1988 Calgary games venue: Olympic _____
14. Exceedingly
15. Body shop guess (abbr.)
19. Terminal letters?
20. Supersonic jet
23. Eur. econ. grp.
25. New Testament book (abbr.)
28. Reddish fruit shrubs (var.)
30. Sick
31. Not Jewish, in slang
32. Description
33. 1967 war peninsula
35. Japanese stringed instrument (var.)
36. Santa _____ River
37. Painter's masterpiece?
38. *The Mill on the Floss* scribe George
39. Cherry and Getty
42. Pâté pot
43. Convenience stores
45. Canadian Olympian Clara Hughes, in summer
47. Confucian concept
49. "Vengeance is mine … _____ the Lord"
51. More diaphanous
53. Close by
54. Intrepid, say?
55. Mystery writers' award
56. 1992 vote type in Canada
57. Masons' mugs?
62. Quick swim
63. Obvious, like an heir?
64. Eatons or Roots, say
66. Portuguese royal
67. Pronoun in Québec
69. By hook or by crook
70. Detect
73. Milk-related
75. Maiden name marker
76. _____-Sainte-Anne QC
77. In this instant
79. American author Philip
80. 2008 Theory of a Deadman hit: "_____ My Life"
81. Footnote word
82. *Delta of Venus* author Anaïs
83. *The Marilyn Denis* _____
85. Palish
86. "Guilty," e.g.
87. '84 Howard Engel mystery: *Murder _____ the Light*
88. Tic-_____-toe
89. Gametes

Canada Cornucopia 33

ACROSS

1. Shop 'til you _____
5. 1,501 to a Roman
8. Cleave onto
14. Aunt or daughter
16. Carcinogenic compound
17. Some Middle East areas
18. Giller-winning author Margaret
19. Neophyte
20. Gum buildup
22. Stoney _____ ON
23. Canadian dollar currency code
24. Killer whales
27. "Sunglasses at Night" Juno recipient Corey
28. Two-faced Roman god
30. Pickle type
31. Thomas and Thaddeus
34. "Sprechen _____ Deutsch?"
35. Ships out from a CFB
38. Licorice flavouring
40. Bublé song: "_____ Got You Under My Skin"
41. '98 Ontario/Québec weather event
43. Small rodents
45. The skies, to a bard
46. Did well, colloquially

50. Urban blights
52. Long-time *All My Children* character Martin
53. Got behind the wheel
54. Harper or Mulcair
56. Beaver's kin
57. Like pencil ends
59. *Barney Miller* was set in the 12th one
61. The Maritimes, in its early days
62. You'd give these for that?
63. Did grammar class work
64. River that empties into Lake Winnipeg
65. Impudence

DOWN

1. Soak
2. Fish that fastens
3. Ontario premier Mowat (1872–96)
4. Cranial lobe
5. Arachnid
6. John's deer?
7. Type of replay
8. Jewish month
9. "Likewise"
10. '80s Manitoba premier Pawley
11. Defeat the devil

12. Orinoco, e.g.
13. _____ of the line
15. Bulletin board pin
21. Flattered excessively
23. Audio tape
25. What George Washington could not tell
26. Musher's transport
28. '70s CTV talk show host Davidson
29. Spanish Mr.
32. Luau food
33. Title for 3-D
35. Fades
36. Vile
37. Strange
39. Popular Canadian candy
42. More acute
44. Fixes
47. Lens covering
48. Removes a renter
49. Obits, say
51. Debussy contemporary Erik
53. Tube
55. Pair
56. Require
57. Dad's drivel?
58. South American tuber
60. Canadian Club whisky type

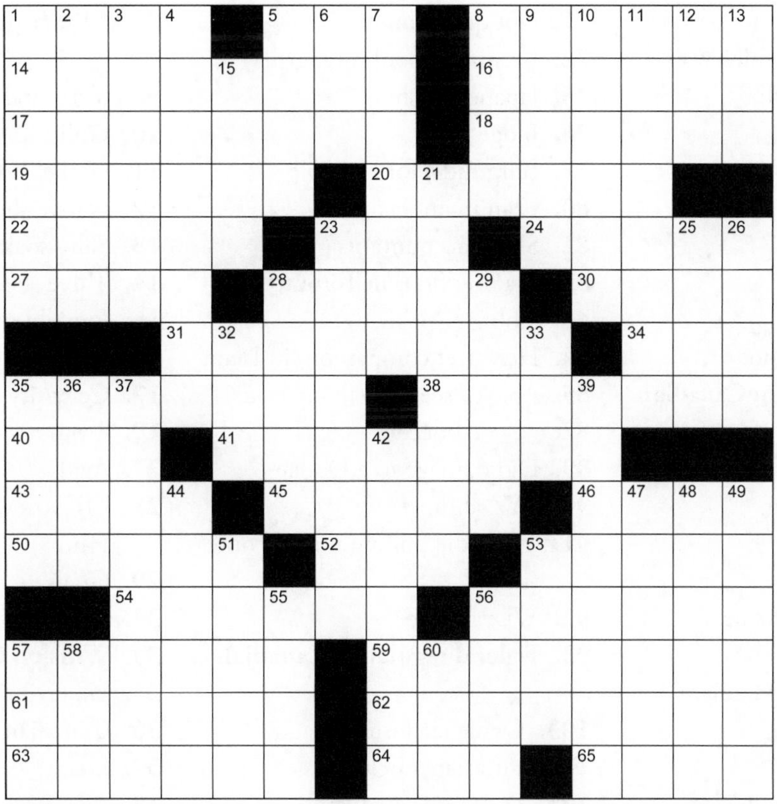

Solution on page 232

ACROSS

1. Oil cartel org.
5. Foam rubber trademark
9. Nincompoops
14. Saskatchewan premier Wall
18. Chanel's hot quaff?
19. "Try" band: Blue _____
20. Arm bones
21. Overdue
22. Gull's cousin
23. Command
24. Ratify a motion, say
25. _____ in a blue moon
26. **Ottawa attraction: Canadian _____**
30. Does lace work
31. Oahu-to-Maui dir.
32. Got lured in?
33. Mutton necks
36. Big name in magazine publishing
38. Business process paradigm
44. Genetic duplicate
45. Knock sharply
46. South American wildcats
48. Spawn
49. Vienna residents
51. Mennonite subgroup
52. Oft seen machine on snowy streets
53. Steve Nash league (abbr.)
54. Puerto _____
55. **Music group: Canadian _____**
56. *Norma Rae* star Field
57. Sidekick
59. Deke
60. Pulley
61. Peevish, old style
64. Uninterested
65. QC-born Oscar winner Norma
66. Twenty–forty connector
67. Wears well

68. Bee-related
69. Wanders
70. **Airline: Canadian _____**
71. Not quite round
72. Evening school mtg. grp.
75. Japanese sashes
76. Judge
77. Burgundy, for example
80. Clan members
81. Ships' accountants
83. Trading floor in Toronto (abbr.)
84. Hereafter companion, in Islam
85. Able to see high-flying birds?
87. _____ bucco
89. Did damage to a Dodge
90. YYZ abbr.
91. "A needle pulling thread" note (var.)
92. Wise mystic
93. **Federal regulator: Canadian _____**
103. Ovule enclosure
104. Eurasian antelope
105. Lacquer ingredient
106. Prosodic foot
108. Man or Capri
109. Former felon
110. Formal napkin material
111. Marineland mammal
112. Canada's '98 snowboard gold Olympian Rebagliati
113. Bread ingredient
114. Morgue arrivals (abbr.)
115. Bangladesh bread

DOWN

1. '70 Canadian crisis mo.
2. Canadian McCrae's "In Flanders Fields"
3. Hosiery shade
4. '92 k.d. lang hit: "_____ Craving"

5. Standards
6. Taro tuber
7. Coral formation
8. **Military group: Canadian _____**
9. Horizontal beam
10. Gully, in Ghana
11. "Rebel Yell" rocker Billy
12. Native shelter (var.)
13. Salty soak
14. Three sheets to the wind
15. Punjabi princess
16. AB natural gas company
17. Celebrity chef Paula
19. Trounces
27. Avid
28. "To Know Him _____ Love Him"
29. Goals
33. Take a look
34. **Whisky: Canadian _____**
35. US civil rights figure Parks
36. Canadian skiing icon Greene
37. Lhasa _____
38. Aggressive request
39. High-and-mighty invitees, say
40. Throw a horseshoe
41. **Currency: Canadian _____**
42. Develop
43. Mulroney's pre-prime minister occupation
45. Lightfoot hit: "_____ Day People"
47. Tooth decay
50. Scorning device, in literature
52. Song of thanksgiving
55. Docking spot
56. Former New York stadium name
57. Mythological agriculture goddess
58. Soaks, as flax

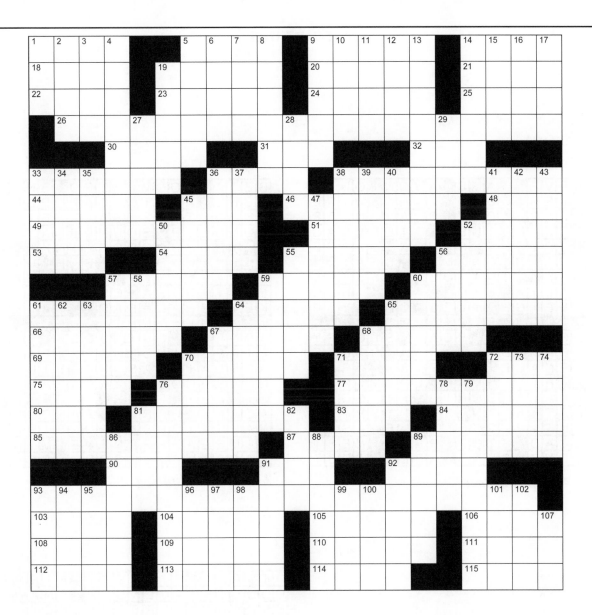

59. Long-time voice of hockey Hewitt
60. Manitoba military base
61. Golfer's caress?
62. Aversion
63. **Magazine: Canadian** _____
64. Pushed (with "in")
65. Body-shaping undergarment manufacturer
67. Evil entomologist?
68. French naval boat
70. Not a soul, say
71. Chooses

72. Unfunny face
73. **Store: Canadian** _____
74. Like the Sahara
76. Dairy cattle breed
78. At that location
79. Not affiliated, in the trades
81. *Frasier* co-star Gilpin
82. Fireplace carbon
86. Soup servers
88. **Craton: Canadian** _____
89. Ate with gusto
91. Minimal
92. Trivial pursuits?

93. Equitable, at the CNE?
94. Guesstimate phrase
95. Lubricates
96. Old German duchy name
97. Typewriter type
98. Self-images
99. Mélange
100. She sang "99 Luftballons" in '83
101. *Fame* star Irene
102. One of these opened in Montréal in 1851
107. Prohibit

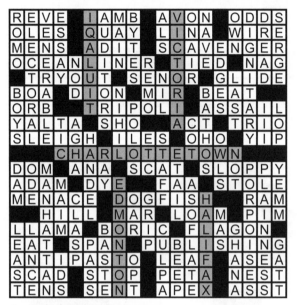

1 ■ *Capital Places*

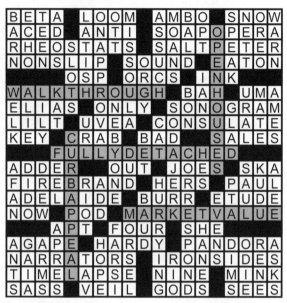

2 ■ *House Hunting*

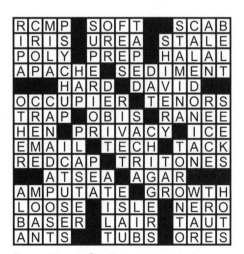

3 ■ *Canada Cornucopia 1*

4 ■ *Bird's-eye View*

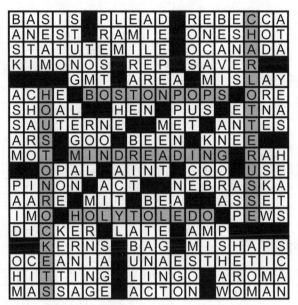

5 ▪ *All-American*

6 ▪ *Canada Cornucopia 2*

7 ▪ *By the Numbers*

8 ▪ *Give Yourself a Hand*

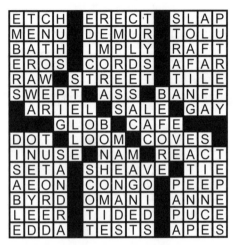

9 ▪ *Canada Cornucopia 3*

10 ▪ *His Own Way to Rock*

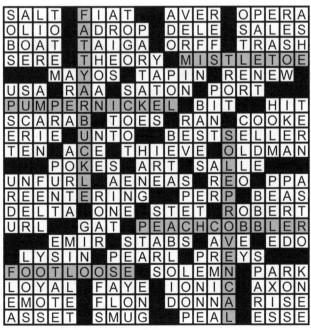

11 ▪ *Willie's Shoemaker*

12 ▪ *Canada Cornucopia 4*

13 ▪ *Into the Water*

```
ABBOT   ETAT   RPM   FACE
BRAVO   NOVA   ARIZONAN
RULER   DRIB   MONOXIDE
ACER   VITAL   STONE
MESH   EVENED   ERE   FCC
    EIRE        OHMS   PIER
UNGAVA   MANGE   TEENY
BEERS   TITI   SECHELT
OURS   RESEAL   LOURDES
ATM   CASTIGATING   GSA
TRIDENT   NATION   COIL
  ACADIAN   RENT   ALAMO
CLINE   OVARY   AVALON
OLDS   LINE   ERAS
BYE   BAN   GEORGE   SAGA
    BASTE   AVERS   MAAM
ANDERSON   TILE   TARSI
BAILBOND   ONES   STOPS
EVEL   SES   NETS   BENES
```

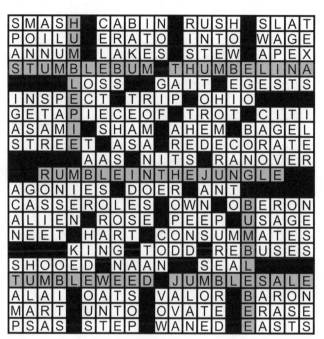

14 ▪ *That's the Way the Cookie Crumbles*

```
SMASH   CABIN   RUSH   SLAT
POILU   ERATO   INTO   WAGE
ANNUM   LAKES   STEW   APEX
STUMBLEBUM   THUMBELINA
    LOSS     GAIT   EGESTS
INSPECT   TRIP   OHIO
GETAPIECEOF   TROT   CITI
ASAMI   SHAM   AHEM   BAGEL
STREET   ASA   REDECORATE
    AAS   NITS   RANOVER
RUMBLEINTHEJUNGLE
AGONIES   DOER   ANT
CASSEROLES   OWN   OBERON
ALIEN   ROSE   PEEP   USAGE
NEET   HART   CONSUMMATES
    KING   TODD   REBUSES
SHOOED   NAAN   SEAL
TUMBLEWEED   JUMBLESALE
ALAI   OATS   VALOR   BARON
MART   UNTO   OVATE   ERASE
PSAS   STEP   WANED   EASTS
```

15 ▪ *Canada Cornucopia 5*

```
SHES   BACCA   CRES
TOME   OGLES   HERO
ROIL   WHORL   AGIN
URGED   AUTOCRACY
NARCOS   TIPPET
GHETTOS   FEASTED
    SEAWAY   TAME
BAD   SKILIFT   SUB
EPIC   TENURE
TECHNIC   GRANDPA
    TRUTHS   SITARS
STAIRHEAD   LETUP
HATS   ADIOS   RIDE
ALOT   CONDO   AVEC
WARY   ANTON   TEST
```

16 ▪ *Eponymous Edibles*

```
BARDS   SITU   SHAFT   GIT
USUAL   HOIST   TABLE   ACH
RESTIGOUCHESALMON   SHA
RATATAT   SAGER   SUNSPOT
    SMUT   PANEL   TATERS
SAP   EPICENTRES   NOS
RAREFY   MOD   SUBTOTAL
IDEAL   REX   BASELY   DENE
CLARE   ALAMODE   MEDIATE
HYSTERIA   AGORA   BUNKER
    CALGARYREDEYE
TANDEM   SLIME   DAEDALUS
HEARSES   ONEROUS   ADAME
AONE   AUSTEN   ACT   TANIA
INASMUCH   CHI   AEGEAN
IDI   HOREHOUNDS   ESK
LAMEME   WOMAN   GOTO
IRONORE   WILDS   WIGWAMS
LAB   SASKATOONBERRYPIE
ASA   ASSIN   SNAIL   ELORA
CHR   SEEMS   EGGS   SEDER
```

17 ■ *Mix and Match*

18 ■ *Canada Cornucopia 6*

19 ■ *Words and Images*

20 ■ *Put it in Reverse*

21 ▪ *Canada Cornucopia 7*

22 ▪ *Recipe for Good TV*

23 ▪ *Armed and Musical*

24 ▪ *Canada Cornucopia 8*

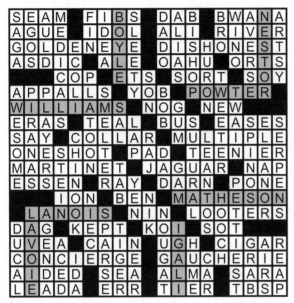

25 ▪ *Oh Danny Boys*

26 ▪ *Ode to Vivaldi*

27 ▪ *Canada Cornucopia 9*

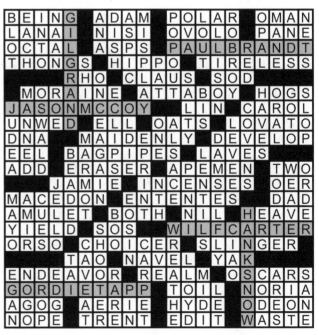

28 ▪ *Country Gentlemen*

29 ■ *Orienteering*

30 ■ *Canada Cornucopia 10*

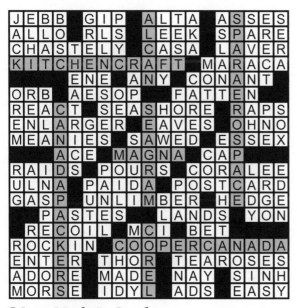

31 ■ *Made It Good*

32 ■ *Stop Your Sobbing*

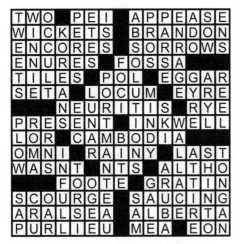

33 ■ *Canada Cornucopia 11*

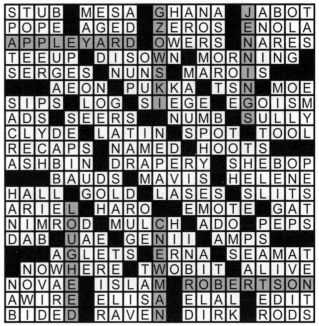

34 ■ *For Pete's Sake*

35 ■ *Tops-y-turvy*

36 ■ *Canada Cornucopia 12*

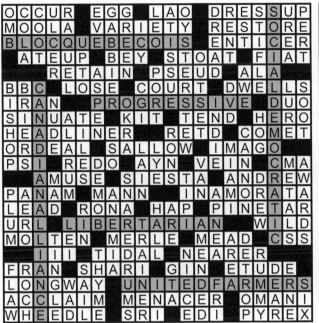

37 ■ *The Party Line*

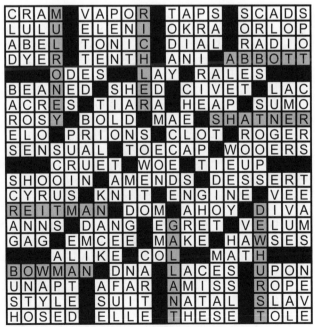

38 ■ *Red, White and Blue*

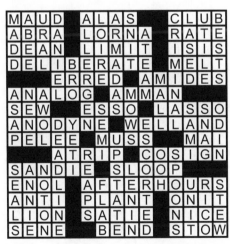

39 ■ *Canada Cornucopia 13*

40 ■ *They Hail from Montréal*

41 ■ *An Apple a Day*

42 ■ *Canada Cornucopia 14*

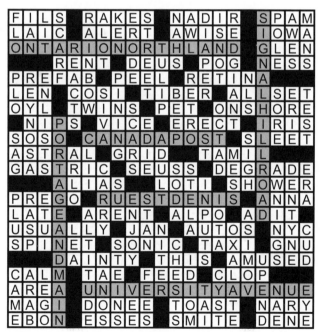

43 ■ *Are You Game*

44 ■ *Cross-eyed?*

45 ▪ *Canada Cornucopia 15*

46 ▪ *Big Mac Attack*

47 ▪ *Games People Play*

48 ▪ *Canada Cornucopia 16*

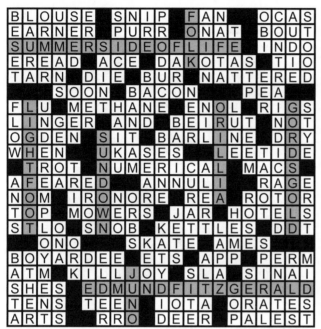

49 ■ *Who Am I? 1*

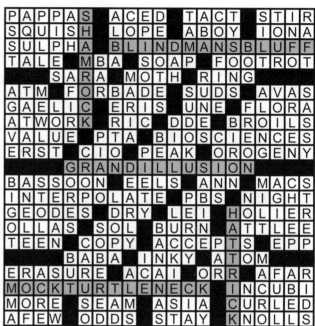

50 ■ *Let's Pretend*

51 ■ *Canada Cornucopia 17*

52 ■ *How Sweet It Is*

53 ■ *For the Birds*

54 ■ *Canada Cornucopia 18*

55 ■ *Canadian Singalong*

56 ■ *Double Up*

57 ■ *Canada Cornucopia 19*

58 ■ *Ekal Lake, et al.*

59 ■ *We All Fall Down*

60 ■ *Canada Cornucopia 20*

61 ▪ *CanadianZ*

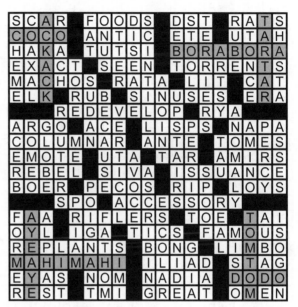

62 ▪ *Repetitious*

63 ▪ *Canada Cornucopia 21*

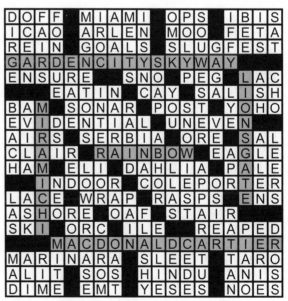

64 ▪ *Bridging the Gaps*

65 ▪ *Book of the Month Club*

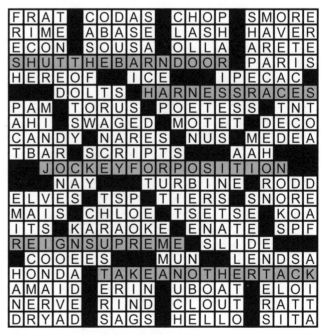

66 ▪ *Canada Cornucopia 22*

67 ▪ *Hill Billies*

68 ▪ *Horsing Around*

69 ▪ *Canada Cornucopia 23*

70 ▪ *Pick a Number*

71 ▪ *You Can Bank on Them*

72 ▪ *Canada Cornucopia 24*

73 ■ *And the Territory Is . . .*

74 ■ *Sweets and Starches*

75 ■ *Canada Cornucopia 25*

76 ■ *Canadian Combos*

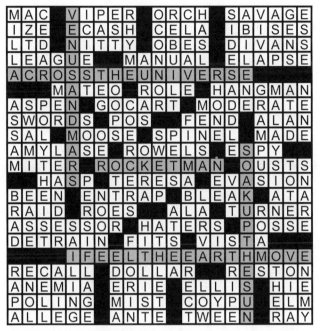

Grid 77:

```
MAC VIPER ORCH SAVAGE
IZE ECASH CELA IBISES
LTD NITTY OBES DIVANS
LEAGUE MANUAL ELAPSE
ACROSSTHEUNIVERSE
   MATEO ROLE HANGMAN
ASPEN GOCART MODERATE
SWORDS POS FEND ALAN
SAL MOOSE SPINEL MADE
AMYLASE ROWELS ESPY
MITER ROCKETMAN OUSTS
 HASP TERESA EVASION
BEEN ENTRAP BLEAK ATA
RAID ROES ALA TURNER
ASSESSOR HATERS POSSE
DETRAIN FITS VISTA
   IFEELTHEEARTHMOVE
RECALL DOLLAR RESTON
ANEMIA ERIE ELLIS HIE
POLING MIST COYPU ELM
ALLEGE ANTE TWEEN RAY
```

77 ▪ *Up in the Air*

Grid 78:

```
UPSTREAM LOESS
REHEARSE ONSETS
BROADEST CATNAP
ADAMS ORGANISMS
NUTS DROOL VIP
   PATSY TATER
PROMOTE BETIDE
LEVERED SLEEVED
ALERTS PONDERS
NARCS SLOGS
 YEA MOONS MDIV
TRAPPINGS GOODE
RATTAN GOVERNOR
ICEAGE IRANIANS
ERNES ASSENTTO
```

78 ▪ *Canada Cornucopia 26*

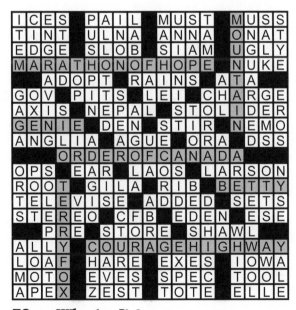

Grid 79:

```
ICES PAIL MUST MUSS
TINT ULNA ANNA ONAT
EDGE SLOB SIAM UGLY
MARATHONOFHOPE NUKE
 ADOPT RAINS ATA
GOV PITS LEI CHARGE
AXIS NEPAL STOLIDER
GENIE DEN STIR NEMO
ANGLIA AGUE ORA DSS
  ORDEROFCANADA
OPS EAR LAOS LARSON
ROOT GILA RIB BETTY
TELEVISE ADDED SETS
STEREO CFB EDEN ESE
 PRE STORE SHAWL
ALLY COURAGEHIGHWAY
LOAF HARE EXES IOWA
MOTO EVES SPEC TOOL
APEX ZEST TOTE ELLE
```

79 ▪ *Who Am I? 2*

Grid 80:

```
TACO GUSH CELA SPAY
OMAN ONCE ANIK ORSO
AMSTERDAM MAKI WISH
TOTALDEBASEMENT MAO
 PAIR NILES OARS
ATM NAPA ZOLOFTDOSE
WHIP NIL ETS RUSSIA
NONOS NOR CAP ENR
SUDOKU HEIRESS PSS
 HIGHANNEXIETY
ODS ARSENIC RELISH
IVE INS NET DORIA
TETRAD ABA SAC NITS
TRAUMATTIC SILD SET
 LIMB HASTE LEIF
FAN STEVESMCGARRETT
OREM ERIC CHANTEUSE
OGEE REST EATS ERAS
LESE ISMS EPEE DORS
```

80 ▪ *What the Ell?*

81 ▪ *Canada Cornucopia 27*

82 ▪ *Talking to Thespians*

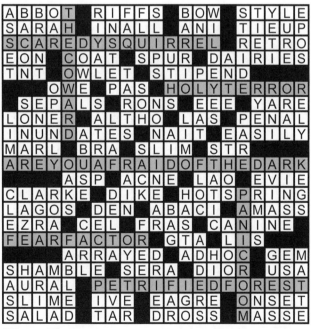

83 ▪ *Terrorisms*

84 ▪ *Canada Cornucopia 28*

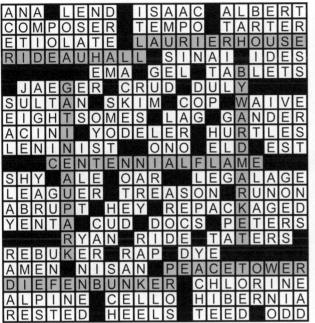

85 ▪ *Destination: Ottawa*

86 ▪ *Piracy?*

87 ▪ *Canada Cornucopia 29*

88 ▪ *Hometown Glory*

89 ■ *Skipping a Long*

90 ■ *Canada Cornucopia 30*

91 ■ *Canadian Boys of Summer*

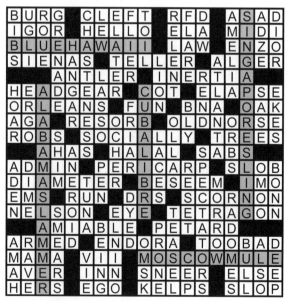

92 ■ *Cartographers' Cocktails*

93 ▪ *Canada Cornucopia 31*

94 ▪ *For the Foodies*

95 ▪ *Sayonara to Cinema*

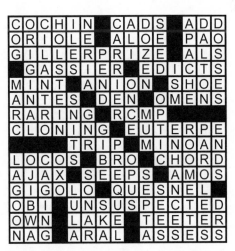

96 ▪ *Canada Cornucopia 32*

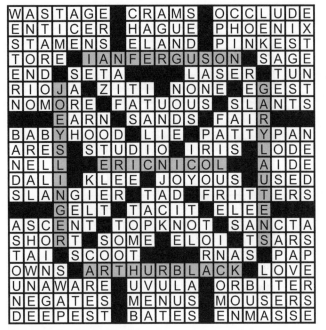

97 ■ *By Their Wits*

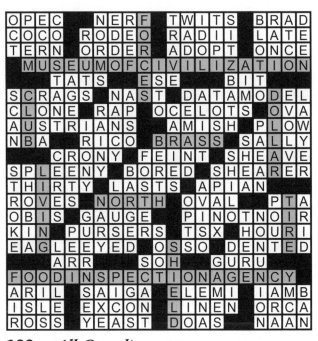

98 ■ *Dinner in Blackpool*

99 ■ *Canada Cornucopia 33*

100 ■ *All-Canadian*